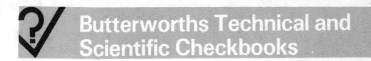

Butterworths Technical and Scientific Checkbooks

Electrical and Electronic Applications 2 Checkbook

D. W. Tyler
CEng, MIEE

Butterworths

London   Boston   Sydney   Wellington   Durban   Toronto

First published 1982
© Butterworth & Co (Publishers) Ltd 1982

British Library Cataloguing in Publication Data
Tyler, D. W.
  Electrical and electronic applications 2 Checkbook.
  (Butterworths Checkbook Series)
  1. Electric engineering
  I. Title
  621.3   TK145

ISBN 0-408-00661-7
ISBN 0-408-00616-1 Pbk

Typeset by Tunbridge Wells Typesetting Services Limited
Printed and bound in Scotland by Thomson Litho Ltd., East Kilbride

Contents

Note to Reader

As textbooks become more expensive, authors are often asked to reduce the number of worked and unworked problems, examples and case studies. This may reduce costs, but it can be at the expense of practical work which gives point to the theory.

Checkbooks if anything lean the other way. They let problem-solving establish and exemplify the theory contained in technician syllabuses. The Checkbook reader can gain *real* understanding through seeing problems solved and through solving problems himself.

Checkbooks do not supplant fuller textbooks, but rather supplement them with an alternative emphasis and an ample provision of worked and unworked problems. The brief outline of essential data—definitions, formulae, laws, regulations, codes of practice, standards, conventions, procedures, etc—will be a useful introduction to a course and a valuable aid to revision. Short-answer and multi-choice problems are a valuable feature of many Checkbooks, together with conventional problems and answers.

Checkbook authors are carefully selected. Most are experienced and successful technical writers; all are experts in their own subjects; but a more important qualification still is their ability to demonstrate and teach the solution of problems in their particular branch of technology, mathematics or science.

Authors, General Editors and Publishers are partners in this major low-priced series whose essence is captured by the Checkbook symbol of a question or problem 'checked' by a tick for correct solution.

Preface

This textbook of worked problems covers the Technician Education Council level 2 double unit in Electrical and Electronic Applications (syllabus U76/361). However It can also be regarded as a basic testbook in such applications for a much wider range of courses.

Each topic considered in the text is presented in a way that assumes in the reader only the knowledge attained in the Physical Science 1 unit.

The aim of the book is to provide a broadly based introduction to applications in electronic and power systems.

The book contains nearly 200 illustrations, some 75 detailed worked problems followed by 200 short questions and 275 further problems with answers.

I wish to thank the Institution of Electrical Engineers for permission to quote from Regulations for the Electrical Equipment of Buildings. Any interpretation of those Regulations is mine alone.

D. W. Tyler
Reading College of Technology

Butterworths Technical and Scientific Checkbooks

General Editors for Science, Engineering and Mathematics titles:
J.O. Bird and A.J.C. May, Highbury College of Technology, Portsmouth.

General Editor for Building, Civil Engineering, Surveying and Architectural titles:
Colin R. Bassett, lately of Guildford County College of Technology.

A comprehensive range of Checkbooks will be available to cover the major syllabus areas of the TEC, SCOTEC and similar examining authorities. A comprehensive list is given below and classified according to levels.

Level 1 (Red covers)
Mathematics
Physical Science
Physics
Construction Drawing
Construction Technology
Microelectronic Systems
Engineering Drawing
Workshop Processes & Materials

Level 2 (Blue covers)
Mathematics
Chemistry
Physics
Building Science and Materials
Construction Technology
Electrical & Electronic Applications
Electrical & Electronic Principles
Electronics
Microelectronic Systems
Engineering Drawing
Engineering Science
Manufacturing Technology
Digital Techniques
Motor Vehicle Science

Level 3 (Yellow covers)
Mathematics
Chemistry
Building Measurement
Construction Technology
Environmental Science
Electrical Principles
Electronics
Microelectronic Systems
Electrical Science
Mechanical Science
Engineering Mathematics & Science
Engineering Science
Engineering Design
Manufacturing Technology
Motor Vehicle Science
Light Current Applications

Level 4 (Green covers)
Mathematics
Building Law
Building Services & Equipment
Construction Technology
Construction Site Studies
Concrete Technology
Economics for the Construction Industry
Geotechnics
Engineering Instrumentation & Control

Level 5
Building Services & Equipment
Construction Technology
Manufacturing Technology

1 Transmission and distribution of electrical energy

A SUMMARY OF FORMULAE AND DEFINITIONS ASSOCIATED WITH TRANSMISSION AND DISTRIBUTION SYSTEMS

1   Nearly electrical energy generation throughout the world is produced by 3-phase synchronous generators. Almost invariably the synchronous generator has its magnetic field produced electrically by passing direct current through a winding on an iron core which rotates between the three windings or phases of the machine. These windings are embedded in slots in an iron stator and one end of each winding is connected to a common point and earthed. The output from the generator is taken from the other three ends of the windings. Therefore, the output from a three-phase generator is carried on three wires. All generators connected to a single system must rotate at exactly the same speed, hence the term 'synchronous' generator.

Generators are driven by prime movers using steam which is produced by:

burning coal or oil, or
nuclear reactions;
water falling from a higher to a lower level (hydraulic), or
aircraft gas turbines burning oil or gas.

A very small amount of generation is carried out using diesel engines.

2   **Synchronous generators** range in size from 70 MVA (60 MW at 0.85 power factor) at a line voltage (i.e. the voltage between any pair of output lines) of 11 kV which were mostly installed in the 1950s, through an intermediate size of 235 MVA (200 MW at 0.85 power factor) to the recent machines rated at 600 MVA (500 MW) which generate at 25.6 kV line. There are generators rated at 660 MW and 1000 MW but these are rare at present.

3   The power in a single-phase circuit $= VI \cos \phi$ watts where V and I are the r.m.s. values of circuit voltage and current respectively and ϕ is the phase angle between them. As an example, consider a power of 1 MW at 240 V and a power factor of 0.8 lagging. (1 MW $= 1000$ kW $= 10^6$. Transposing gives

$$I = \frac{10^6}{240 \times 0.8} = \textbf{5208 amperes}$$

By increasing the voltage to say 20 000 V, the required value of current falls to 62.5 A. The voltage drop in a transmission line due to the resistance of the line $= IR$ volts. Therefore, the power loss

$=$ voltage drop $\times$ current

$= IR \times I = I^2R$ **watts**

It follows therefore that by increasing the working voltage (thus reducing the current required) the losses in a given size of cable will be reduced or if the losses

1

in both cases are to be the same, a smaller diameter cable may be used in the high voltage case since with a smaller current a higher resistance can be tolerated.

4   In the UK major transmission is carried out at 400 kV, this voltage being achieved by the use of **transformers** directly coupled to the generator output terminals. The voltage is reduced to the value required by the consumer using transformers local to the point of consumption. To economise on transformers it would seem that generation could best be carried out at 400 kV but so far it has not been found possible to develop insulation for use in rotating machines which will withstand such a high voltage whilst allowing the heat produced in the winding to be dissipated. In particular there are problems where the conductors leave the slots and emerge into the gas filled spaces at each end of the stator.

5   Since the power transmitted from a single power station may be in excess of 2000 MW, the high cost of insulation and switchgear required to handle 400 kV is justified by the considerable reduction in conductor size. At distribution level the supply for a single factory or for housing from an individual transformer represents a relatively small power so that even at much lower voltages the current involved is quite small. The cost of extra-high voltage switchgear would not be justified and the land area for the substation might well be restricted. As local demands decrease the voltage at which they are fed is reduced; a large factory demanding 100 MW might well be fed directly from the 132 kV system whereas a smaller factory with a demand of 1 MW would probably be fed from the 33 kV or 11 kV system (see *Fig 1*).

6   Typical **transformer ratings** and **voltage levels** at different points in the transmission and distribution system in the UK are as follows:
   (i)   Generation at 25.6 kV stepping up to 400 kV, rating 600 MVA;
   (ii) From major transmission voltage 400 kV to local distribution at 132 kV, rating 150–250 MVA;
   (iii) From 132 kV to 33 kV for further distribution or industrial consumers, rating 50–75 MVA;
   (iv) From 33 kV to 11 kV at which voltage power is taken to street corner and factory substations, rating 10–15 MVA;
   (v)   From 11 kV to 415/240 V at which voltage commercial premises and houses are fed, rating 250–500 KVA.

7   **Overhead lines** for power transmission are usually made of aluminium with a steel core. The bare conductors are supported by insulators of porcelain or glass which are fixed to wooden poles or steel lattice towers. *Fig 2* shows some typical British line supports together with the associated insulators.

   All the steel lattice towers use suspension insulators whilst the wooden poles employ either type. Three conductors comprise a single circuit of a 3-phase system so that the 33 kV single circuit tower has three cross arms and three sets of suspension insulators. Towers with six cross arms carry two separate circuits.

   Wood supports are of red fir impregnated with creosote and may be in the form of single poles or two poles made into an A or H. In the UK they are used for circuits up to 33 kV but in other countries lines working at up to 250 kV using 50 m poles have been erected. Each pole is, in fact, a complete tree trunk and as these have to be imported into the UK large ground clearances using poles proves to be very expensive. Towers are made of steel angle section and may easily be fabricated up to almost any height by adding bottom sections or trestles.

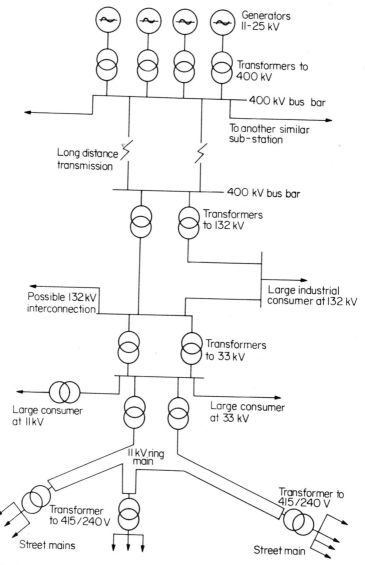

Fig 1

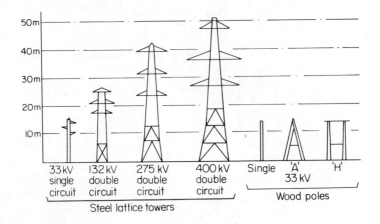

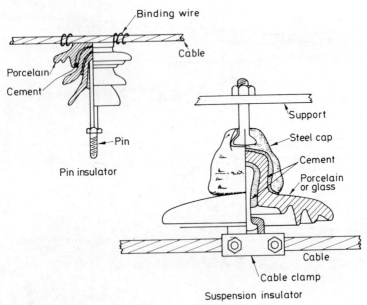

Fig 2

8 **Comparison between overhead lines and underground cables**

Cost The h.v. overhead line is made of steel cored aluminium and is supported by insulators mounted on towers or poles which are between 100 and 400 m apart. The underground h.v. cable is made of copper to reduce the resistance of a given cross-sectional-area cable. The cable is fully insulated and armoured to protect it against mechanical damage and is covered with a corrosion resistant material (see *Fig 2*, chapter 4 on page 45). The high cost of copper, insulation, armouring and corrosion protection together with that of taking out a suitable trench and refilling it, make the high-voltage cable many times more expensive than the overhead line. The price difference at 415/240 V using aluminium cored cables is not so great and underground cables may be chosen on environmental grounds.

Environment The underground cable is invisible. However there can be no building or large trees planted over it since it must be readily accessible in the event of a fault. Also, the heat produced by an extra-high-voltage cable can affect the soil around it thus modifying the plant growth in the immediate vicinity. The overhead line has supports and these, together with the line itself, are often visible for long distances. Electrical discharges from the lines can cause radio interference.

Reliability There is little difference in the reliability of the overhead and underground systems. The overhead line can be struck by lightning whereas the underground cable is at the mercy of earth moving equipment. Occasionally a cable will develop a small hole in its outer sheath due to movement over a stone, for example, giving rise to water ingress followed by an explosion but this is thankfully rare.

Fault finding Overhead lines are patrolled regularly on foot or by helicopter. Broken insulators can be seen and by using infra-red detecting equipment local hot spots, possibly in compression joints where two lengths of conductor have been joined, can be detected. If an underground cable develops a fault, electrical methods have to be used to locate it. When the fault has been found the repair is expensive.

9 A **circuit breaker** is a mechanical device for making and breaking a circuit under all conditions. Two examples of the positions where circuit breakers are used are:
(i) to connect a generator transformer to the 400 kV system;
(ii) to connect an industrial consumer taking a supply at 33 kV or 11 kV to the system at that voltage.
   When a circuit breaker opens to interrupt a circuit an arc is drawn between the contacts. At domestic voltages the arc is small and arc extinction occurs quickly in the atmosphere. At extra-high voltages the arc is much more difficult to extinguish and air or oil, often under pressure have to be used.

10 A **switch** is a device for making and breaking a circuit which is carrying current of value not greatly in excess of normal loading. Typical uses are:
(i) in the home for making and interrupting the supply to an appliance, light fitting, fire, etc.
(ii) in a factory, for starting and stopping an electric motor. In this case the operation will probably be by electrical means rather than manual when the switch will be known as a contactor.

11 An **isolator** is a means of isolating or making dead a circuit which is not carrying current at the time (like pulling out a fuse in the home so that work may be carried out safely on a circuit). The isolator may be used to close a circuit on to

load. Isolators are often used in series with high voltage circuit breakers so that having opened the circuit breaker it can be isolated from the supply to enable work to be carried out on it.

12 The small substation shown in *Fig 3* is typical of the thousands of such installations feeding factories, housing and commercial premises. It is connected to the 11 kV ring main as shown in *Fig 1*. The ring main is equipped with two isolators at each tap-off point and these are normally closed making the ring complete. The transformer is fed through a circuit breaker of the oil-immersed or air-break type. The transformer will be rated at 11 000 V to 433 V nominally. On the high-voltage side there will be a tap changer which is used to alter the number of operational turns in the winding and this has the effect of maintaining

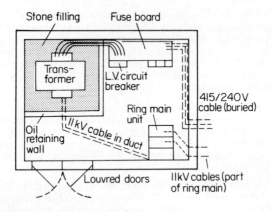

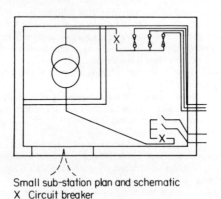

Small sub-station plan and schematic
X Circuit breaker
—⌐Isolator
Fig 3   o–o Fuse

6

the output voltage at the desired level over a fairly wide range of the input voltage.

Such transformers employ paper insulation and are oil filled. The heat produced in the windings and core is carried by the oil to cooling tubes on the outside of the transformer whence it is convected away by natural air circulation. For this reason the building must be adequately ventilated and louvres are fitted in the doors and high up in the walls. The transformer is either mounted on a plinth in the centre of a large pit filled with stones or there is a small wall built around it. If the transformer suffers a fault and oil leaks out it must be contained to minimise the risk of fire spreading.

In a large substation with many circuit breakers, fire resistant barriers are used to create small sections and automatic fire-fighting equipment is fitted in each section using either carbon dioxide gas or fine water spray.

B. WORKED PROBLEMS ON TRANSMISSION AND DISTRIBUTION

Problem 1   Each core of a two cable feeding a load 200 m distant from the supply point has a resistance of 0.1 Ω. The cross-sectional area of each of the two cores in the cable is 0.35 cm². The voltage at the supply end of the cable is 240 V. The input power to the cable is 20 kW at 0.85 power factor lagging.
(a) Calculate: (i) the current in the cable; (ii) the cable losses; (iii) the power in the load.
(b) Calculate the required cross-sectional area of each core of a two-core cable which will have the same losses as in (a) above when the input power is 200 kW at the same power factor.
(c) What would be the value of the losses in the cable in (a) if it were used with an input of 200 kW again at 0.85 lagging power factor?

(a) (i)   Power in a single-phase circuit = $VI \cos \phi$ watts. ($\cos \phi$ = power factor).
Hence $20\,000 = 240 \times I \times 0.85$

$$I = \frac{20\,000}{240 \times 0.85} = 98 \text{ A}$$

(ii)   Losses in the cable = $I^2 R$ watts,
where R = total resistance, go and return
$= 2 \times 0.1 \ \Omega$
losses $= 98^2 \times 0.2 = \mathbf{1921 \ W}$

(iii)   Power at the load = Input power to the cable – cable losses
$= 20\,000 — 1921 = \mathbf{18\,079 \ W}$

(b) Again power = $VI \cos \phi$ watts

$$I = \frac{200\,000}{240 \times 0.85} = 980 \text{ A}$$

The cable losses are to be the same as in (a) (ii) above, i.e. 1921 W

$980^2 \times R = 1921$

$$R = \frac{1921}{980^2} = \mathbf{0.002 \ \Omega}$$

Therefore each core must have a resistance of 0.001 Ω.

The resistance of a cable is inversely proportional to its cross-sectional area. For example, doubling the cross-sectional area halves the resistance.

The total cable resistance is to be reduced from 0.2 Ω to 0.002 Ω i.e. by a factor of 100. The cross-sectional area will therefore need to be 100 times that in (a), i.e. $100 \times 0.35 = 35$ cm^2

(c) The losses with 200 kW input to the cable in (a) = $980^2 \times 0.2 = 192\,100$ W. The voltage at the load would be very small, almost all the power input being absorbed by the cable which would become very hot. This illustrates the point that to transmit large powers at low voltages requires very large conductors.

Problem 2 Discuss the changes in transmission costs which occur as voltage levels are raised.

As voltage levels are increased, the conductor cross-sectional area for a given power may be reduced. This means that the cost of conductor material, generally copper for underground cables and aluminium for overhead lines, is reduced. Alternatively for given sizes of conductor much more power may be transmitted at high voltages hence reducing the effective cost of transmission per kW transmitted. The same arguments apply to the cost of supporting towers or poles since these do not have to be so strong to carry smaller conductors at extra-high voltage.

However, as the voltage levels are raised the cost of cable insulation is increased, it becomes thicker and oil is used which must often be maintained under pressure which involves the use of more plant. Very expensive cable terminations or sealing ends must be used to contain the pressure.

Switchgear for use at high voltages becomes more complicated, bulkier and hence more expensive than that for use at medium or low voltages. High pressure air, or oil is used to extinguish the arc produced when a circuit is opened. In addition all the electrical parts must be kept well away from earth and these clearances are much greater when high voltages are used.

The provision of land must also be considered. The additional bulk of extra-high voltage gear means that substations may occupy many thousands of square metres.

To increase and decrease voltages transformers are required and these again add to land area and cost. They contain oil, the condition of which must be monitored and which must be filtered or replaced at intervals.

Problem 3 Compare the use of steel lattice towers and wooden poles for supporting overhead lines in an electricity transmission system.

Overhead line supports must be capable of supporting the line without movement in the ground when both the line and supports are carrying specified wind and ice loadings. Safety factors must be allowed and under the worst *probable* conditions the line must not approach collapse conditions.

Occasionally under very adverse conditions a line will break or a support will give way. In these cases the line must be reconstructed but this is cheaper than erecting the whole line with such strength as to be safe in weather conditions which might occur only once in a century.

Wood supports are of red fir impregnated with creosote and may be in the form of single poles or two poles made into A or H. Wood poles carry either suspension or pin-type insulators. In the UK they are used for circuits up to 33 kV.

Towers are made from mild-steel angle section and may easily be fabricated up to almost any height using extra bottom sections or trestles. The four legs of a lattice tower lie on the corners of a 2–8 m square so that it is a very stable structure especially when the legs are fixed to steel reinforcing bars set into a concrete base. Some large towers may have 40 tonnes of concrete forming the base. A single wooden pole however is less stable and if situated where a line changes direction will almost certainly have to be guyed.

C. FURTHER PROBLEMS ON TRANSMISSION AND DISTRIBUTION

(a) SHORT ANSWER PROBLEMS

1 What is the function of the 400 kV system in the UK?

2 What is the function of the 132 kV and 33 kV systems in the UK?

3 What type of insulation is used in extra-high voltage underground cables?

4 Define the terms: (i) circuit breaker; (ii) isolator; (iii) switch.

5. Name three types of prime mover used to drive electricity generators.

6 Give three typical ratings of synchronous generators used in the UK.

7 Why is generation not carried out at the level of the major transmission voltage?

8 When a circuit breaker interrupts a circuit an arc is drawn. How is this extinguished in e.h.v. circuit breakers?

9 Why has the aluminium conductor, used in overhead transmission systems, a steel core?

10 What is meant by the term 'Safety Factor' as applied to overhead line supports?

11 Why must the route of an underground cable be kept clear?

12 In the UK domestic premises are supplied at 240 V whilst in other parts of the world 110 V systems are used. What advantages and disadvantages are there to using a lower voltage system?

13 What advantages are there to using steel lattice towers as compared with wooden poles in connection with a transmission system?

14 What is the upper voltage limit usually applicable to wooden poles in the UK?

15 What difference in design would you expect to find in an outdoor circuit breaker as compared with one situated indoors?

16 What is the function of the stone-filled pit under an oil-filled transformer?

17 Why are large indoor substations often sectioned?

18 What is the function of a tap-changer?

19 How is ventilation achieved in a small indoor substation?

(b) MULTI-CHOICE PROBLEMS (answers on page 213)

1 The conduction (copper) losses in a particular cable are 150 kW when the load transmitted is 200 MW. A load of 400 MW is transmitted through a second cable of the same material, each core having twice the cross sectional area of those on the first cable. The conduction losses in the second cable will be:
(i) 150 kW;   (ii) 300 kW;   (iii) 600 kW;   (iv) 1200 kW?

2 Most extra-high-voltage transformers for use in power-supply systems have windings insulated using:
(i) PVC;   (ii) Rubber;   (iii) Paper;   (iv) PTFE?

3 Transmission voltages are made as high as practicable in order to:
(i)   minimise the size of generators;
(ii)   reduce the cross sectional area of overhead transmission lines;
(iii) allow circuit breakers to be more efficient since they will be handling smaller currents;
(iv)   minimise the cost of underground cables in the system.

4 Overhead lines are often made of aluminium and employ a central steel core. The steel core is present:
(i)   To increase the strength of the conductor;
(ii)   To increase the overall conductivity of the conductor since the resistance of steel is less than that of aluminium,
(iii) To increase the circuit inductance;
(iv)   To assist in the process of joining two sections of conductor together since it is difficult to weld aluminium.

5 (a) and (b) following are two definitions of electrical switchgear. Couple these with the correct names from (i) to (iv) beneath.
(a)   A device for making a circuit dead which is not carrying current at the time but which may be used for energising a circuit under any conditions.
(b)   A device for making and breaking a circuit under all circumstances.
(i) Circuit breaker, (ii) Switch, (iii) Isolator, (iv) Contactor.

6 The stone-filled pit under an oil-filled transformer is provided:
(i)   Since it is cheaper than a solid concrete floor;
(ii)   It facilitates cable laying and renewal when required;
(iii) It assists in fire prevention and fire fighting.

7 A transformer tap changer allows:
(i)   The oil to be changed periodically;
(ii)   the output voltage to be maintained at the correct value;
(iii) the input voltage to be changed;
(iv)   the input power factor to be changed.

(c) CONVENTIONAL PROBLEMS

1 Discuss the effect of voltage level on the cost of distribution and distribution of electrical energy. Clearly differentiate between capital and running costs.

2 Make a single-line diagram showing a section of transmission and distribution system. Indicate typical generation, transmission and distribution voltages. Explain why transmission is carried out at extra-high voltage whilst distribution is carried out at reduced voltages.

3 Discuss the various merits of using overhead lines or underground cables for (a) major transmission; (b) local distribution.

4 Draw suitable sketches of a typical indoor distribution substation showing: (i) the transformer; (ii) h.v. switchgear; (iii) l.v. switchgear; (iv) provision for the prevention of the spread of fire and (v) the ventilation arrangements.

5 (a) A two-core cable, 100 m in length supplies a current of 85 A to a load which operates at unity power factor. The resistance of each core of the cable is $0.06\ \Omega$. If the voltage at the load is to be 240 V, determine: (i) the load power; (ii) the voltage required at the sending end; (iii) the cable losses.

(b) What would be the value of the load voltage if the sending end voltage in (a) (ii) were maintained and a new cable was used which had a core area 1.5 times that in (a)? (Assume the load current is unchanged.)

(a) (i) 20 400 W; (ii) 250.2 V; (iii) 867 W; (b) 243.4 V.

6 Although desirable on environmental grounds, major transmission is not carried out in the main using underground cables. Discuss the reasons for this.

2 L.V. distribution, earthing and simple circuit protection

A. SUMMARY OF FORMULAE AND DEFINITIONS ASSOCIATED WITH L.V. DISTRIBUTION, EARTHING AND SIMPLE CIRCUIT PROTECTION

1   *Fig 1* shows a schematic diagram of a **generator,** its windings physically displaced from each other by 120° and with one end of each winding connected to earth. Because of its appearance this is known as the star connection. The supply lines are labelled red, yellow and blue respectively and the wire connected to the common or star point is known as the neutral. The voltage from any output line to the neutral is called the phase voltage and the voltage between any pair of supply lines is called the line voltage. Grid voltages quoted at 400 kV, 132 kV, 33 kV etc. are all line values. The line voltage in a three-phase star-connected system = $\sqrt{3}$ × the phase voltage.

   Single phase loads are connected between any line and the neutral wire and this is the normal situation in the home.

2   **Load balancing**   Consider the case of the three single phase loads shown in *Fig 1*. Let each of the loads draw the same value of current and operate at the same power factor. *Fig 2* shows the three phase voltages R, Y and B, and three current phasors each of the same magnitude which lag their respective voltages by an angle $\phi°$. All these currents flow from their respective lines to the neutral. The neutral current must therefore be the sum of these three currents. *Fig 3* shows the phasor addition and it can be seen that the resulting neutral current is zero. There is no current flowing in the neutral wire back to the supply generator when the loads are balanced.

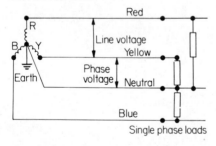

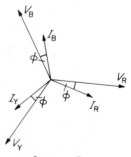

Fig 1 (above)

Fig 2 (right, above)

Fig 3 (right, below)

It s desirable that over the country as a whole the loads shall be balanced over the phases since this minimises the cable losses and voltage drops in the supply lines. (No current in the neutral results in the I^2R loss in this wire being zero.) In addition there are problems in the generators themselves when the three phases are not equally loaded.

3 **General arrangement of an industrial installation** A substation for a factory is usually situated on the factory premises. In *Fig 4* a substation as in *Fig 3* (chapter 1) is shown supplying a number of loads. Metering of energy consumption and the maximum demand made by the factory on the supply system is carried out using meters fed by current transformers fitted in or adjacent to the main low voltage circuit breaker or fuses. At 415/240 V the voltage elements of meters are fed directly.

The main fuseboard is equipped with switches incorporating fuses rated at 400 A, but the actual size will depend on the rating of the equipment used in the factory. Some large single loads may be fed directly from this board, the control being achieved by local contactors. There will be several circuits feeding further fuseboards in particular workshops. These will feed individual loads or further fuseboards for lighting, heating, small tools and processes.

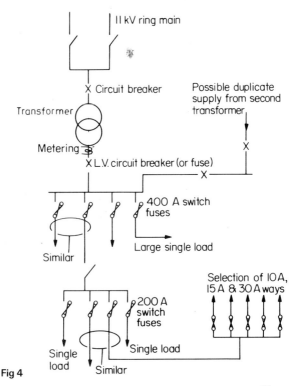

Fig 4

4 **Earthing** Both the Institution of Electrical Engineers' Regulations and the Electricity Supply Regulations require one point on a transformer-fed system to be earthed. In the UK, the supply transformer neutral is connected to a plate or rod buried in the earth. Such a connection provides a return path for leakage currents so facilitating clearance of faulty circuits (see also *Problem 1*).

5 **Protective Multiple Earthing** (PME) This system involves earthing the neutral wire on the distribution network at a number of points instead of just at the supply transformer. In addition, consumers have their earth and neutral terminals connected together on their premises and these in turn are bonded to the gas and water systems to prevent the potential of these services rising above that of earth. The advantages claimed for this system are:

(a) Four core cable need not be used. Three core cable with armouring or metallic sheathing which becomes the neutral/earth conductor is cheaper and there is a weight saving.

(b) If the neutral/earth conductor becomes discontinuous at any point, say at a joint in the cable, current can continue to flow between the disconnected sections through the ground because of the regular earthing points.

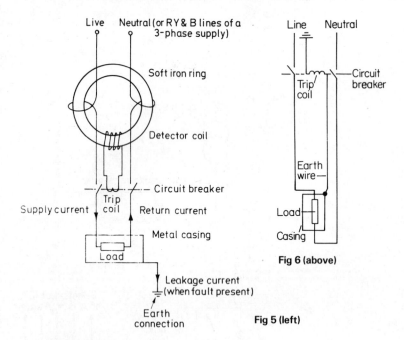

Fig 6 (above)

Fig 5 (left)

6 **Earth leakage circuit breakers**

(a) *Current balance* The live and neutral wires pass once or twice round the soft-iron core in opposite directions as shown in *Fig 5*. When the currents in live and neutral wires have the same value the net magnetomotive-force in the

14

ring is zero and no magnetic flux links with the detector coil. When the two currents differ as they will do if an earth fault is present at the load then there will be resultant magnetisation of the ring and a voltage will be induced in the detector coil. This will drive a current in the trip coil and the circuit breaker will open. An out-of-balance current of only a few milli-amperes will cause operation.

(b) *Voltage operated*   If a fault develops in the load such that the potential of the casing rises above that of earth, a current flows in the earth wire through the trip coil and the circuit breaker opens. Less than 40 V is required for operation (see *Fig 6*).

7 **The H.B.C. fuse**   The High Breaking Capacity or High Rupturing Capacity fuse comprises a ceramic tube filled with fine sand, with plated brass end caps of various shapes suitable for clipping or bolting into its fuse carrier. The fusible

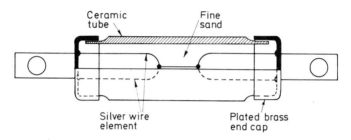

Part sectioned view of an H.B.C. fuse

Fig 7

element is made from silver and may consist of one strand or several strands in parallel. A three-strand element is shown in *Fig 7*.

The current rating marked on the fuse is that value of current which it can carry continously without melting or in any way deteriorating. The rated minimum fusing current is the least value of current which will cause the element to melt.

$$\text{Fusing factor} = \frac{\text{Rated minimum fusing current}}{\text{Current rating}}$$

Fuses may be used to provide either close or coarse protection. With close protection the fuse operates when the circuit current is marginally above the current rating whilst with coarse protection a larger overload is permitted. H.B.C. fuses are grouped into classes:

Class P.   Fusing factor 1.25 or less. These provide protection for a circuit in which virtually no overload is permitted.

Class Q.   Group 1. Fusing factor between 1.25 and 1.5.
Group 2. Fusing factor between 1.5 and 1.75.
These provide protection for circuits which can withstand some degree of overloading.

Class R. Fusing factors between 1.75 and 2.5. Generally these fuses are used as back-up protection for some other form of protection which should normally operate first.

8 **The thermal relay** Current flowing either through a heating coil wound on a bi-metal strip or through the strip itself causes it to be distorted upwards so lifting the cross beam. This occurs becauses brass, when heated, expands more than iron or Invar. Lifting the beam releases a trip lever which either mechanically

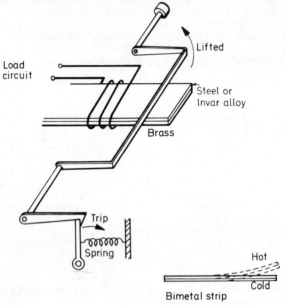

Fig 8

unlatches the associated contactor or closes a pair of tripping contacts which gives an electrical supply to a tripping coil (see *Fig 8*).

9 **The instantaneous relay** The load current or the output from a current transformer passes through the coil casing the iron core to become magnetised. At a certain value of current the magnetic field is strong enough to lift the armature so closing the tripping contacts (*Fig 9*).

10 **The magnetic relay** Current flowing in the coil of the relay shown in *Fig 10* attracts an iron plunger upwards against the force of gravity. When a pre-determined value of current is reached, tripping occurs by lifting the beam as in the thermal relay. For the first few millimetres of travel the piston moves slowly as it is pulled through the oil, the valves being automatically closed by this action. As the piston moves into the wide section of the dashpot the speed increases due to less drag and the trip bar is pushed upwards.

The dashpot prevents instantaneous operation during very short periods of overcurrent. The valves automatically open as the plunger falls allowing the relay to reset very rapidly.

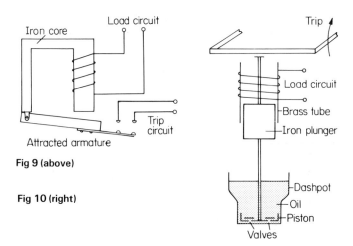

Iron core

Load circuit

Trip

Attracted armature

Fig 9 (above)

Fig 10 (right)

Load circuit

Brass tube

Iron plunger

Dashpot

Oil

Piston

Valves

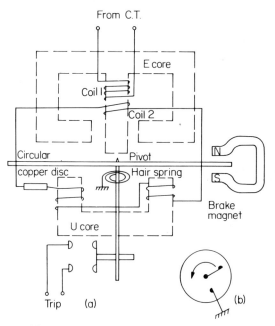

From C.T.

E core

Coil 1

Coil 2

Circular
copper disc

Pivot

Hair spring

Brake
magnet

U core

Trip   (a)

(b)

Fig 11

11 **The induction overcurrent relay**   The output from a current transformer is fed
to coil 1 (*Fig 11*) on the laminated E core. This current sets up a magnetic flux in
the core, across the air gap in which a circular copper disc is situated, and into
the bottom U core which is also of laminated construction. Coils 1 and 2 make
up a transformer and the alternating flux set up by coil 1 induces a voltage in coil
2 which is 90° out of phase with the flux. (See also chapter 5 for the phasor
diagram of the transformer). This voltage drives a current through the two coils
on the U core setting up a magnetic flux which crosses the gap into the top E
core.

There are now two fluxes linking with the copper disc, both alternating and
differing in phase. Under these conditions a torque is set up in the disc which
would cause it to rotate if it were free to do so. The device is in fact a small
inductor motor. The disc is restrained by hairsprings and at a predetermined
current the torque produced by the disc overcomes that of the springs and the
disc turns so closing a tripping circuit.

12 **Operating characteristics of fuses and relays**   *Fig 12* shows typical
characteristics of H.B.C. fuses, induction relays, thermal and magnetic relays.

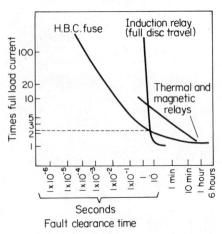

There are many different types
designed for specific purposes
so that it is only possible to
make general comments.
Assuming that the fuse rating
and full load currents for the
relays are the same it may be
seen from the curves that for
currents greater than 2.5 times
the full-load value the fuse will
clear a fault faster than any of
the relays. For currents below
this the induction relay is
faster.

Fig 12

There is a similar cross-over point between the induction relay and the other
relays in the region of ten times the full load current. The induction relay cannot
operate much faster above this level of current due to magnetic saturation effects
in the relay and in the current transformer which supplies it. The characteristic is
very nearly vertical above this level of current.

13 **Radial distribution systems**   A radial system for the distribution of electrical
energy is shown in *Fig 13*. A substation supplies consumers (C) through radial
distributors which fan out from the substation. A fuse or circuit breaker protects
each distributor. Some distributors have subsidiary fuses somewhere along their
length; these fuses are of a lower rating than the main fuse. In the event of a fault

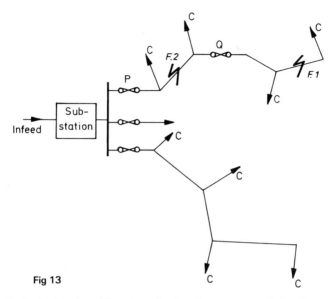

Fig 13

on the feeder the relevant fuse clears, leaving all consumers on that section without a supply. In *Fig 13* a fault F.1 would cause fuse (Q) to clear leaving two consumers without a supply. A fault F.2 would cause fuse (P) to clear leaving all four consumers without a supply. Since there is no alternative method of supply to these consumers, repairs to the line have to be carried out before the consumers can be reconnected.

The consumer at the end of each distributor suffers voltage reductions as the load on the distributor increases. In order to minimise these, the cross-sectional area of the conductors must be large. The radial distribution system is therefore expensive to install and offers poor security of supply.

14 **The ring system** The addition of further substations feeding the other ends of the radial feeders and the interconnection of these substations converts the system into a ring. This substantially reduces the voltage drops along the distributors and enables savings in conductor cross sectional areas and cost to be made. In *Fig 14* a fault F.1 would result in fuses (Q) and (R) clearing leaving two consumers without a supply. A fault F.2 would result in fuses (P) and (Q) clearing again only two consumers losing their supply.

At 11 kV a ring system employing isolators at each load point enables greater security of supply to be achieved. In *Fig 15* a fault F.1 can be cleared by opening

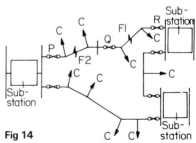

Fig 14

19

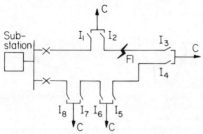

I = isolator (all isolators normally closed)   **Fig 15**

isolators I_2 and I_3 and no other section need be disconnected provided that a second fault does not occur. Meanwhile repairs can be carried out.

15 Distributor calculations

(i) Radial feeder

Fig 16 (a) shows two loads B and C respectively being fed from a power source at A. Single line representation is generally used and this is shown in *Fig 16 (b)*.

$R_1 = (R_a + R_b)$ i.e. R_1 = the sum of go and return resistances to the load at B.

Similarly $R_2 = (R_c + R_d)$.

In *Fig 16 (b)*,

Current in section BC = I_2A

Current in section AB = $(I_1 + I_2)$A (Apply Kirchhoff's first law at point B. This states that the algebraic sum of the currents at a point is zero)

Voltage V_1 = Supply voltage − volt drop to B = $V_s - (I_1 + I_2)R_1$ volts

Voltage V_2 = Voltage V_1 − volt drop from B to C = $V_1 - I_2R_2$ volts

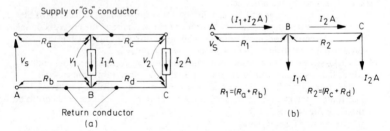

Fig 16

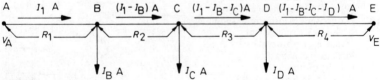

Fig 17

20

Power loss in section AB $= (I_1 + I_2)^2 R_1$ watts
Power loss in section BC $= (I_2)^2 R_2$ watts
Load power at B $= V_1 I_1$ watts   Load power at C $= V_2 I_2$ watts
Input power $= V_s(I_1 + I_2)$ watts

The efficiency of the system $= \dfrac{\text{Total load power}}{\text{Total input power}} = \dfrac{V_1 I_1 + V_2 I_2}{V_s(I_1 + I_2)}$ per unit.

(*See Problem 3*)

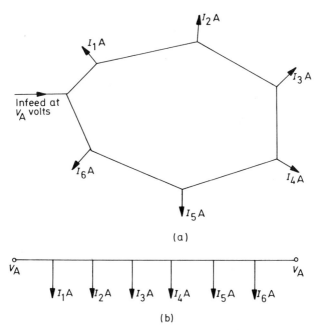

Fig 18

(ii) Feeder fed at both ends
R_1, R_2, R_3 and R_4 are the sums of the go and return resistances for the relevant sections of the feeder shown in *Figure 17*. The feeder is fed at V_A volts at A and V_E volts at E.

Let the current entering at end A be I_1 A. Then the current in section AB $= I_1$ A. After feeding load B with I_B A, the current in section BC will be $(I_1 - I_B)$ A. Section CD carries $(I_1 - I_B - I_C)$ A and section DE carries $(I_1 - I_B - I_C - I_D)$ A. The voltage V_E = Voltage V_A – all volt drops along the line.
$V_E = V_A - I_1 R_1 - (I_1 - I_B)R_2 - (I_1 - I_B - I_C)R_3 -$
$(\mathbf{I}_1 - I_B - I_C - I_D)R_4$
Using this equation the value of I_1 and hence the currents in each of the sections may be found. The load voltages and powers and hence efficiency may be determined as for the radial reeder. (*See Problem 4*)

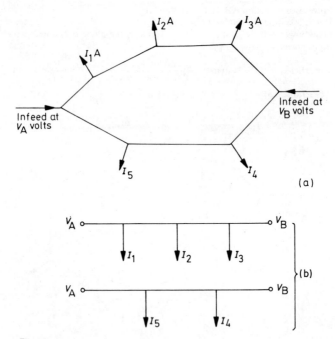

Fig 19

(iii)The ring main

(a) Fed at one point

Calculations on the ring main shown in *Fig 18* are best performed by considering it to be a feeder fed at both ends at the same voltage. It should be redrawn as in *Fig 18 (b)* when the approach is identical to that in (ii) above.

(b) Fed at two points

The ring main fed at two points should be considered as two feeders as shown in *Fig 19 (b)* when the calculations are again as in (ii) above. (See *Problem 5*).

B. WORKED PROBLEMS ON L.V. DISTRIBUTION, EARTHING AND SIMPLE CIRCUIT PROTECTION

Problem 1 Explain why British practice in the distribution of electrical energy is to earth the supply transformer neutral and the metal casings of electrical equipment.

Supply transformer secondaries are star connected and the star point is earthed as shown in *Fig 20*. If the live conductor or part of the winding of a piece of equipment comes into contact with the metal casing of the equipment this becomes potentially dangerous. A person standing on the ground and touching the casing will receive an electric shock due to the potential difference between that of the casing and earth. It only requires a few milli-amperes on a route which includes the chest cavity to cause death. Earthing the casing allows a current to flow through the earth connection back to the supply transformer neutral.

The circuit may be protected by either a fuse or a current balance earth-leakage circuit breaker. In the case of the fuse, if the impedance of the earth path

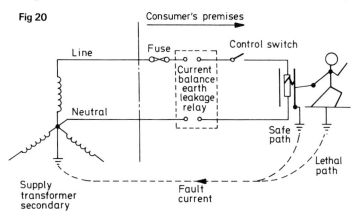

Fig 20

is small, sufficient current will flow to melt the fuse in the supply line. A high earth loop impedance is dangerous since the metal casing will remain connected to the supply if insufficient current flows to cause clearance. The earth leakage circuit breaker operates with a very small earth leakage current so that high earth loop impedance is not so important.

In certain situations equipment is run without an earth wire. In this case the equipment must be completely enclosed in a layer of insulating material or so disposed in an insulated box that it is impossible for the box to become alive or for a person to push a finger in and so touch live metal.

Problem 2 Discuss the merits of electrical protection using fuses as compared with relays and contactors or circuit breakers with regard to (i) personnel; (ii) circuits and equipment.

A fuse operates when the protected circuit carries more current than it should. A fuse is an overload device. In the event of an earth fault on a circuit, if the earth loop impedance is small, sufficient current flows to melt the fuse. (See also *Problem 1*).

Should a person come into contact with a live conductor, so creating an earth fault through himself, the resulting shock may well be fatal but the current flowing would almost certainly be too small to clear the fuse. The current balance earth-leakage circuit breaker overcomes this problem since it will operate with only a few milli-amperes of leakage current regardless of the value of current in the main circuit.

Where overcurrents arise due to overloading of circuits or short-circuit faults the protection has to prevent overheating and mechanical damage due to the forces produced between current-carrying conductors. Overcurrents which are transient, as created by motors starting for example, should not cause operation of the protection and thermal or magnetic relays associated with contractors are suitable since they have inverse-time characteristics. Transmission lines may be protected using induction-type relays controlling circuit breakers. When operation does occur, the circuit breaker or contactor can be reclosed after checking the circuit. Fuses have to be replaced which can be very expensive.

In the event of a short circuit fault the current will be very many times greater than normal and H.B.C. fuses, where fitted, are very much faster acting than any relay under this condition. For this reason fuses and relays are fitted to many circuits, the relays taking care of overcurrents up to two or three times normal, the fuses acting faster than the relays for currents in excess of these values.

Problem 3 The details of a radial feeder are shown in *Fig 21*. Calculate: (a) the load voltages; (b) the power lost in the cable; (c) the power developed by each load; (d) the efficiency of the system.

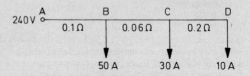

Fig 21   Resistances are go and return (loop) valves

Kirchhoff's first law is applied to each load point.
The current in section CD of the feeder = 10 A
Section BC carries load currents C and D = 30 + 10 = 40 A
Section AB carries the total load currents = 40 + 50 = 90 A
The volt drop between A and B = $I_{AB} \times R_{AB} = 90 \times 0.1 = 9$ V
Voltage at load B = 240 - 9 = 231 V
Power loss in section AB = $(I_{AB})^2 R_{AB} = 90^2 \times 0.1 = 810$ W
Power developed by load B = $V_B I_B = 231 \times 50 = 11550$ W

Repeating for section BC gives:
Voltage drop from B to C = $40 \times 0.06 = 2.4$ V
Voltage at load C = 231 - 2.4 = 228.6 V
Power loss in section BC = $40^2 \times 0.06 = 96$ W
Power developed by load C = $228.6 \times 30 = 6858$ W

Repeating for section CD gives:

Voltage drop from C to D = $10 \times 0.2 = 2$ V

Voltage at load D = $228.6 - 2 = 226.6$ V

Power loss in section CD = $10^2 \times 0.2 = 20$ W

Power developed by load D = $226.6 \times 10 = 2266$ W

Total load powers = $2266 + 6858 + 11550 = 20674$ W

Total losses = $20 + 96 + 810 = 926$ W

$$\text{Efficiency} = \frac{\text{Power in loads}}{\text{Total power input}} = \frac{20674}{20674 + 926} \text{ or } \frac{20674}{240 \times 90}$$

$$= \textbf{0.957 p.u.}$$

Problem 4   Re-calculate the quantities (a) to (d) in *Problem 3* for the feeder reinforced from a supply point at D as shown in *Fig 22*.

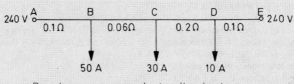

Fig 22   Resistances are go and return (loop) valves

In this case we firstly have to determine how much current is supplied from each end of the feeder. Consider a current I_1 to be entering at the left hand end, as shown in *Fig 23*.

The current in the section AB = I_1 A and the volt drop between A and B = $I_1 \times 0.1$ V. At point B a load current of 50 A is supplied so that the current flowing on in section BC must be $(I_1 - 50)$ A. The volt drop from B to C = $(I_1 - 50) \times 0.06$ V. Similarly the current in section CD = $(I_1 - 50) - 30 = (I_1 - 80)$ A and the volt drop from C to D = $(I_1 - 80) \times 0.2$ V In section DE the current = $(I_1 - 90)$ A and the volt drop from D to E = $(I_1 - 90) \times 0.1$ V.

The voltage at A − (all the volt drops along the line) = voltage at E.

The voltage at E is given as 240 V.

Therefore:

$$240 - I_1 \times 0.1 - (I_1 - 50) \times 0.06 - (I_1 - 80) \times 0.2 - (I_1 - 90) \times 0.1 = 240$$

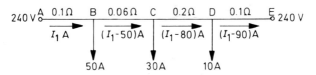

Fig 23

Multiplying out the brackets gives:
$240 - 0.1I_1 - 0.06I_1 + 3 - 0.2I_1 + 16 - 0.1I_1 + 9 = 240$ V
Transposing gives:
$240 - 240 + 3 + 16 + 9 = 0.1I_1 + 0.06I_1 + 0.2I_1 + 0.1I_1$
$$28 = 0.46I_1. \ I_1 = \mathbf{60.86\ A}$$
Fig 23 may be redrawn showing the actual currents in each section. This is shown in *Fig 24*.

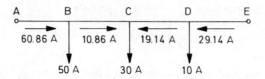

Fig 24

In section BC we have $(60.86 - 50) = 10.86$ A
In section CD we have $(60.68 - 80) = -19.14$ A. The negative sign indicates a reversal of current direction from that shown in *Fig 23* and this is seen to be logical since the 30 A load receives 10.86 A from end A and 19.14 A from end E.
Voltage at B = $240 - 60.86 \times 0.1 = 233.9$ V.
Power loss in section AB = $60.86^2 \times 0.1 = 370.4$ W.
Power in the load B = $233.9 \times 50 = 11695$ W.
Voltage at C = $233.9 - 10.86 \times 0.06 = 233.25$ V.
Power loss in section BC = $10.86^2 \times 0.06 = 7.08$ W.
Power in load C = $233.25 \times 30 = 6997.5$ W.
Voltage at load D. Since the current flows from D to C, the voltage at D must be greater than that at C. The minimum voltage on this distributor is at load C and currents flow from both ends to this point.
Voltage at D = $233.25 + 19.14 \times 0.2 = 237.08$ V.
Power loss in section CD $- 19.14^2 \times 0.2 = 73.27$ W.
Power in load D = $237.08 \times 10 = 2370.8$ W.
We know that the voltage at E = 240 V. Let us check the calculations by adding the voltage drop from E to D to the voltage at D.
$237.08 + 29.14 \times 0.1 = 240$ V
Power loss in section DE = $29.14^2 \times 0.1 = 84.91$ W.
Total load powers = $11695 + 6997.5 + 2370.8 = 21063.3$ W.
Total losses = $370.4 + 7.08 + 73.27 + 84.91 = 535.66$ W

Efficiency $= \dfrac{21063.3}{21063.3 + 535.66} = \mathbf{0.975\ p.u.}$

Problem 5 For the ring main shown in *Fig 25* determine the value of current in each section and the minimum load voltage

Fig 25 is redrawn putting in the go and return resistances. A 100 m length of two core cable has a resistance of $2 \times 0.05 = 0.1\ \Omega$. A ring may be considered as a feeder fed at both ends at the same voltage as shown in *Fig 26*.

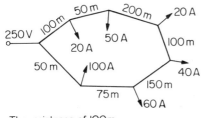

The resistance of 100m
of single conductor = 0.05 Ω

Fig 25

Starting with I_1 A entering at the left hand end.
$250 - 0.1I_1 - 0.05(I_1 - 20) - 0.2(I_1 - 70) - 0.1(I_1 - 90) - 0.15(I_1 - 130) - 0.075(I_1 - 190)$
$- 0.05(I_1 - 290) = 250$
$250 - 0.1I_1 - 0.05I_1 + 1 - 0.2I_1 + 14 - 0.1I_1 + 9 - 0.15I_1 + 19.5 - 0.075I_1 + 14.25$
$- 0.05I_1 + 14.5 = 250$
$72.25 = 0.725I_1$. $I_1 = \textbf{99.66 A}$

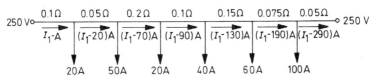

Fig 26

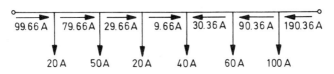

Fig 27

The currents in each section are shown in *Fig 27*. The minimum voltage occurs at
the 40 A load since current flows towards it from both ends.
Starting from the left:
$250 - 99.66 \times 0.1 - 79.66 \times 0.05 - 29.66 \times 0.2 - 9.66 \times 0.1 = \textbf{229.15 V}$
or starting from the right:
$250 - 190.34 \times 0.05 - 90.34 \times 0.075 - 30.34 \times 0.15 = \textbf{229.16 V}$

C. FURTHER PROBLEMS ON L.V. DISTRIBUTION, EARTHING AND SIMPLE CIRCUIT PROTECTION

(a) SHORT ANSWER PROBLEMS

1 Why is a ring main used for power distribution wherever possible?

2 How are faults detected on overhead lines?

3 Why have accurate records to be kept of the route of an underground cable?

4 What is meant by the term 'Fault level'? Why is its value important?

5 What is 'Protective-multiple earthing'?

6 What is 'Current-balance earth leakage protection'?

7 Draw a simple sketch showing the construction of an H.B.C. fuse.

8 Give three advantages of the H.B.C. fuse as compared with the rewireable type.

9 Define the term 'Fusing factor' as applied to an H.B.C. fuse.

10 Why do we often find an instantaneous relay fitted in series with a thermal type to protect a circuit?

11 How does a magnetic type of overcurrent relay discriminate between a short-term overcurrent and a prolonged overload?

12 A three-phase distribution system has a line voltage of 11 kV. What is the value of the phase voltage (one line to neutral)?

13 The domestic voltage in the UK is generally 240 V. What is the value of the line voltage of the three-phase system from which it is derived?

14 Why is care taken to balance the loads across the phases of a three-phase system?

15 What is the name given to an electrically operated switch used to control motors?

16 What might be the outcome of a high earth loop impedance on an installation?

17 Why are gas and water pipes bonded to the supply neutral in a P.M.E. system?

18 A fuse with a fusing factor of 1.25 has a rating of 30 A. What is the value of the minimum fusing current?

19 Why might an H.B.C. fuse be used to back up relay protection?

(b) MULTI-CHOICE PROBLEMS (answers on page 213)

1 A three-phase, four-wire system has a line voltage of 66 000 V. Its phase voltage is:
(i) 66 000 V; (ii) 38 105 V; (iii) 114 315 V.

2 A two-wire system carries 50 A to a single load. The resistance of each wire is 0.05 Ω. The total conduction loss in the system is:
(i) 2.5 W; (ii) 125 W; (iii) 250 W.

3 Each phase of a 440 V, three-phase, star connected load carries 20 A at 0.7 power factor lagging. The current returning to the supply transformer neutral is
(i) 87.5 A; (ii) 60 A; (iii) zero; (iv) 28.6 A.

4 A three-phase, four-wire system supplies a three-phase star connected load. The load is balanced and each phase draws 25 A. The resistance of each wire is 0.1 Ω. The total system losses are:
(i) 62.5 W; (ii) 187.5 W; (iii) 375 W.

5 Where motors are controlled by contactors, H.B.C. fuses are normally provided in series with the contactor because:
(i) the fuse will normally operate first on motor overload and so save the contactor from undue wear;
(ii) the contactor will operate too slowly on a short circuit fault at the motor;
(iii) the fuse will protect the main circuit breaker from damage in the event of a fault in the contactor.

6 Current balance earth leakage protection of a single-phase circuit operates:
(i) at a much lower current;
(ii) at a slightly higher current; than a suitably rated H.B.C. fuse. It operates when:
(iii) the live and neutral currents differ slightly;
(iv) a current is detected in the earth connection; (v) a person or earthed substance touches the neutral wire.
Select (i) or (ii) together with (iii), (iv) or (v) to make a correct statement.

7 Circuit protection may be accomplished by using:
(i) H.B.C. fuses;   (iv) magnetic relays;
(ii) instantaneous relays;   (v) induction relays.
(iii) thermal relays;
Which *one* of these pieces of equipment does *not* have inverse-time characteristics?

8 The supply to electrical loads with a minimum of cable losses and the greatest security is best achieved using:
(i) a radial system; (ii) a feeder fed at both ends; (iii) a ring system.

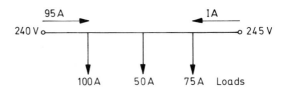

Fig 28

9 *Fig 28* shows a two-wire feeder fed at both ends at the voltages specified. The load at which the voltage has the least value is:
(i) 50 A load; (ii) 100 A load; (iii) 75 A load.
The value of the current *I*, entering at the right hand end is:
(iv) 55 A; (v) 130 A; (vi) 125 A.

10 A fuse has a fusing factor of 1.5 and a rating of 15 A. It will melt when a current of:
(i) 10 A; (ii) 15 A; (iii) 22.5 A; (iv) 30 A passes through it.

(c) CONVENTIONAL PROBLEMS

1 Explain why it is desirable to balance the loads across the phases of a three-phase distribution system.

2 Draw a connection diagram showing a supply transformer connected to a load. Include any protective devices you consider necessary and explain how a consumer is protected against the effects of an earth fault on his apparatus.

3 Explain what is meant by the term 'Protective Multiple Earthing'. What advantages are claimed for this system over that in which the supply transformer is earthed at one point only. Why are the other house services bonded together and connected to the supply earth?

4 Describe the operation of: (i) a thermal relay; (ii) a magnetic relay; (iii) an induction overcurrent relay; (iv) an H.B.C. fuse. Which of these devices would operate most quickly in the event of a short circuit fault on the system which they are protecting?

5 Calculate the currents in each section of the networks shown. Hence determine (i) the potential difference at each load; (ii) the overall efficiency of the system.
(a) *Fig 29*; (b) *Fig 30*; (c) *Fig 31*; (d) *Fig 32*; (e) *Fig 33*.
(a) $I_{AB} = 75$ A, $I_{BC} = 25$ A, $V_B = 246.25$ V, $V_C = 243.75$ V. Efficiency 0.98 p.u.
(b) $I_{AB} = 88.46$ A, $I_{BC} = 38.46$ A, $I_{DC} = 61.54$ A, $I_{ED} = 86.54$ A, $V_B = 231.15$ V, $V_C = 228.27$ V, $V_D = 231.35$ V. Efficiency = 0.96 p.u.
(c) $I_{AB} = 47.86$ A, $I_{BC} = 37.86$ A, $I_{DC} = 62.14$ A, $I_{ED} = 132.14$ A, $I_{EF} = 157.14$ A, $V_B = 236.17$ V, $V_C = 231.63$ V, $V_D = 241.56$ V, $V_E = 246.85$.
Effciency = 0.96 p.u.

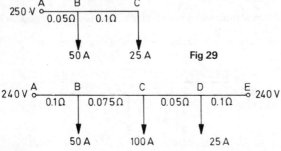

Fig 29

Fig 30

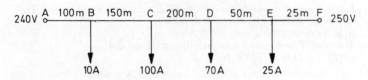

Fig 31   Resistance of 100m of cable (both conductors) = 0.08Ω

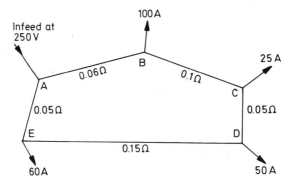

Fig 32   Resistances go and return

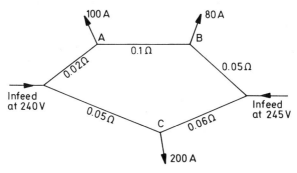

Fig 33   Resistances go and return

(d) $I_{AB} = 132.32$ A, $I_{BC} = 32.32$ A, $I_{CD} = 7.32$ A, $I_{ED} = 42.68$ A, $I_{AE} = 102.68$ A, $V_B = 242.06$ V, $V_C = 238.83$, $V_D = 238.46$ V, $V_E = 244.87$ V.
Efficiency $= 0.97$ p.u.

(e) 240 V infeed to A, $I = 82.35$ A. $I_{AB} = 17.65$ A. 245 V infeed to B $= 97.65$ A.
240 V infeed to C, $I = 63.63$ A. 245 V infeed to C $= 137.37$ A.
$V_A = 238.35$ V, $V_B = 240.12$ V, $V_C = 236.82$ V.
Total load powers $= 90408.6$ W. Efficiency $= 0.98$ p.u.

6   A radial feeder ABCD is fed at 200 V. The loads are 20 A, 10 A, and 10 A at B, C and D respectively. The resistances of go and return conductors are: AB $= 0.1$ Ω, BC $= 0.15$ Ω, CD $= 0.05$ Ω. Calculate the efficiency of the system.
[0.972 p.u.]

7   A feeder ABCD is fed at A and D at 220 V. A load of 20 A is situated at B which is 100 m from A. A load of 30 A is situated at C which is 120 m from D. The feeder is 420 m long. The resistance of 100 m of *single* conductor is 0.025 Ω.

Determine the current in each section of the feeder and the value of the minimum voltage.

$$[I_{AB} = 23.8 \text{ A}, I_{BC} = 3.81 \text{ A}, I_{DC} = 26.2 \text{ A}. \text{ Min. p.d. at } C = 218.43 \text{ V}].$$

8 For the feeder shown in *Fig 34,* determine the value of power in the load which has the minimum potential.

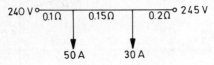

Fig 34 Resistances go and return

[50 A load power = 11.79 kW]

9 The ring main ABCDEFGA is fed at A at 250 V.
AB = 50 m, BC = 50 m, CD = 100 m, DE = 75 m, EF = 75 m, FG = 150 m, GA = 100 m. 100 m of single conductor has a resistance of 0.05 Ω.
The loads are as follows: B = 20 A, C = 30 A, D = 10 A, E = 50 A, F = 20 A and G = 25 A.
Determine the value of current in each section of the ring and the value of the minimum load potential.
$I_{AB} = 89.6$ A, $I_{BC} = 69.6$ A, $I_{CD} = 39.6$ A, $I_{DE} = 29.6$ A, $I_{FE} = 20.4$ A.
$I_{GF} = 40.4$ A, $I_{AG} = 65.4$ A. Min. p.d. at E = 235.9 V.

3 Regulations, tariffs and power factor correction

A. SUMMARY OF FORMULAE AND DEFINITIONS ASSOCIATED WITH REGULATIONS, TARIFFS AND POWER FACTOR CORRECTION

1 Over the years regulations applying to suppliers and consumers have been drawn up to prevent dangerous situations and accidents as far as is reasonably practicable. The regulations are as follows.

(a) **The Electricity Supply Regulations** These are issued by the Department of Trade and Industry. They apply to the electricity distribution system covering construction, operation, protection, maintenance and safety up to the consumer's terminals. Certain sections relate to the consumer's installation in as much as they give the Area Boards powers to insist on certain standards of work in these installations before the supply can be connected. The supply may be withdrawn from installations which subsequently become unsafe. The Area Board has to declare the voltage of the supply and maintain this within 6% of that value. Area and Generating Boards have very strict sets of safety rules and operate a 'Permit-to-Work' system which ensures an extremely low accident rate.

(b) **The Electricity (Factories Act) Special Regulations** These deal with factory installations and the operation of electrical plant. They ensure safe working in factories and are necessary to prevent unsafe installations and practices. The Health and Safety at Work Act 1974 is used to enforce the Regulations and places responsibilities for safe working on both management and employee. There are thirty-two Regulations in all so that only a brief extract can be quoted here. Further to para. 12, chapter 1: a substation is defined as '. . . any premises in which energy is transformed or converted to or from a pressure above medium pressure except for the purpose of working instruments, relays or similar apparatus, if such premises are large enough for a person to enter after the apparatus is in position'.

Regulation 20 'Where a high-pressure or extra-high pressure supply is transformed to above low pressure suitable provision shall be made to guard against danger by reason of the lower pressure system becoming accidentally charged above its normal pressure by leakage or contact from the higher voltage system. Permanent connection of one part of the lower voltage system to earth is the best method of complying with the regulation and in the case of the public supply the provision is usually made by the Supply Authority . . .'. (The neutral point is earthed).

Regulation 30 Every substation shall be substantially constructed and shall be so arranged that no person other than an Authorised person can obtain access thereto otherwise than by the proper entrance or can interfere with the apparatus therein from outside; and shall be provided with an efficient means of ventilation and be kept dry'.

The Factory Inspectorate can issue improvement notices in respect of substandard equipment or methods of working requiring them to be brought up to standard within a certain period of time. In extreme cases prohibition notices are issued which take effect immediately. Prosecution can result from contravention of these notices and also in accident cases where it can be proved that the accident has been caused or contributed to by contravention of the Regulations.

(c) **The Institution of Electrical Engineers' Regulations for the Electrical Equipment of Buildings** The IEE Regulations are designed '. . . to ensure safety, especially from fire and shock, in the utilisation of electricity in and about buildings.' They relate to consumers' installations and specify conductor and cable types, methods of installation of wiring and apparatus, safety measures and testing methods. The IEE Regulations are not legally enforceable as in the case of the Factories Act Special Regulations but almost certainly work which did not comply with the IEE Regulations would contravene the Factories Act. The Factories Act often calls for additional safety requirements, for example where work is carried out in coal mines, oil refineries and places of public entertainment. Tables of cable sizes for different currents and groupings are provided together with factors for close and coarse protection. (See *Problem 1*).

4 The cost of generation and transmission of electrical energy is divided into two parts: (i) Capital charges; (ii) Running charges.

Capital charges In order to **build** a power station or transmission line money is borrowed and interest paid annually. Money is put aside so that in theory at least at the end of twenty-five or thirty years the loan can be repaid.

Running charges In order to **operate** a power station personnel must be paid, fuel purchased and repairs carried out. On overhead lines and underground cables, repairs must be made and routine testing and inspections carried out. These costs are very nearly proportional to the amount of energy sold. The cost of losses on the system is also included in the running costs.

Tariffs to industrial consumers are often of a 'two-part' type reflecting both of these charges.

3 **Power factor** Most loads on the electricity supply system comprise resistance and inductance in series so that the supply current lags the voltage by an angle $\phi°$ as shown in *Fig 1(b)*. The value of current which is in phase with the voltage and therefore capable of doing work is called the active component of current, I_a. The component of current at right angles to the voltage is I_r, the reactive current so called because it is present due to circuit reactance. Taking the triangle in *Fig*

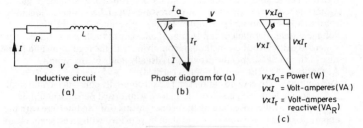

Inductive circuit
(a)

Phasor diagram for (a)
(b)

$V \times I_a$ = Power (W)
$V \times I$ = Volt-amperes (VA)
$V \times I_r$ = Volt-amperes reactive (VA_R)
(c)

Fig 1

34

1(b) and multiplying each side by V, the circuit voltage, gives a similar triangle showing the relationship between power (VI_a), volt-amperes (VI) and volt-amperes reactive (VI_r). Since in this case the current lags the voltage these are known as lagging volt-amperes reactive (*Fig 1(c)*).

Power factor is defined as $\dfrac{\text{Power in watts}}{\text{Volt-amperes}}$

which from *Fig 1(c)* can be seen to be equal to cosine ϕ.

4 **Maximum demand**   When industrial consumers buy energy from the Area Boards or the Area Boards buy from the Generating Board the amount of plant involved and hence the capital charges are determined by measuring the maximum demand. This may be on a kW or kVA basis. In the former case a kilowatt-hour meter has its advance measured during each half hour of the year. The number of kWh used in one half hour multiplied by two gives the hourly rate in kWh/h. (kWh/h = kW). The largest value of kW demand in a given period (month, quarter or year) is the maximum demand for the period. Where charges on a kVA basis are made then the power factor must also be measured.

5 **Diversity factor** = $\dfrac{\text{Demand of equipment actually connected at any instant}}{\text{Maximum demand}}$

6 **Load factor** = $\dfrac{\text{Energy consumed in a given period}}{\substack{\text{Energy that would have been consumed had the maximum}\\ \text{demand been sustained during that period.}}}$

7 **Power factor correction**   Where a tariff incorporates a maximum demand charge based on kVA, savings can be achieved by improving a low power factor. Such tariffs seek to discourage low power factor since this involves a larger current than necessary to perform a given amount of work. Conductors, transformers and switchgear must therefore all be larger than for the same load at unity power factor.

The improvement may be brought about by the use of capacitors connected across the supply either at the load point itself or in the substation feeding the factory. A capacitor draws current which leads the supply voltage by 90° and therefore has no active component. It is totally reactive and multiplying the

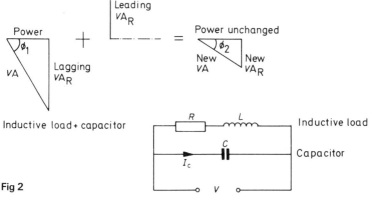

Inductive load + capacitor

Fig 2

current by the supply voltage gives VI_C, leading volt-amperes reactive. Adding a capacitor to the system as shown in *Fig 2* does not affect the load power but since the leading and lagging volt-amperes reactive are in direct phase opposition the arithmetic difference may be taken.

The new value of VA_R = lagging VA_R − leading VA_R. The overall phase angle has been reduced from ϕ_1 to ϕ_2 and the value of VA has been reduced.

Correction to unity power factor is rarely done since the improvement from about 0.9 to unity costs more in capacitors than the resulting saving brought about by the corresponding reduction in kVA. (See *Problem 4*).

B. WORKED PROBLEMS ON REGULATIONS, TARIFFS AND POWER FACTOR CORRECTION

Problem 1   What is the difference in scope between the Factories' Acts and the IEE Regulations?

The Electricity (Factories Act) Special Regulations deal with factory installations and the operation of factory electrical plant. They have been drawn up to ensure safe working in factories and are necessary to prevent unsafe installations and practices which might otherwise be employed either out of ignorance or for cost saving. The Health and Safety at Work Act 1974 places responsibility for safe working on both management and employees. The Act has the force of law behind it and there are Factory Inspectors who may visit any plant at any time. If they have reason to suppose they might be impeded in their duty they may bring a police officer with them.

They may issue improvement notices in respect of substandard equipment or methods of working requiring them to be brought up to standard within a certain period of time. In extreme cases prohibition notices are issued which take effect immediately. Prosecution can result from contravention of these notices and in accident cases where it can be proved that the accident has been caused or contributed to by a contravention of the regulations.

The Institution of Electrical Engineers' Regulations for the Electrical Equipment of Buildings are designed to ensure safety and relate to consumers' installations. The IEE Regulations specify conductor and cable types, methods of installation of wiring and apparatus, safety measures and testing methods. These regulations are not legally enforceable as in the case of the Factories' Act but almost certainly, work which did not comply with the IEE Regulations would contravene the Factories Act. The Factories Act often calls for additional factors in specially hazardous situations.

Problem 2   A private house contains the following equipment:
Electric lamps, total power 1200 W   Food mixed 500 W
Television set 120 W   Electric cooker 15000 W
Electric iron 750 W   Electric kettle 3000 W
Two electric fires, total 3000 W   Home workshop equipment 2500 W
Washing machine with heater 4500 W

Assuming the maximum demand is equivalent to 60% of that of all the equipment installed calculate:

(a) the diversity when (i) 500 W of lighting, the television set and both electric fires are operating and (ii) the cooker is operating at half full power whilst the home workshop equipment is being fully utilised and the electric kettle is switched on.

(b) the load factor for the installation over one quarter of a year if in that quarter 1560 kWh were consumed. (Take 1 year = 365 days).

(c) the electricity charge for the quarter in (b) above and the average cost per kWh on a tariff: £4.40 fixed charge + 3.2 p/kWh for all energy consumed.

(a) (i) Total rating of all the equipment installed
$$= 1200 + 120 + 750 + 3000 + 4500 + 500 + 15000 + 3000 + 2500 = 30570 \text{ W}$$
The maximum demand = 60% of the installed capacity =

$$\frac{60}{100} \times 30570 = 18342 \text{ W}$$

$$= 18.342 \text{ kW}$$

$$\text{Diversity factor} = \frac{\text{Load connected}}{\text{Maximum demand}} = \frac{500 + 120 + 3000}{18342} = \mathbf{0.197}$$

(ii) Diversity factor $= \dfrac{7500 + 2500 + 3000}{18342} = \mathbf{0.709}$

(b) Load factor $= \dfrac{\text{kWh consumed}}{\text{kW of maximum demand} \times \text{hours in the period}}$

$$= \frac{1560}{18.342 \times 24 \times 365/4} = \mathbf{0.0388}$$

(c) Total cost $= £\left(4.4 + 1560 \times \dfrac{3.2}{100}\right)$

$$= £(4.4 + 49.92) = £54.32$$

Average price per kWh $= \dfrac{\text{Cost}}{\text{kWh consumed}} = \dfrac{54.32 \times 100 \text{ p}}{1560}$

$$= \mathbf{3.48 \text{ p/kWh}}$$

Problem 3 The half-hourly advances of a kWh meter are as follows during a working period of 8 hours:
100, 125, 175, 200, 300, 500, 450, 400, 400, 350, 350, 450, 500, 490, 502, 350.
These readings contain the highest value obtained throughout the year. The load factor over the year is 0.2. Assuming the power factor to be 0.8 lagging, calculate the annual cost of energy on tariffs: (i) £15/kVA of maximum demand + 2 p/kWh; (ii) £20/kW of maximum demand + 2.1 p/kWh

The largest advance in any one half hour = 502 kWh
The hourly rate = $2 \times 502 = 1004$ kWh per hour = 1004 kW
The maximum demand = 1004 kW,

At 0.8 power factor, the maximum demand in kVA = $\dfrac{1004}{0.8}$ = 1255 kVA

Load factor = $\dfrac{\text{kWh consumed}}{\text{kW of max. demand} \times \text{hours in period}}$

$0.2 = \dfrac{\text{kWh consumed}}{1004 \times 24 \times 365}$

Hence, kWh consumed = $0.2 \times 1004 \times 24 \times 365 = 1\,759\,008$

(i) Tariff £15/kVA of M.D. + 2 p/kWh

$\text{Cost} = £\left(15 \times 1255 + 1\,759\,008 \times \dfrac{2}{100}\right)$

$= £(18\,825 + 35\,180) = \textbf{£54\,005}$

(ii) Tariff £20/kW of M.D. + 2.1 p/kWh

$\text{Cost} = £\left(20 \times 1004 + 1\,759\,008 \times \dfrac{2.1}{100}\right)$

$= £(20\,080 + 36\,939)$

$= \textbf{£57\,019}$

Problem 4 An industrial load has a maximum demand of 500 kW at a power factor of 0.65 lagging. Calculate the saving in maximum demand charges and the overall saving if a capacitor bank is fitted which draws 150 kVA$_R$. The tariff is £15/kVA of maximum demand. The annual charges for the capacitor are £600.

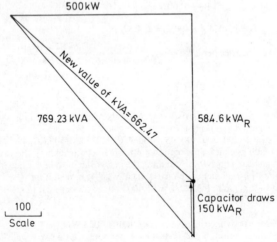

500 kW

New value of kVA = 662.47

769.23 kVA

584.6 kVA$_R$

Capacitor draws
150 kVA$_R$

100
Scale

Fig 3

38

(*see Fig 3*)

$kVA \times \cos \phi = kW$. Hence $\dfrac{kW}{\cos \phi} = kVA$

Original value of $kVA = \dfrac{500}{0.65} = 769.23$

By Pythagoras' theorem: $kVA_R = \sqrt{(kVA)^2 - (kW)^2}$

$kVA_R = \sqrt{769.23^2 - 500^2} = 584.6 \, kVA_R$
The capacitor bank draws $150 \, kVA_R$ leading. The total kVA_R will therefore be reduced to $584.6 - 150 = 434.6 \, kVA_R$.
The new value of kVA (note that the power in kW remains unchanged)

$= \sqrt{500^2 + 434.6^2}$
$= 662.47 \, kVA$

Saving in electricity maximum demand charges = reduction in $kVA \times £15$
$= (769.23 - 662.47) \times £15 = \textbf{£1601.40}$
The actual saving after paying the annual charges on the capacitor bank
$= £(1601.40 - 600) = \textbf{£1001.40}$

C. FURTHER PROBLEMS ON REGULATIONS, TARIFFS AND POWER FACTOR CORRECTION

(a) SHORT-ANSWER PROBLEMS

1 Name the three sets of regulations which have been drawn up to ensure safe working practices in the electrical industry.

2 What are the powers of the Factory Inspectors with respect to the Electricity (Factories Act) Special Regulations?

3 What is the general overall aim of the IEE Regulations for the electrical equipment of buildings?

4 What significance do the IEE Regulations have in a court of law?

5 What is the general objective of the Electricity Supply Regulations?

6 What power does the Electricity Supply Regulations give to the Area Boards with respect to consumers' equipment?

7 What is the difference in scope between the Factories Act and the IEE Regulations?

8 What additional regulations to those already mentioned may have to be complied with in some specially hazardous situations?

9 The cost of generation and transmission of electrical energy is divided into two parts. Name and briefly explain these two components of cost.

10 Define the term 'Maximum Demand'.

11 Why do the Electricity Boards charge industrial consumers on a tariff based on maximum demand?

12 Why is the domestic consumer not charged on a maximum demand tariff?

13 Draw a triangle for a lagging power factor load showing watts, volt-amperes and volt-amperes reactive.

14 Define the term 'Diversity factor'.

15 Explain why it is that improving the load factor on a piece of equipment can lower the cost per kWh of energy consumed.

16 A factory has a maximum demand of 600 kW at 0.75 power factor lagging. How many kVA_R are being drawn from the supply at the time of maximum demand?

17 The basic charge per kWh on a certain industrial tariff is 2 p. There is a fuel adjustment clause whereby the unit charge may be increased by 0.0001 p for every penny that fuel costs rise above £20/tonne. Calculate the cost per kWh when fuel costs £23/tonne.

18 Why is there no incentive for domestic consumers to practice power factor improvement?

19 When a factory improves its power factor to effect savings in its electricity charges it rarely corrects to unity. Why is this?

20 Where a factory has a large consumption, the choice of taking a bulk supply at high voltage may be offered. Why would this be likely to reduce the tariff charged?

(b) MULTI-CHOICE PROBLEMS (answers on page 213)

1 A substation is defined as 'Any premises in which . . .
   (i)   switchgear is housed;
   (ii)   a high/medium voltage transformer is situated and which is large enough for a person to enter;
   (iii) an Authorised person or person acting under his supervision is employed to control power to consumers.

2 The IEE Regulations are designed to:
   (i)   deal with factory plant and ensure its safe working;
   (ii)   ensure safety especially from fire and shock in the utilisation of electricity in and around buildings;
   (iii) secure the safety of the public and to ensure a proper and sufficient supply of electrical energy.

3 There are three sets of Regulations governing the supply and utilisation of electrical energy. These are:
   (a)   The Electricity Supply Regulations;
   (b)   The Electricity (Factories Act) Special Regulations;
   (c)   The IEE Regulations.
   These Regulations cover the following areas:
   (i)   installation of equipment in buildings;
   (ii)   safe operation and practice in workshops and the like;
   (iii) equipment up to the supply point in a factory.
   Link the particular regulation to its application. (Example (a) & (i); (b) & (iii); etc.

4 The capital charges involved in building a power station and associated transmission lines are made up of:

(i)   Interest paid on capital borrowed
(ii) cost of fuel;
(iii) wages paid to operatives;
(iv) depreciation allowance towards the provision of new plant,
(v)   cost of repairs to the plant;
(vi) cost of system losses.

Select *two* of the six alternatives.

5 The power in a single-phase circuit operating at 250 V is 1250 W. The power factor is 0.6 lagging. The value of the reactive current, I_r is:
(i) 5 A; (ii) 8.33 A; (iii) 6.67 A; (iv) 4 A.

6 A factory with a maximum demand of 200 kW has a load factor of 0.3. The energy consumed during a period of 90 days is:
(i) 129 600 kWh; (ii) 60 kWh; (iii) 1.44×10^6 kWh.

7 A factory with a maximum demand of 550 kW at 0.65 power factor lagging improves its power factor to 0.95 lagging by the connection of capacitors. The tariff is £16/kVA of maximum demand per annum. The annual saving in electricity charges is:
(i) £7398; (ii) £2890; (iii) £4275.

8 Domestic electricity is paid for on one of the following tariffs. Which is it?
(i)   maximum demand in kW + charge per kWh;
(ii) maximum demand in kVA + charge per kWh;
(iii) fixed charge + charge per kWh;
(iv) charge per kWh + penalty for poor power factor.

9 A consumer with a poor power factor charged on a tariff with a maximum demand charge per kW should be . . . . . (i) *or* (ii) . . . . his power factor since by so doing he will . . . . (iii) *or* (iv) . . . .
Select statements from (i) to (iv) below to make up a correct statement.
(i)   encouraged to improve;
(ii) discouraged from improving;
(iii) reduce substantially the number of kW of maximum demand so reduce his electricity bill.
(iv) spend money unnecessarily since it will have no effect on the electricity bill.

10 A factory with maximum demand 350 kVA at 0.7 power factor lagging installs a capacitor bank which draws 150 kVA_R leading. The value of the kVA drawn by the factory after adding the capacitor is:
(i) 249.9 kVA; (ii) 245 kVA; (iii) 265 kVA.

11 A factory wishes to expand production. This may be achieved by either (a) increasing the amount of production plant installed or (b) by working existing plant for two shifts instead of one as at present.
   A saving in the electricity bill be achieved by scheme (b) as opposed to scheme (a) since:
(i)   the power factor will be improved;
(ii) the diversity factor will be improved;
(iii) the load factor will be improved;
(iv) the actual energy charge (kWh consumed) will be reduced.

(c) CONVENTIONAL PROBLEMS

1 Write brief notes explaining the purpose of, and the need for, the following regulations:
   (i) The Electricity Supply Regulations;
   (ii) The Electricity (Factories Act) Special Regulations;
   (iii) The IEE Regulations.

2 (a) Calculate the cost of electrical energy supplied to a domestic premise per quarter year given that the load factor is 5% and the maximum demand is 10 kW
   (i) On a quarterly tariff of: Fixed charge £5, first kWh at 6 p/kWh, all units over 150 at 2.5 p/kWh;
   (ii) On a flat rate tariff of 4 p/kWh.
   (b) A family uses 2000 kWh in a winter quarter. The quarterly tariff is: First 100 kWh cost 8 p/kWh, all over 100 kWh cost 2.4 p/kWh. The maximum demand is 12 kW.
   Calculate: (i) the average cost per kWh, (ii) the load factor for the quarter.

$$\left[\begin{array}{l} \text{(a) (i) 1092 kWh used. £37.55; (a) (ii) £43.68;} \\ \text{(b) (i) 2.68 p/kWh; (b) (ii) Load factor} = 0.076 \end{array}\right]$$

3 A factory has a maximum demand of 200 kW, a load factor of 40% and an average operating power factor of 0.7.
   Calculate the annual cost of electricity on the following three tariffs:
   (i) Maximum demand charge £15/kW. Running charge 1.8 p/kWh;
   (ii) Maximum demand charge £12/kVA. Running charge 1.8 p/kWh;
   (iii) Basic maximum demand charge of £15/kW increased by a factor of 10% for each 0.1 the power factor is less than 0.9. Running charge 1.8 p/kWh.

[(i) £15614; (ii) £16042; (iii) £16214]

4 A factory with an annual consumption of 1 million kWh has a load factor of 0.5. The electricity tariff is £14/kW of maximum demand plus 1.7 p/kWh. Calculate the average cost per kWh.

[M.D. 228.3 kW. Average price 2.0196 p/kWh]

5 An industrial load has a maximum demand of 300 kW at a power factor of 0.6 lagging. Calculate the saving in maximum demand charges and the overall saving when a compensating capacitor is fitted which draws 150 kVA$_R$. The tariff is £12/kVA of maximum demand. The annual charges for the capacitor are £500.

[Saving on M.D. £1314. Overall £814.]

6 Calculate the saving in maximum demand charge if a factory with maximum demand 500 kW at a power factor of 0.7 lagging improves this to 0.9 lagging. The maximum demand charge is £14/kVA. What is the overall annual saving if the power factor correction equipment costs £800 per annum?

[£2222; £1422]

7 A factory consumes 1.2 million kWh per annum. It has a load factor of 45% and operates at an average power factor of 0.65 lagging.
   (i) Calculate the total electricity charges on a tariff of £14/kVA of maximum demand plus 1.6 p/kWh.
   (ii) Calculate the savings to be made by improving the power factor to 0.9 lagging. The capital charges on power factor correction equipment are £5/kVA$_R$ per annum.
   (iii) Calculate the additional saving in maximum demand charge which can be made by improving the power factor to unity. What additional cost is

involved in the provision of correcting equipment? Would this final improvement be economically sound?

(i)   £25 756;
(ii) M.D. saving £1821; cost £1042. Overall saving £778.
(iii) M.D. saving £473. Cost £737. Not sound.

8 A factory has a maximum demand of 750 kW at 0.6 power factor lagging. It is to have its power factor improved by the addition of capacitors. The maximum demand charge is £15/kVA of maximum demand and the cost of capacitors is £4/kVA$_R$ per annum. Calculate the overall savings to be achieved by correction from the original power factor to (i) 0.7 lag, (ii) 0.8 lag; (iii) 0.9 lag and (iv) unity power factor. Which of these values might therefore be chosen in practice?

	(i)	(ii)	(iii)	(iv)
Savings on M.D. charges	2685	4687.5	6255	7500
Cost of capacitors	940	1750	2548	4000 ALL £
Overall saving	1745	2937.5	3707	3500

An overall power factor of 0.9 would be chosen to give the best return on cash spent.

4 Materials and their applications

A SUMMARY OF FORMULAE AND DEFINITIONS ASSOCIATED WITH MATERIALS AND THEIR APPLICATIONS IN THE ELECTRICAL INDUSTRY

1 Silver is the best **electrical conductor** known at the present time but this is far too expensive and rare to provide all the conductor material required by the electrical industry. Next, in order of conductivity, are copper and aluminium and these important current carrying materials are used in cable and line manufacture. These materials are compared in *Table 1*.

Table 1

Property	Copper	Aluminium
Weight	87 200 N/m^3	26 700 N/m^3 (0.306 times copper)
Resistivity	1.73×10^{-8} Ωm	2.87×10^{-8} Ωm (1.7 times silver)
Strength	Ultimate: 320 MN/m^2	Ultimate: 144 MN/m^2 (0.45 times copper)
Flexibility	When annealed, quite good. Used hard for cables and overhead lines when it must be stranded to give the required flexibility	Very flexible, can be used solid in cables
Jointing	Soldered ferrules for cables. Compression joints on overhead lines	Compression type on overhead lines. Crimped lugs for cable terminations. Can be soldered or welded using special fluxes but generally more difficult than copper
Resistance to Corrosion	Excellent, virtually none in most circumstances	Poor when in contact with other materials and in particular copper and copper bearing alloys. Special sleeves and fittings required. On overhead lines there is limited deterioration, much of the original 1933 grid is still operational in its original form however

2 The conductivity of both copper and aluminium falls very rapidly even with very small additions of alloying elements. For this reason these materials are generally used pure. In the case of aluminium, the mechanical strength is improved by using a stranded conductor with steel strands at the centre.

Fig 1 shows a **stranded conductor**; this can be made up from either one strand of steel plus six strands of aluminium; seven strands of steel plus twelve strands of aluminium, or by adding a further layer of aluminium strands, seven of steel plus thirty of aluminium.

3 For **underground cables,** up to 3.3 kV, the most commonly used insulating material is polyvinyl chloride (p.v.c.). Street mains use either copper or aluminium conductors insulated with p.v.c. The cable is steel wire armoured and

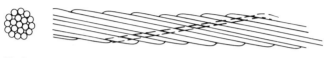

Fig 1

covered overall with p.v.c. to prevent corrosion. House wiring usually comprises copper conductors which are insulated with p.v.c.

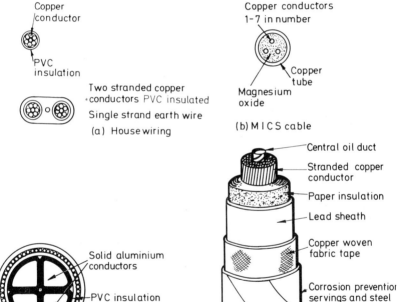

Copper conductor
PVC insulation

Two stranded copper conductors PVC insulated
Single strand earth wire
(a) House wiring

Copper conductors 1-7 in number
Copper tube
Magnesium oxide
(b) M I C S cable

Central oil duct
Stranded copper conductor
Paper insulation
Lead sheath
Copper woven fabric tape
Corrosion prevention servings and steel wire armouring if required

Solid aluminium conductors
PVC insulation
Steel wire armouring
PV C sheath
(c) Aluminium conductor street main

(d) Oil pressure cable suitable for voltages from 60 kV to 400 kV

Fig 2

45

Mineral insulated cables use magnesium oxide which spaces solid copper conductors within a copper tube. Some 11 kV cables have polythene insulation but, in the main, paper is used at this voltage level. At voltages above 11 kV paper insulation with oil or gas filling predominates. *Fig 2* shows some typical cable constructions.

4 Since all conductors in normal service have resistance, the passage of current along the conductor gives rise to a voltage drop. This voltage drop is in phase with the current which produces it so that the power loss is equal to the product of voltage drop and current flowing.

For one core: Volt drop = IR where R = resistance of one core.
Power loss = volt drop × current = $IR \times I = I^2R$ watts per core.

The power heats the core producing a rise in temperature of the conductor and hence of its insulation. In addition to the core loss the leakage current through the insulation must be considered. For example a cable operating at 19 052 V which has an insulation resistance of 200 MΩ will allow $19052/(200 \times 10^6)$ A to pass through the insulation resulting in a power loss of 1.8 W.

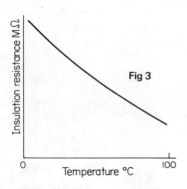

Fig 3

Fig 3 shows that as the temperature of a cable insulating material **rises** its insulation resistance **falls.** Hence at a higher temperature the leakage current is greater so that more heat is produced in the insulation. An unstable situation can be created where more heat increases the temperature which in turn lowers the resistance so allowing more leakage current which produces more heat, etc. The cable eventually fails by burning under these conditions.

5 The amount of heat which can be conducted away from a cable depends on the **temperature difference** between it and the surrounding medium. A cable which can carry 20 A safely when situated in an environment at 25°C may only be able to carry 12 A when the surrounding temperature is 60°C. The IEE Regulations contain de-rating factors which take account of high ambient temperature.

6 Cables which are in ducts or are laid close to each other suffer **mutual heating.** One cable becoming warm heats its neighbours. Where cables touch each other the number of free paths by which heat can escape to the environment is reduced. The general mass of cables may raise the temperature of the surrounding air or ground. For these reasons it is necessary to reduce the current rating of the conductors. A de-rating factor is applied which may be determined experimentally or obtained from such sources as the IEE Regulations or Electrical Research Association data. The following data is from the IEE Regulations:

Number of circuits	2	3	4	5	6	10	14
Factor	0.8	0.69	0.62	0.59	0.55	0.48	0.41

(see *Problem 2*)

7 **Permitted volt drops in cables**

IEE Regulation B.23 states: 'The size of every bare conductor or cable conductor shall be such that the drop in voltage from the consumer's terminals to any point in the installation does not exceed 2.5% of the declared or nominal voltage when the conductors are carrying full load current, but disregarding starting conditions. This requirement shall not apply to wiring fed from an extra-low voltage secondary of a transformer.'

Table 2 is an extract from Table 1M of the IEE Regulations. (See *Problem 3*).

Nominal cross-sectional area mm²	Current rating for 2 cables single-phase a.c. or d.c. bunched and enclosed in conduit or trunking A	Volt drop per ampere per metre run mV
1	11	40
1.5	13	27
2.5	18	16
4	24	10
6	31	6.8
10	42	4.0

8 When two conductors in proximity carry currents there will be a **mechanical force** set up between them. The value of this force is given by the formula:

$$F = 2 \times 10^{-7} \frac{I_1 I_2}{d} \text{N per metre run.}$$

The symbols are defined in *Fig 4*.

Should a short circuit fault occur, the current and resulting force can be extremely large, sufficient in fact to disrupt the cable or conductor system (see *Problem 4*).

9 A current in a conductor sets up a **magnetic field** around it, the strength of which is proportional to the current. This magnetic field may affect other circuits in the vicinity and to prevent this circuit screening is necessary. Where a component is

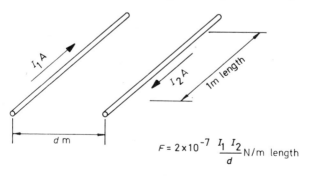

Fig 4

to be screened from a steady magnetic field it is surrounded with a material having low magnetic reluctance. In *Figure 5* the component to be screened is marked C. With the screen in position the magnetic lines of force take the low reluctance path leaving the component in a region of zero flux.

Where alternating currents are involved the conductor carrying the alternating current must be surrounded by the screen. The arrangement is in effect a

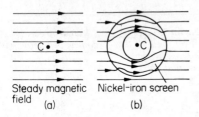

Steady magnetic field (a) Nickel-iron screen (b) **Fig 5**

transformer, the conductor being the primary and the screen a short circuited secondary (see *Fig 6*). The alternating flux induces a voltage in the screen and a current flows which sets up an opposing flux. The two fluxes are very nearly equal so that the magnetic field outside the screen is very nearly zero. The magnetic field around a cable feeding a circuit is eliminated by using the coaxial construction (see *Fig 7*).

Current is supplied to the load along the core of the cable and is returned to

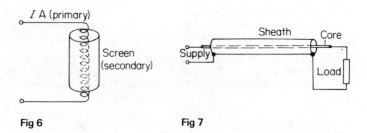

Fig 6   **Fig 7**

the supply through the sheath. Since the go and return currents are in opposite directions, the magnetic fields produced are in opposite directions and completely cancel each other outside the sheath.

10 Now that valves have largely been replaced by transistors and integrated circuits in which the heat generated is relatively small, printed circuit boards have replaced individually wired chassis in electronic equipment. The fixed pattern of components and connections ensures repeatable values of circuit resistance and capacitance. The board provides mechanical support for the components and the means for their interconnection. Modern rigid boards are made of phenolic resins reinforced with woven glass fabric or paper. Flexible boards are available which are made from polyester film or p.t.f.e.

48

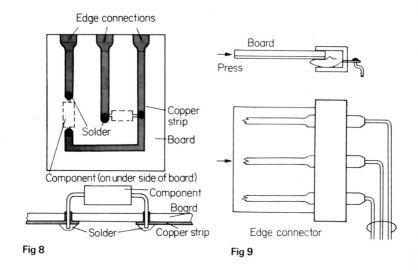

Fig 8

Fig 9

Printed circuit boards use copper foil conductors securely cemented to the laminated board. Holes are drilled through the foil and board and the component tails fixed by soldering. *Fig 8* shows a very simple board with two components, and *Fig 9* shows it connected to a chassis or another board. The current carrying capacity of the copper foil is determined largely by the permissible temperature rise. Foils vary in thickness from 0.035 mm to 0.106 mm and in width from 0.25 mm up to several millimetres. As an example a strip 0.07 mm thick and 0.76 mm wide can carry 3.5 A allowing a 40°C rise in temperature but only 2 A allowing a 10°C rise, both from 15°C. Increasing the strip width gives a less than proportional increase in current carrying capacity so that current for other strips cannot be deduced by proportion. Makers' charts have to be consulted.

Gold is generally used for low-voltage connections, as in the edge connector, since only low contact pressure is required to obtain a good connection. (Only 0.03 times that necessary to obtain the same resistance between brass contacts.) Also gold does not oxidise or corrode. Even a very thin oxide film can cause a virtual open circuit unless the voltage employed is large enough to break it down. The gold, generally less than 50×10^{-6} m thick, is plated over nickel or silver, the former combination being particularly good in hostile environments.

11 Interconnection between boards or pieces of equipment is achieved using insulated wires which are either grouped into **multicore cables** or merely bunched and neatly carried around the chassis of the equipment. Some of the available types of multicore cable are shown in *Fig 10*.

Multicore cables for telecommunications have pairs of fine insulated wires twisted together along their length to form circuits, two pairs then being twisted together. Many such groups of four conductors make up a complete cable.

12 The characteristics of semiconducting devices such as rectifiers and transistors

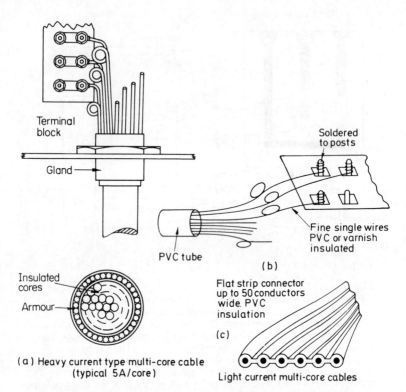

Terminal block

Gland

Soldered to posts

Fine single wires PVC or varnish insulated

PVC tube

(b)

Insulated cores

Armour

(a) Heavy current type multi-core cable (typical 5A/core)

Flat strip connector up to 50 conductors wide. PVC insulation

(c)

Light current multi-core cables

Fig 10

change considerably with rises in temperature so much so that the circuit in which they are connected may cease to operate in the manner intended. Often a device is permanently damaged and the old characteristics are not re-established by cooling. Where excessive currents have been drawn due to these changes, other components in the circuit may have been damaged. To help dissipate the heat generated within a device and so to limit the temperature rise, **heat sinks** (see *Fig 11*) are often employed. These are clip or screw-on additions to a device which effectively increase the surface area available for cooling.

13 Porcelain is most commonly used for **overhead line insulators.** The insulators are shaped from the raw material—a mixture of clay, finely ground feldspar and silica in water, is dried, dipped in liquid glaze and then fired at very high temperature. The glaze forms a glass-like coating providing a surface to which dirt cannot readily stick. It also improves the strength of the insulator so that fracture is more difficult.

One disadvantage of porcelain is that when the glaze is chipped by a power arc or by missiles from vandals, water can soak into the body of the insulator. This causes it to become conducting and an electrical discharge takes place which trips out the line while the heat produced dries out the insulator. Such a fault is immensely difficult to find, the line tripping out each time there is rain.

Glass is an alternative material. Toughened glass insulators have a higher breakdown strength under electrical stress than porcelain and, if damaged, shatter completely. Missing insulators leave gaps which are easily spotted during one of the regular inspections which must be made. The construction is such that although the insulator shatters the line cannot fall down (see *Fig 2,* chapter 1).

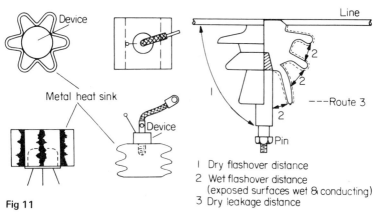

Fig 11

1 Dry flashover distance
2 Wet flashover distance
  (exposed surfaces wet & conducting)
3 Dry leakage distance

Fig 12

Insulators have to withstand both mechanical and electrical stresses. Heavy lines must be held off the ground whilst the electrical potential of the line is considerably above that of earth. Even in wet weather the insulator must function and for this reason it has 'sheds' or 'skirts' to keep at least part of the surface dry in almost any weather conditions. *Fig 12* shows a pin-type insulator supported at the bottom with the line at the top. The steel pin is at earth potential. An electrical breakdown or flashover can occur in one of three ways:

(i)   A dry flashover can occur. This means that the arc will form round the insulator from line to pin along route 1 in *Fig 12.*

(ii) A wet flashover can occur. When the top surfaces of the insulator are wetted by rain they become conducting so that the sheds are so disposed to keep the undersides dry. A flashover can occur along route 2 in *Fig 12.*

(iii) Current can leak from the line over the surface of the insulator along route 3 in *Fig 12.*

Atmospheric pollution causes dirt to accumulate on the surface of the insulator making it partly conducting and a flashover more likely. Fog wets the insulator overall causing surface leakage to occur especially when smoke and sulphur oxides are present. Sea spray carried by the wind also has the same effect.

B. WORKED PROBLEMS ON MATERIALS AND THEIR APPLICATION IN THE ELECTRICAL INDUSTRY

Problem 1 Describe the process whereby the heat produced in a cable may eventually cause a short circuit or earth fault to occur. (Thermal avalanche).

Since all conductors in normal service (not in the superconducting state) have resistance the passage of current along them gives rise to a power loss.

Power loss = I^2R watts.

This power heats the cable cores increasing their temperature and that of the surrounding insulation. In addition, all solid dielectrics have a measurable resistance between conductor to earth and from conductor to conductor within a cable. There will therefore be leakage currents through the insulation which will produce heat within the dielectric again helping to raise the temperature.

The heat is lost to the ground or air. The temperature of the cable rises until the rate of dissipation from the cable sheath is equal to the rate of heat production. There must be a difference in temperature between the insulation and the surrounding medium for there to be any dissipation. Unfortunately good electrical insulators are often good heat insulators and it is quite possible to produce heat in the cable at such a rate that the temperature of the inner layers of insulation would have to be extremely high in order to transfer all the heat through the remaining insulation and sheath. This high temperature can burn the insulation.

Starting from an initially safe condition, an increase in temperature has two effects:
1 The resistance of the conductor itself increases;
2 The resistance of the insulation is reduced.
The former increases the I^2R loss in the conductor whilst the latter increases the leakage current. Both lead to increased heat production which produces further changes in resistance and further heat. If the rate of heat production is sustained at a higher rate than heat dissipation at a safe temperature then the cable fails since charred insulation is a conductor of electricity.

Problem 2 (a) Explain what is meant by proximity or grouping factor as applied to electricity cables. (b) Two p.v.c. insulated cables are drawn into a conduit and feed a single-phase load. The current rating of the conductors is 24 A under these conditions. Using the rating factors given, calculate: (i) the permissible rating per circuit if three more similar pairs are drawn into the conduit, (ii) the maximum number of pairs allowed in the conduit if the rating is to be not less than 14 A per circuit.

Number of circuits:	2	3	4	5	6	10	14
Grouping factor	0.8	0.69	0.62	0.59	0.55	0.48	0.41

(a) Cable cooling depends on the surface area through which heat can be transmitted and on the difference in temperature between the cable and the surrounding material. Where cables are laid close together, one cable becoming warm heats its neighbours. Where cables actually touch each other the number of free paths by which heat can escape to the environment is reduced. The heat from the mass of cables may raise the temperature of the surrounding air or ground thus reducing the capability of the cables to dissipate heat. For these reasons it is necessary to lower the current rating of conductors when they are in close proximity.

(b) (i)   One pair of conductors comprises one circuit.
Adding three similar pairs makes up 4 circuits in all.
The de-rating factor for 4 circuits = 0.62
The rating of each circuit = $0.62 \times 24 = 14.9$ A

(ii)   Rating of each circuit = de-rating factor × current carrying capacity of one circuit alone
14 = de-rating factor × 24

$$\text{De-rating factor} = \frac{14}{24} = 0.583$$

The nearest factor above this is 0.59 for 5 circuits.
The maximum number of pairs = 5
As a check: Rating = $0.59 \times 24 = 14.16$ A. The circuits would be safe carrying 14 A.

Problem 3   A single-phase load of 20 A is to be fed through p.v.c. insulated copper cables as specified in Table 1M of the IEE Regulations. The nominal circuit voltage is 230 V. The load is 40 m from the supply point. Determine the cross-sectional area of a suitable conductor. What is the power loss in the cable when carrying 20 A? (Refer to *Table 2* as quoted in para. 7, page 47.)

The permissible voltage drop is 2.5% of the nominal voltage. 2.5% of 230 = 5.75 V. The voltage drop must not exceed this value when 20 A flows.
By inspection of the *Table 2* the nearest quoted size is 4 mm² which has a rating of 24 A. The volt drop per ampere per metre run is 10 mV.
With 20 A flowing, over a length of 40 m:
volt drop = $40 \times 20 \times 10 \times 10^{-3} = 8$ V
This is greater than 5.75 V so the next larger size must be tried.
Using 6 mm² conductors
volt drop = $40 \times 20 \times 6.8 \times 10^{-3} = 5.44$ V. This is quite satisfactory.
It would therefore be necessary to use conductors with a cross-sectional area of 6 mm² with a nominal current carrying capacity of 31 A.
Power loss = Volt drop × current = $5.44 \times 20 = $ **108.8 W.**
Alternatively use (power input) – (power at the load) to find the losses.
Power input = 230×20 W = 4600 W
Power at the load = $(230 - 5.44) \times 20$ W = 4491.2 W again yielding **108.8 W loss.**

The force between conductors

$$= 2 \times 10^{-7} \times \frac{I_1 I_2}{d} \qquad \text{N/m length (see } Figure\ 4\text{)}.$$

In a single-phase circuit the go and return currents will be the same.

(i) Under normal conditions:

$I_1 = I_2 = 20$ A

$$\text{Force} = 2 \times 10^{-7} \times \frac{20 \times 20}{4 \times 10^{-3} \text{ m}}$$

$\qquad = 0.02$ N/m run.

Power loss $= I^2 R = 20^2 \times 0.05 = \mathbf{20\ W.}$

(ii) Under short circuit conditions: $I_1 = I_2 = 2500$ A

$$\text{Force} = 2 \times 10^{-7} \times \frac{2500 \times 2500}{4 \times 10^{-3} \text{ m}}$$

$\qquad = 312.5$ N/m run.

Power loss $= 2500^2 \times 0.05 = \mathbf{312\,500\ W.}$

On short circuit, after a few cycles of the supply voltage, sufficient heat will be generated to soften the p.v.c. which will allow the forces created to disrupt the cable. Since go and return currents are in opposite directions the cores will be forced apart. An H.B.C. fuse which has an extremely short clearance time under short circuit conditions would prevent such damage.

With the individually wired chassis, low resistance electrical connections between the circuit components are made by using insulated copper wire or bare copper or aluminium strip. In equipments with many components there are several problems to overcome. One is that of the dry joint, when the soldering looks sound but in fact has not made good contact and the joint has a high resistance. Another problem with individual hand wiring is that it is difficult to reproduce a circuit accurately in successive equipments. There may be errors in connections and slightly different lengths and routing for wiring taken. Circuit response is thereby affected. Fault finding can be very difficult and it may be necessary to unsolder connections to make tests.

Mounting components on an insulating board to a fixed pattern is one solution to these problems. This is especially true now that valves have been largely replaced by transistors and integrated circuits in which the heat produced is relatively small. The fixed pattern ensures repeatable values of circuit resistance and capacitance.

The board provides mechanical support for the components and the means for their interconnection. The layout of the components is much clearer than with individually wired equipment and the values of the components are often marked on the board. Soldering becomes much simpler. In addition servicing of the equipment is easier since faulty boards may be replaced to get it working when the components on the faulty boards are replaced at a central workshop where expertise and sophisticated testing equipment will be available.

Problem 6   Calculate the current density in a conductor with a cross section 0.2 mm × 1.5 mm which is carrying 4.5 A.

Current density = $\dfrac{\text{current}}{\text{area}}$

$= \dfrac{4.5}{0.2 \times 1.5}$ = **15 amperes per square millimetre (A/mm^2)**

Problem 7   Briefly describe two processes available for the production of printed circuit boards.

To construct a printed circuit board it is necessary to draw a master circuit diagram. Larger areas of foil have to be allowed for parts of the circuit which will carry the heaviest currents. The master circuit can be drawn directly on the board in the case of a prototype or it can be printed on using a photographic process when large numbers of individual circuits are required. The two processes available are:

1   *The subtractive method*   A board is obtained which has foil completely covering one side. The diagram is drawn or printed on the foil using acid-resisting paint and the board is dipped in acid which dissolves the copper which is not protected. Only the required circuit is left on the board and the necessary holes can be drilled for circuit assembly.

2   *The additive method*   Insulating board is used with no foil covering. The circuit is drawn or printed on the board using electrically conducting paint. Copper is deposited from a plating bath over the treated area. Other additive methods include the use of metallic powder and heat or foil strips and mechanical force.

C. FURTHER PROBLEMS ON MATERIALS AND THEIR APPLICATIONS IN THE ELECTRICAL INDUSTRY

(a) SHORT ANSWER PROBLEMS

1   Although silver is the best electrical conductor it is not used in cable manufacture. Why is this?

2   How is the low tensile strength of aluminium compensated for in the construction of aluminium overhead lines?

3   Hard-drawn copper is not very flexible. How is the required flexibility built into cables and lines made from copper?

4   Why would p.v.c. insulation not be used in a hot situation?

5   Using *Table 2* as quoted in para. 7, page 47, determine the power loss per metre run of a single circuit comprising two conductors each of 2.5 mm^2 cross-sectional area when the circuit current is 15 A.

6   Using grouping factors as quoted in *Problem 2* determine the permissible circuit current for each of three circuits in a conduit if the rating for a single circuit alone in the conduit is 15 A.

7   A single-phase circuit carrying 50 A has a power loss of 1 W per metre run due to conductor heating. There is a force of 0.1 N per metre run due to the magnetic effect. Show that the power loss = 10 kW and the force between the conductors = 1000 N when a short circuit occurs and the current rises to 5000 A.

8   Why is it often necessary to use co-axial cables when interconnecting equipments operating at high frequencies?

9   What advantages are there to using printed circuit boards in a television receiver as compared with individually wired chassis?

10 Name two processes which are available for the production of printed circuit boards.

11 What is the function of a heat sink?

12 Show with the aid of simple sketches: (i) a method of screening a component from a steady magnetic field (ii) a method of preventing the magnetic field produced by a device carrying alternating currents from affecting other components.

13 A printed circuit board with conducting strips 0.1 mm thick and 1.5 mm wide has a maximum current rating of 6 A. Two, re-designed boards are produced:
(i) with strips 0.2 mm thick and 1.5 mm wide.-(Width unchanged);
(ii) with strips 0.1 mm thick and 3 mm wide. (Thickness unchanged.)
Thus in both cases the cross sectional area of the strip has been doubled. Each of the circuit boards is tested using a current of 10 A. State with a reason which one you would expect to run hotter.

14 Name the two principal insulating materials used in overhead line construction. (Other than air).

15 Name two materials with voltage levels used in the insulation of underground cables.

16 What is the difference between a pin and a suspension insulator?

17 Why is flashover on an overhead line more likely to occur on a rainy day than on a dry day.

1 Copper and aluminium are used as electrical conductors in a virtually pure state since the addition of alloying elements:
   (i)   makes them too soft;
   (ii) makes them too hard;
   (iii) increases their electrical resistance;
   (iv) makes it more difficult to machine them or draw out into wire.

2 One of the reasons that aluminium is chosen in preference to copper for overhead lines is that for a given resistance the aluminium line is:
   (i)   smaller in cross section than copper;
   (ii) more flexible than copper;
   (iii) although larger than copper, is lighter;
   (iv) the aluminium strands are easier to lay round the steel core than copper strands which are much harder.

3 Lengths of overhead line are joined together using:
   (i)   crimped terminals and bolting;
   (ii) compression sleeves;
   (iii) split ferrules and solder;
   (iv) welding.

4 Two, single-phase circuits in a conduit each have a rating of 25 A. Adding an extra circuit to the conduit making three circuits in all would cause the rating of each circuit to be reduced to:
   (i) 17.25 A; (ii) 21.56 A; (iii) 20 A. (Use the rating factors quoted in *Problem 2*)

5 At 132 kV, underground cable insulation is almost invariably:
   (i) paper; (ii) p.v.c.; (iii) polythene.

6 For cables which are to operate at 415/240 V in a situation where fire resistance is required, a suitable insulating material is:
   (i)   p.v.c.;
   (ii) Polychloroprene;
   (iii) Paper;
   (iv) Magnesium oxide (mineral);
   (v)   Polythene.

7 The magnetic force between conductors may be disruptive under short circuit conditions. The force may be reduced by:
   (i)   spacing the circuit conductors closer together;
   (ii) increasing the spacing between conductors;
   (iii) using different insulating materials, e.g. replacing p.v.c. with oil impregnated paper;
   (iv) putting the conductors inside a plastic conduit.

8 Co-axial cable is used to interconnect pieces of equipment when:
   (i)   very large currents are involved;
   (ii) the effect of cable heating is to be minimised;
   (iii) it is essential that no magnetic field shall exist round the cable;
   (iv) extra-high voltages are to be used.

9 Gold is often used for multi-contact connections in low voltage circuits. This is because:
   (i)   it has very low resistivity; (ii) it is soft and ductile;
   (iii) it gives low contact resistance at low pressures;
   (iv) it is easily soldered to the connecting wires joining it to another piece of equipment.

10 Pre-stressed glass is used as an insulating material for overhead lines because:
   (i)   it has better electrical properties than porcelain;
   (ii) although the surface layer may be punctured, it cannot absorb water;
   (iii) it may be formed into an insulator with a much larger flash-over distance so
         has better performance in foggy weather;
   (iv) when damaged it completely shatters;
   (v)   is much better than porcelain when used in pin insulators since it is more
         flexible and so less likely to fracture when subject to cross pull (by wind for
         example);
   (vi) the manufacturing cost are considerably less.
   Select *two* of these reasons.

(c) CONVENTIONAL PROBLEMS

1 State, giving your reasons, what materials are used for the conductors and
   insulation for underground cables operating at (i) 415/240 V; (ii) 132 kV.

2 Draw simple sketches to show the construction of the following cables:
   (i)   240 V twin core with earth, p.v.c. insulated;
   (ii) M.I.C.S.
   (iii) 415/240 V, 3-phase employing solid aluminium conductors.

3 Explain why it is necessary to decrease the current rating of cables when they
   operate
   (i)   in a region of high ambient temperature;
   (ii) bunched together in a conduit or trunking.

4 Determine the required cross-sectional area of the conductors in a two-core cable
   feeding a single-phase load for a maximum current of 15 A when the length of
   run is 50 m and the nominal voltage is 240 V. (Use *Table 2,* para. 7, page 47).
   Determine the power loss in the cable under these conditions.   [6 mm^2; 76.5 W]

5 Select suitable conductors from *Table 2* (page 00) for the following loads:
   (i)   15 A over a distance of 10 m from a 250 V supply;
   (ii) 30 A over a distance of 25 m from a 200 V supply;
   (iii) 24 A over a distance of 22 m from a 220 V supply.

$$\begin{bmatrix} \text{(i) 2.5 mm}^2 \\ \text{(ii) 10 mm}^2 \\ \text{(iii) 4 mm}^2 \end{bmatrix}$$

6 A printed circuit board has one circuit formed from foil 0.035 mm thick and
   0.5 mm wide. The permitted current density for a 40°C temperature rise is
   50 A/mm^2. Calculate the value of the maximum permissible circuit current.
   [0.875 A]

7 Calculate the current densities in the following printed circuit board conductors:
   (i)   0.07 mm $\times$ 1 mm carrying 5 A;
   (ii) 0.106 mm $\times$ 2 mm carrying 4 A;
   (iii) 0.35 mm $\times$ 2 mm carrying 10 A.

$$\begin{bmatrix} \text{(i) 71.3 A/mm}^2 \\ \text{(ii) 18.86 A/mm}^2 \\ \text{(iii) 14.28 A/mm}^2 \end{bmatrix}$$

8 Draw a simple sketch of one form of multi-core cable together with its termination. What is the function of such a cable?

9 Draw a sketch showing a printed circuit board and an edge-type connector. Why are the contacts in the connector often gold plated?

10 Describe two processes available for the construction of a printed circuit board. What differences are there in the method of marking out the circuit board in the case of (i) a prototype board; (ii) part of a production run?

11 Draw a sketch of an overhead line insulator showing on it:
    (i)   the dry flashover distance;   (iii) the dry leakage distance.
    (ii) the wet flashover distance;

12 Why is flashover on an overhead line insulator more likely to occur in an industrial as opposed to a country area? What design changes might be made in an attempt to overcome the problem?
                        [Longer sheds or skirts, more insulators in the string].

13 What features are built into an overhead line insulator to minimise the occurence of flashover in wet conditions?

5 Single-phase transformers

A. SUMMARY OF FORMULAE AND DEFINITIONS ASSOCIATED WITH SINGLE-PHASE TRANSFORMERS

1 **The transformer open circuit test** The normal rated voltage is applied to one of the windings whilst the other is connected to a high-resistance voltmeter. The input voltage, power and current are measured using suitable-range instruments connected as shown in *Fig 1*. Since the secondary winding is delivering virtually

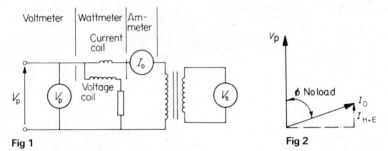

Fig 1

Fig 2

no current and the current in the winding being fed is very small, the total input power to the transformer as indicated on the wattmeter may be considered to be the core hysteresis and eddy current loss. The in-phase component of current is I_{H+E} (where H = hysteresis, E = eddy) and this relates to I_a in Chapter 3, *Fig 1* (see page 34). Using the test results the no-load phasor diagram can be constructed.

In *Fig 2*, I_o = reading on the ammeter in *Fig 1*.

The power factor $= \cos \phi = \dfrac{\text{Power delivered to the transformer}}{V_p I_o} = \dfrac{V_p I_{H+E}}{V_p I_o}$

2 **The transformer short-circuit test** The short circuit test is used to determine the power loss in the transformer windings.

The winding power loss $= (I_s')2R_p + I_s^2 R_s$, where $I_s' = I_s \dfrac{N_s}{N_p}$

I_s' is the current which flows in the primary because of the load current in the secondary.
R_p and R_s are the resistances of the primary and secondary windings respectively.

One winding of the transformer is short circuited through an ammeter whilst the other is fed from a variable-voltage supply through a wattmeter and ammeter as shown in *Fig 3*. The input voltage is raised gradually from near zero to a value at

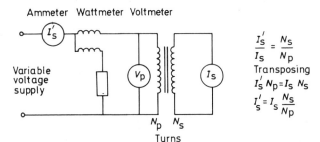

Ammeter   Wattmeter   Voltmeter

$$\frac{I'_s}{I_s} = \frac{N_s}{N_p}$$

Transposing

$$I'_s N_p = I_s N_s$$

$$I'_s = I_s \frac{N_s}{N_p}$$

Fig 3

which full-load currents are circulating in both windings. Usually only 10–20% of normal rated voltage is required to accomplish this so that the core magnetic flux density is low. Since the core losses are very nearly proportional to the square of the maximum flux density, these will be extremely low and the input power is considered to be that due to winding losses only.

The winding losses are proportional to the square of the current (losses $= I^2R$) so that from the full-load loss, the value of loss at any other load can be predicted. At one half full-load the loss wil be $(\frac{1}{2})^2 \times$ full load value. Generally, for a proportion (x) of full load the losses will be $(x)^2 \times$ full load losses.

3 **Rating**   A transformer has a nameplate rating which, in effect, indicates how much current the transformer windings can carry without overheating. The rating is quoted in volt-amperes (VA) at the full-rated voltage. For example a transformer with a rating of 10000 VA and a ratio of 500 : 100 V can carry 10000/500 = 20 A in its 500 V winding and 10000/100 = 100 A in its 100 V winding.

4 When a transformer is supplied at full rated voltage the energised winding (the primary) carries a current of I_o amperes the value of which is determined from the open circuit test results. When the other winding (the secondary) is connected to a load such that it supplies I_s amperes a current I'_s flows in the primary in addition to I_o.

The total primary current $I_p = I_o + I'_s$ (phasorially)

Consider a transformer supplying a current of I_s amperes which lags on the secondary voltage V_s by an angle ϕ_L. Thje primary balancing current will lag on its driving voltage V_p by the same angle. The input conditions are shown in *Fig 4*.

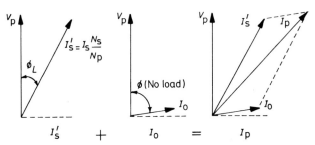

Fig 4 I'_s + I_o = I_p

The balancing current is added to I_o either by using the parallelogram method or by resolution of both currents into vertical and horizontal components.

5 **Transformer efficiency**

$$\text{Efficiency} = \frac{\text{Output power}}{\text{Input power}} = \frac{\text{Output power}}{\text{Output power} + \text{internal losses}}$$

$$= \frac{\text{Output VA} \times \text{power factor}}{\text{Output VA} \times \text{power factor} + \text{core loss} + \text{winding losses}}$$

6 The maximum efficiency of a transformer occurs at a load at which the winding copper loss is equal to the core loss. *Fig 5* shows the core and winding losses of a transformer and a typical efficiency curve. The maximum efficiency generally lies between 0.95 and 0.99 depending on type and rating. The core losses are kept small by: (i) using high grade steel to minimise hysteresis losses, (ii) laminating the core to increase its resistance to eddy currents. (See also chapter 9, para. 5).

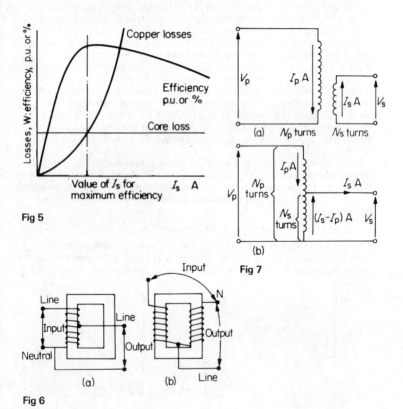

Fig 5

Fig 7

Fig 6

7 Auto transformer construction and operation

The auto transformer has only one winding part of which is common to both primary and secondary. *Fig 6* shows the possible arrangements of coils and core. The inputs and outputs are reversible providing for a voltage increase or decrease.

Considering ideal operation, the double wound auto-transformer action is compared in *Fig 7*. *Fig 7 (a)* shows the current directions in the primary and secondary of a double-wound transformer. When the secondary is in fact part of the primary, the current in the secondary section becomes $(I_s - I_p)$ as shown in *Fig 7 (b)*. The cross-sectional area of this part may therefore be reduced, so saving copper.

8 Advantages of the auto connection

(i) *Less copper is required*   The volume of copper in the winding is proportional to the number of turns and to the cross-sectional area of the wire used, which is in turn proportional to the current to be carried. Therefore:

Volume of copper $\alpha N \times I$ ampere turns.
From *Fig 7 (b)*: I_p flows in $(N_p - N_s)$ turns.
Ampere turns $= I_p(N_p - N_s)$
$\qquad\qquad = I_p N_p - I_p N_s$
Also: I_s flows in N_s turns. Ampere turns $= I_s N_s$
Total ampere turns in the auto transformer $= I_p N_p - I_p N_s + I_s N_s$
If we assume ideal operation: $I_p N_p = I_s N_s$, hence total ampere turns $= 2I_p N_p - I_p N_s$
In the double-wound transformer, ampere turns $= I_p N_p + I_s N_s = 2I_p N_p$ assuming ideal operation.

$$\frac{\text{Volume of copper in the auto transformer}}{\text{Volume of copper in the double-wound transformer}} = \frac{2I_p N_p - I_p N_s}{2I_p N_p}$$

$$= 1 - \frac{N_s}{N_p}$$

Transposing: Volume of copper in the auto transformer

$$= (1 - \frac{N_s}{N_p}) \times \text{volume of copper in a double-wound transformer.}$$

When N_s approaches N_p (V_s approaches V_p) the saving in copper is greatest.

(ii) *The weight and volume of the auto transformer* is less.

(iii) *The auto transformer* has a higher efficiency and suffers less voltage variation with changing load due to the better magnetic linkage between the primary and secondary sections of the winding.

(iv) *A continuously variable output voltage* is obtainable using the arrangement shown in *Fig 8*.

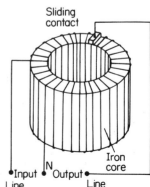

Sliding contact

Iron core

N
Fig 8   Input Line   Output Line

9 **Disadvantages of the auto connection**
   (i)   Since the neutral connection is common to both primary and secondary, earthing the primary automatically earths the secondary. Double-wound transformers are sometimes used to isolate equipment from earth.
   (ii) If the secondary suffers a short-circuit fault, the current which flows will be very much larger than in the double-wound transformer due to the better magnetic linkage.
   (iii) A break in the secondary section of the winding stops the transformer action and the full primary voltage will be applied to the secondary circuit.
10 **Current transformers** The current required to give **full-scale deflection** of a d.c. moving-coil ammeter is very small being typically only a few milli-amperes. When large currents are to be measured a shunt or bypass resistor is used in conjunction with the meter. Alternatively a moving iron meter may be used. In either case the meter coil is at the potential of the circuit in which the current is being measured. With very large currents the size of the conductor and meter terminals will be large and the internal wiring of control and metering panels made very unwieldy.

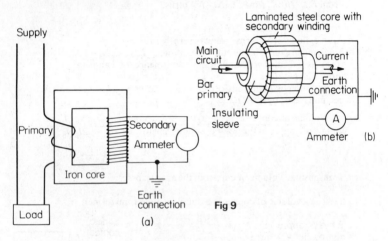

Fig 9

Where alternating currents are involved, a shunt cannot be used since the proportion of the current which flows in the meter will depend on its impedance, which varies with the frequency. A small change in frequency would upset the calibration of the meter. These problems are overcome by the use of current transformers which isolate the meter from the main circuit and allow the use of a standard range of meters giving full-scale deflections with 1, 2 or 5 A irrespective of the value of current in the main circuit. Two types of current transformer are shown in *Fig 9*.

The primary of the current transformer is connected in series with the load on the circuit, replacing an ammeter, and has an extremely small voltage drop. The core flux is therefore small. The value of the primary current is determined solely by the load on the main circuit and not by the load on its own secondary which is typically between 2.5 VA and 30 VA. Since the core flux is small, I_o is small so that $I_s = I_p$ (closely) and $I_p N_p = I_s N_s$. The magnetic fluxes set up by the m.m.f.s. $I_p N_p$ and $I_s N_s$ may individually be quite large but are very nearly equal and are in opposite directions.

The secondary of a current transformer must never be open circuited whilst the primary is carrying current since under these conditions $I_s N_s$ will be zero but the load current will continue to flow creating an m.m.f. of $I_p N_p$ ampere turns. This will set up a large flux which is unopposed and in linking with the secondary turns will induce a large voltage in them. This may be a danger to life and to the insulation within the current transformer. The large flux will cause an increase in the hysteresis and eddy current losses in the core with subsequent heating and further damage to the insulation.

The secondary of the current transformer is earthed to prevent its potential rising above that of earth due to the capacitance between windings. Also in the event of an insulation failure between primary and secondary, the earth connection would allow fault current to flow which should cause the circuit to be isolated. (Electricity Supply Regulation 20).

Typical current transformer ratings given in BS 3938 are 10, 15, 20, 30, 50 or

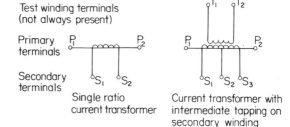

Fig 10

Test winding terminals
(not always present)

Primary terminals

Secondary terminals

Single ratio
current transformer

Current transformer with
intermediate tapping on
secondary winding

75 A in the primary with 1, 2 or 5 A in the secondary. Current transformers are made for circuits carrying several thousands of amperes. Typical terminal markings for current transformers are shown in *Fig 10*.

11 **Voltage or potential transformers** A d.c. ammeter is converted into a voltmeter by the addition of a series resistor or multiplier which limits the current at full circuit voltage to that required to give full-scale deflection of the movement. This arrangement is quite satisfactory up to about 1000 V. Insulating the meter movement, the terminals and the multiplier from the case and the panel in which the meter is situated presents no special problems.

Above 1000 V various difficulties start to appear. The cables to the meter may be long and are vulnerable to damage. Insulation becomes difficult and increasingly expensive as voltages rise.

Where alternating voltages are to be measured, the voltage transformer is used to reduce the voltage at the meter to 63.5 V or 110 V typically. The voltage transformer is essentially a power transformer designed to have a very small core loss when

$$\frac{V_p}{V_s} = \frac{N_p}{N_s} \text{(Closely)}$$

Fig 11 shows a voltage transformer connected to one phase of an 11 kV system. The transformer has a ratio of 100 : 1. The dial of the voltmeter is

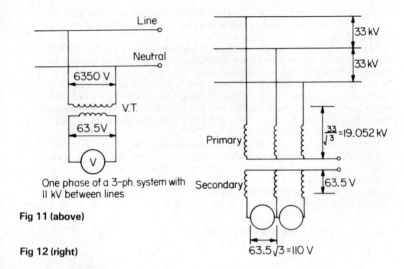

One phase of a 3-ph. system with
II kV between lines

Fig 11 (above)

Fig 12 (right)

$63.5\sqrt{3} = 110$ V

marked to indicate the voltage on the high-voltage side allowing for the transformer ratio. Where voltage transformers are used to measure the line voltages on a three-phase system as shown in *Fig 12* the secondaries are star connected giving line voltages of $63.5 \times \sqrt{3} = 110$ V at the meters.

12 Current and voltage transformers are used to isolate wattmeters from the high-

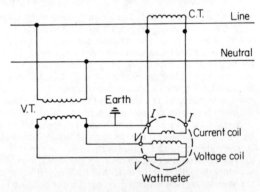

Fig 13

voltage system in which the power is to be measured. The connections for a single-phase wattmeter are shown in *Fig 13*. The voltage and current coils are connected on one side to earth, for safety reasons, as already outlined in para. 10.

B. WORKED PROBLEMS ON SINGLE-PHASE TRANSFORMERS

Problem 1   An open-circuit test on a 240 V : 440 V single-phase transformer gave the following results with the 240 V winding connected to a 240 V supply: Input current = 1.8 A (I_o). Input power = 85.54 W.

Calculate: (i) the no-load power factor and phase angle; (ii) the value of the iron loss current, I_{H+E} (where H = hysteresis loss and E = eddy current loss); (iii) the value of the magnetising current I_m. Draw a phasor diagram showing these quantities.

(i) $VI \cos \phi$ = power. Transposing gives

$$\frac{\text{power}}{VI} = \cos \phi$$

which is also known as the power factor (see para. 1).

Power factor = $\cos \phi = \dfrac{85.54}{240 \times 1.8} = 0.198$. Hence $\phi = \textbf{78.58}°$

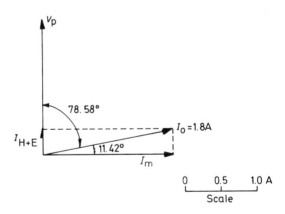

Fig 14

In *Figure 14*, I_o is drawn at 78.58° from the primary voltage phasor V_p. The component of I_o in phase with the voltage (I_{H+E}) provides the core losses.

The component of I_o lagging V_p by 90° (I_m) does no work but magnetises the core.

(ii) $\dfrac{I_{H+E}}{I_o} = \sin 11.42°$ Hence: $I_{H+E} = I_o \sin 11.42° = 1.8 \times 0.198 = \textbf{0.356 A}$

(iii) $\dfrac{I_m}{I_o} = \cos 11.42°$ Hence: $I_m = I_o \cos 11.42° = 1.8 \times 0.9802 = \textbf{1.76 A}$

67

Problem 2 A single-phase transformer with ratio 440 V : 110 V has a core loss of 190 W at full rated voltage. The magnetising current is 2 A in the 440 V winding. The transformer delivers a current of 75 A from its 110 V winding at a power factor of 0.85 lagging. Determine: (i) the iron loss component of current I_{H+E}; (ii) the no-load current of the transformer; (iii) the balancing current in the primary winding; (iv) the total primary current; (v) the power factor of the primary input at this load.

(i)   As stated in *Problem 1*, I_{H+E} provides the core loss which we know to be 190 W. Hence $V_p \times I_{H+E} = \mathbf{190}$
We are told that the magnetising current = 2 A in the 440 V winding so that we need to determine the loss current in the same winding, i.e. at 440 V

$$440 \times I_{H+E} = 190 \qquad I_{H+E} = \frac{190}{440} = 0.432 \text{ A}$$

(ii) $I_o = \sqrt{I_{H+E}^2 + I_m^2}$ (Pythagoras) $= \sqrt{0.432^2 + 2^2}) = \mathbf{2.046\ A}$
(see *Fig 15*)

$$\cos\phi_o = \frac{I_{H+E}}{I_o} = \frac{0.432}{2.046} = 0.211. \text{ Therefore } \phi_o = \mathbf{77.82°}$$

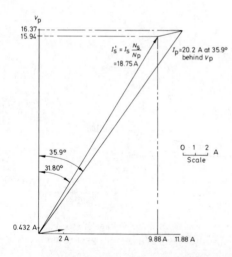

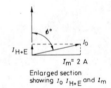

Enlarged section
showing I_o I_{H+E} and I_m

Fig 15

(iii) $I_s' = 75 \times \dfrac{N_s}{N_p} = 75 \times \dfrac{E_s}{E_p} = 75 \times \dfrac{110}{440} = \mathbf{18.75\ A}$

(iv) The load power factor = 0.85 so that I_s' lags on V_p by 31.8°.
These quantities are shown to scale in *Fig 15*.
I_s' is added to I_o using scale drawing and the parallelogram method or by resolution into vertical and horizontal components.
Vertical component of $I_s' = 18.75 \cos 31.8° = 15.94$ A

Adding to I_{H+E} which is in the same direction gives $15.94 + 0.432 = 16.37$ A
Horizontal component of $I_s = 18.75 \sin 31.8° = 9.88$ A
Adding to I_m which is in the same direction, gives $9.88 + 2 = 11.88$ A
By Pythagoras' theorem: $I_p = \sqrt{(16.37^2 + 11.88^2)} = 20.2$ A

$$\cos \phi_p = \frac{16.36}{20.2} = 0.81 \quad \text{Therefore } \phi_p = \textbf{35.9°}$$

Problem 3 A single-phase transformer rated at 15 kVA has a core loss of
400 W and a winding loss of 540 W when full load current flows in the windings.
Calculate the efficiency of the transformer for each of the following loads. (i)
Full load at unity power factor; (ii) Full load at 0.6 power factor lagging; (iii)
Half full load at unity power factor; (iv) Three eighths of full load at 0.7 power
factor lagging.

(i) $\text{Efficiency} = \dfrac{\text{output}}{\text{output} + \text{core loss} + \text{winding loss}}$

15 kVA at unity power factor = 15 kW

Therefore efficiency $= \dfrac{15000}{15000 + 400 + 540} = \textbf{0.94}$

(ii) At 0.6 power factor lagging, output $= 15000 \times 0.6 = 9000$ W

Efficiency $= \dfrac{9000}{\textbf{9000} + \textbf{400} + \textbf{540}} = \textbf{0.905}$

Note that although the output *power* is different at 0.6 power factor, the
number of kVA and hence current and winding losses are the same as in (i).

(iii) At one half full load the winding losses will be reduced to $(\frac{1}{2})^2$ of their full
load value since the losses are proportional to I^2 (see para. 2).
Winding loss on half full load $= \frac{1}{4} \times 540 = 135$ W. The core loss does not
change.

The load is $\dfrac{15000}{2} = 7500$ VA which at unity power factor = 7500 W

Efficiency $= \dfrac{7500}{7500 + 400 + 135} = \textbf{0.93}$

(iv) Winding losses $= (3/8)^2 \times 540 = 76$ W
Power output $= 3/8 \times 15000 \times 0.7 = 3938$ W

Efficiency $= \dfrac{3938}{3938 + 400 + 76} = \textbf{0.89}$

Problem 4 A single-phase, 25 kVA, 3300 V:240 V transformer has a core loss of 500 W. The winding (copper) loss was determined by performing a short circuit test with full-load current in each winding. This loss was 660 W. Determine the value of load at which the maximum efficiency occurs and the efficiency at that load assuming unity power factor.

For maximum efficiency, copper loss = core loss (see *Fig 5*).
At a proportion 'x' of full load, the copper losses are x^2 times their full-load value.

$$x^2 \times 660 = 500$$

$$x^2 = \frac{500}{660} = 0.758 \qquad \text{Therefore } x = \sqrt{0.758} = 0.87$$

The maximum efficiency occurs at $0.87 \times$ full load $= 0.87 \times 25$ kVA
$= 21.75$ kVA. ($= 21.75$ kW at unity power factor.)
At this load the core loss = copper loss, both being 500 W

$$\text{Efficiency} = \frac{21\,750}{21\,750 + 500 + 500} = \textbf{0.956 p.u.}$$

Problem 5 With the aid of simple sketches show the construction of an auto-transformer. Discuss the advantages of this connection as compared with a double-wound transformer.

The sketches required are as shown in either *Fig 6 (a)* or *(b)* together with *Fig 7 (b)*. The auto-transformer has only one winding. Part of this winding is common to both primary and secondary which are therefore magnetically and electrically linked. *Fig 6 (a)* or *(b)* shows one possible arrangement of the winding which is wound on a laminated iron core similar in construction to that used in the double-wound transformer. Using a toroidal arrangement a continuously variable output may be obtained via a sliding brush (see *Fig 8*).

ADVANTAGES OF THE AUTO CONNECTION

1 *Less copper is required* The volume of copper in a winding is proportional to the number of turns and to the cross-sectional area of the wire used which, in turn, is a function of the current to be carried. This can be demonstrated by using the currents as shown in *Fig 16*.

In the double-wound transformer, 50 turns of wire of cross section suitable to carry 5 A and 25 turns capable of carrying 10 A are required. In the auto transformer, since the secondary is part of the primary only 50 turns capable of carrying 5 A are required. Thus a saving in copper has been achieved in this case equivalent to the volume of the complete secondary in the double-wound transformer. The saving is greatest for small ratios, 2 : 1, 3 : 1 for example. For large ratios, say 10 : 1 the secondary of the double-wound transformer would have relatively few turns so that there is little saving to be made.

2 *The weight and volume of the auto-transformer is less* Auto-transformers are used to interconnect the 400 kV, 275 kV and 132 kV sections of the British grid system. When transporting very large, high-voltage transformers by road the

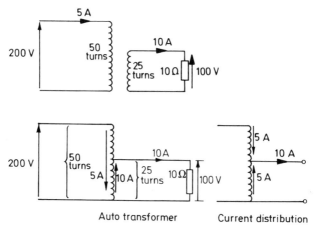

Fig 16

weight has to be carefully considered and quite often before major power system construction is commenced, roads and bridges have to be specially reinforced to carry such loads.

3 *High efficiency and less voltage variation*   The auto-transformer has a higher efficiency and suffers less voltage variation with changing load due to the better magnetic linkage between the primary and secondary sections of the winding.

4 The continuously variable voltage obtainable using the special arrangement shown in *Fig 8* is particularly useful in laboratories for test purposes and indeed for obtaining the reduced voltage used in the transformer short circuit test.

Problem 6   A voltage transformer of ratio 100:1 and a current transformer of ratio 100:5 are used to measure the power and power factor in a single-phase circuit using a wattmeter as shown in *Fig 17*. The potential difference across the wattmeter voltage coil is 63.5 V and the current in the current coil is 4.3 A. The wattmeter reading is 245 W.

  Calculate, for the primary circuit (i) the current; (ii) the phase voltage; (iii) the power factor; (iv) the power.

(i)   The current transformer ratio = 100:5, i.e. with 100 A in the main (primary) circuit, 5 A will flow in the wattmeter current coil.

  With 4.3 A in the secondary, primary current = $4.3 \times \dfrac{100}{5} = \textbf{86 A}$

(ii) The voltage transformer ratio = 100:1
  Therefore the primary voltage = $100 \times 63.5 = \textbf{6350 V}$

71

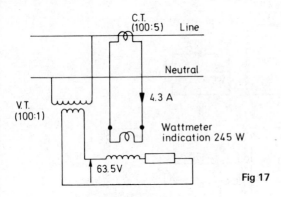

C.T.
(100:5)   Line

Neutral

4.3 A

V.T.
(100:1)

Wattmeter
indication 245 W

63.5 V

Fig 17

(iii) The power factor in the secondary circuit is the same as that in the primary circuit assuming perfect transformers.

$$\text{Power factor} = \frac{\text{Power}}{\text{Volt-amperes}} = \frac{245}{63.5 \times 4.3} = \mathbf{0.897}$$

(iv) Power in the primary $= VI \cos \phi$ watts

$$= 6350 \times 86 \times 0.897 = \mathbf{490\,000\ W}$$

This is the same as secondary power × voltage transformer ratio × current transformer ratio

$$= 245 \times \frac{100}{1} \times \frac{100}{5} = \mathbf{490\,000\ W.}$$

Problem 7   A single-phase auto-transformer has a ratio of 1000:750 V and supplies a load of 45 kVA at 750 V. Calculate the value of current in each section of the winding. Assume ideal operation.

45 kVA at   750 V requires a current of $\dfrac{45000}{750} = \mathbf{60\ A}$

45 kVA at 1000 V requires a current of $\dfrac{45000}{1000} = \mathbf{45\ A}$

The current in the secondary section of the winding $= 60 - 45 = \mathbf{15\ A}$
The current in the primary section of the winding $= \mathbf{45\ A}$
(see *Fig 7(b)*)

Problem 8   Compare the volume of copper in a single-phase auto transformer with that in a double-wound transformer for ratios (i) 440:400 V; (ii) 440 V:40 V

(i) Volume of copper in the auto transformer $= (1 - \dfrac{400}{440}) \times$ volume in the double wound transformer $= \mathbf{0.091\ times.}$

72

(ii) Volume of copper in the auto transformer $= (1 - \frac{40}{440}) = \mathbf{0.91}$ times that in the double wound transformer.

C. FURTHER PROBLEMS ON SINGLE-PHASE TRANSFORMERS

(a) SHORT ANSWER PROBLEMS

1   What is the purpose of the open-circuit test as performed on a transformer?

2   What is the purpose of a short-circuit test as performed on a transformer?

3   The input to the 240 V winding of a 240:110 V, 5 kVA, single-phase transformer is 150 W when the secondary is open circuited and full voltage is applied to the 240 V winding. What will be the value of the core loss when the transformer is supplying its full rated load?

4   A transformer has a copper loss of 50 W when supplying one half its rated load. What will be the value of the copper loss when it is carrying full load?

5   A transformer has a core loss of 100 W at full rated voltage. What will be the value of the copper loss when the transformer is operating at its maximum efficiency?

6   A single-phase transformer has a ratio of 440:240 V. It supplies a load of 10 kVA from its 240 V terminals. What are the values of the primary and secondary currents assuming that the magnetising and loss currents may be ignored?

7   A 2 kVA transformer has an iron loss of 200 W and a copper loss of 250 W on full load. Calculate the value of the maximum efficiency possible when operating at unity power factor.

8   Draw a sketch showing a schematic arrangement of an auto-transformer.

9   List three advantages and two disadvantages of the auto connection as opposed to the double-wound type.

10   What proportion of the copper used in a double-wound transformer could be saved under the auto connection given a ratio of 231 kV:76.2 kV?

11   A current transformer with a bar primary has 150 secondary turns. Determine the value of primary current necessary to give full-scale deflection of 5 A on an ammeter connected to the secondary.

12   Why is the secondary winding of a current transformer normally connected to earth?

13   Draw a connection diagram showing a current transformer and a voltage transformer connected to a wattmeter so as to measure power in a single-phase circuit.

(b) MULTI-CHOICE PROBLEMS (answers on page 213)

1   The iron core of a transformer is laminated in order to:
   (i)   Reduce hysteresis loss;   (iii) Increase the resistance of the core
   (ii) Improve magnetic linkage between   and so reduce eddy currents;
       primary and secondary windings; (iv) Make fabrication easier since it is
                                         simpler to stack many thin sheets
                                         into the required shape than to
                                         fabricate it from a solid piece.

2   The open circuit test on a transformer is carried out at:
   (i)   Normal operating voltage;
   (ii) A voltage slightly in excess of normal;
   (iii) A very much reduced voltage to reduce the current.
   The test is used to determine:
   (iv) the winding losses;
   (v)   the hysteresis and eddy current losses in the core.
   Select *one* from (i), (ii) and (iii) and *one* from (iv) and (v) to make a correct
   statement.

3   A single-phase transformer has a ratio 240:110 V. On no load it draws a current
   of 2 A at 0.2 power factor lagging from a 240 V supply. When the secondary
   (110 V) winding is carrying a current of 21.82 A at unity power factor, the
   primary current is:
   (i) 20.5 A; (ii) 10.6 A; (iii) 11.97 A; (iv) 12 A; (v) 22 A.

4   A 2.5 kVA, single-phase transformer has an iron loss of 50 W and a copper loss
   on one half full load of 15 W. Maximum efficiency occurs when the load on the
   transformer is:
   (i) 2.08 kVA; (ii) 0.75 kVA; (iii) 2.28 kVA; (iv) 4.56 kVA.

5   A double-wound transformer of ratio 440:220 V contains a mass of 50 kg of
   copper in its two windings. An auto transformer of the same rating would
   contain (closely):
   (i) 50 kg; (ii) 100 kg; (iii) 18 kg; (iv) 25 kg of copper?

6   Auto transformers are used to interconnect the 400 kV and 132 kV transmission
   systems in the UK since:
   (i)   double-wound transformers are unsuitable;
   (ii) auto transformers are more reliable than double wound transformers;
   (iii) auto transformers weigh less than double wound transformers of similar
        ratio and rating;
   (iv) auto transformers deliver less current into a short circuit fault should one
        occur.

7   Should the secondary section of the winding in a step-down auto transformer
   fracture the voltage at the secondary terminals would:
   (i) rise; (ii) fall; (iii) remain substantially constant.

8   A current transformer is used when measuring
   (i)   alternating currents;
   (ii) direct currents.
   It has advantages over the shunt in that:
   (iii) it is cheaper;
   (iv) it isolates the measuring instrument from the main circuit;

74

(v)   the accuracy is not affected by small changes in frequency;
(vi) the meter may be connected to and disconnected from the current
      transformer with no special precautions since the output voltage from the
      current transformer is very low.
Select (i) *or* (ii) together with *two* from (iii) to (vi) to make a correct statement.

9   Single-phase power is measured using a current transformer with ratio 50:5 A
    and a voltage transformer with ratio 3300:110 V. The wattmeter indicates 300 W.
    The power in the primary circuit is
    (i) 3 kW; (ii) 90 kW; (iii) 9 kW; (iv) 12 kW.

(c) CONVENTIONAL PROBLEMS

1   A single-phase transformer has a ratio of 3300:240 V. It supplies a current of
    550 A at 240 V. Calculate the value of the balancing current in the 3300 V
    winding.

                                                                                  [40 A]

2   A 440:110 V, single-phase transformer draws a magnetising current of 1 A and
    an iron loss current of 0.25 A, both in the 440 V winding. The secondary load
    supplied at 110 V is 10.7 A at a power factor of 0.85 lagging. Calculate:
    (a) the no load current of the transformer;
    (b) the balancing current in the primary (440 V) winding;
    (c) the total primary current;
    (d) the phase angle between the primary current and the supply voltage.

$$\begin{bmatrix} \text{(a) 1.03 A} \\ \text{(b) 2.675 A} \\ \text{(c) 3.5 A} \\ \text{(d) 43.7}° \end{bmatrix}$$

3   Determine the rated current in each winding of a 1100:240 V single-phase
    double-wound transformer with a rating of 25 kVA.   [22.73 A 104.2 A]

4   A 480:240 V, 20 kVA, single-phase transformer has a core loss of 200 W and a
    copper loss of 45 W when one half of full load current flows in the windings.
    Calculate the efficiency of the transformer when it is delivering:
    (a) 10 kVA at 0.8 power factor lagging;
    (b) 20 kVA at unity power factor;
    (c) 15 kVA at 0.75 power factor lagging.

$$\begin{bmatrix} \text{(a) 0.97 pu;} \\ \text{(b) copper loss = 180 W, 0.98 pu} \\ \text{(c) copper loss = 101.3 W, 0.974 pu} \end{bmatrix}$$

5   A single-phase auto transformer has a ratio 500:400 V and supplies a load of
    30 kVA at 400 V. Calculate the value of current in each section of the
    winding.
    Assume ideal operation. [Secondary 15 A, Input 60 A, Load current 75 A]

6   Compare the volume of copper in a single-phase auto transformer with that in a
    double-wound transformer for the following ratios:
    (a) 400:300 V; (b) 400:50 V.   [(a) 0.25; (b) 0.875]

7 A current transformer has a primary winding of 2 turns and a secondary winding of 100 turns. The secondary winding is connected to an ammeter with a resistance of $0.2\,\Omega$. The resistance of the secondary of the current transformer is $0.3\,\Omega$. The value of the current in the primary winding is 250 A. Calculate:
(a) the value of current in the current transformer secondary;
(b) the potential difference across the ammeter terminals;
(c) the total e.m.f. induced in the secondary;
(d) the total load in VA on the current transformer secondary.
(For parts (b) and (c) use Ohm's law)

$$\begin{bmatrix} \text{(a) 5 A} \\ \text{(b) 1 V} \\ \text{(c) 2.5 V} \\ \text{(d) 12.5 VA} \end{bmatrix}$$

8 A current transformer has a bar primary (1 turn). The secondary is connected to an ammeter which indicates 4.3 A when the current in the primary circuit is 344 A. Determine the number of turns on the current transformer secondary.

[80 turns]

9 A voltage transformer of ratio 100:1 and a current transformer of ratio 100:5 are used in conjunction with a wattmeter to measure the power and power factor in a single-phase circuit. The potential difference across the wattmeter voltage coil is 190.52 V and the current in the current coil is 3.9 A. The power in the primary circuit is 900 kW. Determine:
(a) the primary current;   (c) the power factor;
(b) the primary voltage;   (d) the indication on the wattmeter.

$$\begin{bmatrix} \text{(a) 78 A} \\ \text{(b) 19052 V} \\ \text{(c) 0.606} \\ \text{(d) 450 W} \end{bmatrix}$$

10 A load of 25 kVA with power factor 0.6 lagging is fed at 450 V from a single-phase supply. A voltage transformer with ratio 4:1 and a current transformer with ratio 100:5 together with a wattmeter are used to measure the power in the circuit. Determine: (a) the potential difference across the wattmeter voltage coil; (b) the current in the wattmeter current coil; (c) the indicated power on the wattmeter.

$$\begin{bmatrix} \text{(a) 112.5 V} \\ \text{(b) 2.78 A} \\ \text{(c) 187.5 W} \end{bmatrix}$$

11 Calculate the efficiency of a single-phase transformer on full load at 0.8 power factor lagging given the following data:
Ratio 500 V:100 V, Rating 20 kVA
Short circuit test results. 100 V winding short circuited. Power input to the 500 V winding = 35 W when the current in this winding = 20 A.
Open circuit test results. 500 V winding open circuited. 100 V applied to the 100 V winding. Input 5 A at 0.2 power factor lagging.
(Start by deciding what proportion of full load current 20 A is in the 500 V winding)   [0.985]

12 A 50 kVA, 11 kV:240 V, single-phase transformer draws 1.2 A at 0.3 power factor lagging from the 11 kV system when the 240 V winding is open circuited.

For the transformer on full load at 0.75 power factor lagging, calculate:
(a) the secondary current;   (c) the primary power factor;
(b) the primary balancing current;   (d) the primary current.

$$\begin{bmatrix} \text{(a) 208.33 A} \\ \text{(b) 4.545 A} \\ \text{(c) 0.673} \\ \text{(d) 5.6 A} \end{bmatrix}$$

13 An open-circuit test on a 6360 V:240 V, 150 kVA, single-phase transformer yielded the following results:
6360 V winding connected to a 6360 V supply with the 240 V winding open circuited, input power = 2500 W at 0.24 power factor lagging.
Determine the value of the primary current and power factor when the secondary (240 V) winding is carrying full load current at 0.85 power factor lagging.

$$[I_p = 24.8 \text{ A; p.f.} = 0.825]$$

6 D.C. machines

A. SUMMARY OF FORMULAE AND DEFINITIONS ASSOCIATED WITH D.C. MACHINES

1   A d.c. machine is made up of the following parts:
(a) Magnetic poles which are electrically produced by coils of wire wound on laminated soft-iron cores and which carry direct current;
(b) A steel yoke which supports the poles;
(c) An armature which is also formed from steel laminations. This carries coils in slots; the ends of which are connected to the copper segments of a commutator;
(d) Carbon brushes which bear on the commutator supplying current to or taking current from the machine;
(e) Bearings to support the shaft and armature.
Fig 1 shows the general arrangement, the armature being shown with only one

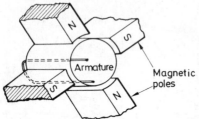

Fig 1

coil (the commutator is not shown). Driving the armature in either direction will result in the coil cutting through the flux produced by the poles with consequent generation of an e.m.f. Feeding the coil with current from an external source will result in forces being produced as the coil passes under the pole faces. This is known as the **motoring action.** To get continuous motion more than one coil is necessary, unless an external starting torque and inertia are provided. *Fig 2* shows an elevation together with the method of exciting the field poles and *Fig 3* shows a section of a commutator.

2   **The ring-wound armature**
In *Fig 4* the laminated iron core is wound with ten coils each having two turns. The commutator has ten segments, one for each coil. The magnetic flux produced by the coils crosses the air gap into the core. Only the outsides of the turns directly under the poles cut the flux and the directions of the induced e.m.f.s shown are deduced using Fleming's right-hand rule. In both the top and bottom halves of the winding this direction is towards the right hand brush which is therefore positive.

With this particular arrangement there are six conductors cutting the magnetic

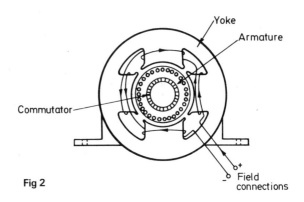

Yoke

Armature

Commutator

Field connections

+

–

Fig 2

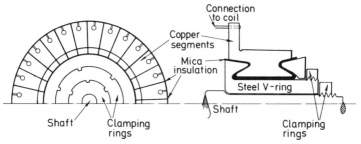

Connection to coil

Copper segments

Mica insulation

Steel V-ring

Shaft

Shaft

Clamping rings

Clamping rings

Fig 3   The commutator

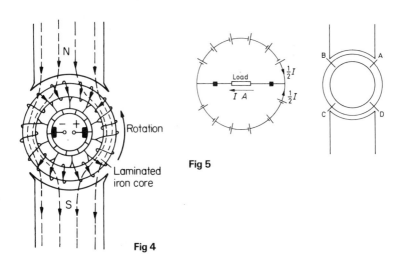

N

Rotation

Laminated iron core

S

Fig 4

Load

I A

$\frac{1}{2}I$

$\frac{1}{2}I$

B   A

C   D

Fig 5

flux from each pole at any instant. Representing the e.m.f induced in each conductor by a cell, each half of the winding has six cells in series. Both halves of the winding are in parallel and, when a load is connected, each half carries one half of the load current. As a coil passes under a pole from point A to point B (see *Fig 5*) the induced voltage is nearly constant. Whilst moving from point B to point C the voltage falls to zero since no flux is being cut. The waveform of the voltage in a single coil is shown in *Fig 6*.

We will now look at the function of the commutator. With the armature in the position shown in *Fig 4* each brush is shorting out one coil which has no e.m.f. induced in it since it is not cutting the flux. The flux at this instant is passing directly through the coil. The action of the commutator is to allow each coil in turn to pass through this position, moving from being under the influence of a north pole, where the current in the coil is in one direction, to being under a

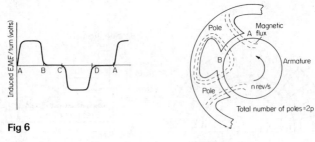

Fig 6

Fig 7

south pole where the current is reversed. The current in the external circuit is uni-directional being unaffected by the reversals within the machine. The process of current reversal in a particular coil is called **commutation** and ideally this should take place with no sparking although large currents may be involved.

3 **Other windings** The ring winding has two disadvantages, these are
   (i) The ring winding is difficult to wind since each turn must be taken round the core by hand;
   (ii) Only a small part of the winding is active at any one time;
   To overcome these problems two alternative windings have been developed known as the **lap winding** and the **wave winding**. (See *Problem 1*).

4 **The e.m.f. and speed equations**
   Fig 7 shows part of a d.c. machine. Consider a single conductor on the armature as it moves from position A to position B.
   Let ϕ = total flux per pole in webers;
   n = speed of the armature in revolutions per second;
   P = number of *pairs* of poles on the yoke;
   Z = total number of conductors on the armature;
   c = number of parallel paths through the armature.
   There are $2P$ poles on the armature and at n rev/s the particular conductor shown will pass $2Pn$ poles every second.

   Time taken to pass one pole = $\dfrac{1}{2Pn}$ s

This is the time taken for the conductor to move from A to B in *Fig 13* and during this time the flux ϕ from one pole is cut. Average voltage induced in the

$$\text{conductor} = \frac{\text{flux}}{\text{time}} = \phi / \frac{1}{2\,Pn} = 2\,Pn\phi \text{ volts}$$

On the armature there are Z conductors arranged in c parallel groups. [See *Problem 1*].

There are therefore $\dfrac{Z}{c}$ conductors in series in each group.

Hence, total e.m.f. $= 2Pn\phi \times \dfrac{Z}{c}$ volts

Transposing gives

$$n = \frac{E}{2P\phi\frac{Z}{c}} = \frac{E_C}{2P\phi Z} \text{ rev/s.}$$

or, since 1 revolution $= 2\pi$ radians

$$= \frac{2\pi Ec}{2P\phi Z} = \frac{\pi E_C}{P\phi Z} \text{rad/s}$$

5   In the d.c. motor the force created by the current flowing in the armature conductors causes acceleration from rest of the armature if it is free to move. The motion of the conductors through the field causes an e.m.f. to be generated. By Lenz's law, the generated e.m.f. opposes the supply voltage. For this reason it is called the **back e.m.f.** At a certain speed dependent on the mechanical forces involved, the strength of the magnetic field and the applied voltage, equilibrium will be reached between the applied voltage and the back e.m.f.

The applied voltage is given the symbol V. The back e.m.f. is given the symbol E. In order that current shall flow into the motor to produce the necessary force and torque to sustain rotation, E must be less than V.

$$V - E = I_a R_a$$

where I_a = armature current in amperes;
R_a = armature resistance in ohms.

If the mechanical load on the motor is increased it will slow down thus reducing the velocity of the conductors through the field. This reduces the back e.m.f. so causing the current to increase. The increase in current provides the extra force necessary to keep the motor turning against the increased load.

If a d.c. machine, connected to a supply and running as a motor, has the speed of its armature raised above that at which it operates as a motor by driving it with an external engine whilst keeping the field constant, the value of the generated e.m.f. will increase since this is proportional to speed. As E becomes greater than the supply voltage V, a current will flow from the machine which has now become a generator, receiving power from the driving engine and delivering power to the electrical system. Again the difference between E and V is $I_a R_a$ but now $V - E = -I_a R_a$ since the current has reversed in direction. Transposing gives
$$E = V + I_a R_a$$

6 **The torque equation**

For a motor $E = V - I_a R_a$

Multiplying throughout by I_a gives: $EI_a = VI_a - I_a^2 R_a$ (all watts)

VI_a = total input to the armature. (Supply voltage × current)

$I_a^2 Ra$ = power loss in the armature as heat.

Hence EI_a must be the power available in the armature to produce torque.

Now $E = \dfrac{2P\phi Zn}{c}$ volts and power = $2\pi nT$ watts

Therefore

$$EI_a = 2\pi NT = \frac{2P\phi Zn}{c}$$

Transposing gives

$$T = \frac{2P\phi Zn}{c2\pi n}I_a = \frac{P\phi Z}{c\pi}I_a \text{ newton metres.}$$

P, Z, c and π are constant so that the torque developed is proportional to flux and armature current I_a. Not all the torque is available to drive an external load however since there will be friction in the motor bearings and between the armature surface and the air in the casing. The armature may be driving a fan to assist its own cooling.

7 **The shunt connection**

Figure 8 shows the shunt connection. The field winding comprises many turns of fairly fine wire and it is connected in series with a control rheostat directly across the supply. It is therefore in parallel with, or shunting, the armature. The field current is independent of the armature current. For a particular rheostat setting the field current and hence flux are constant. Consider firstly the motoring condition.

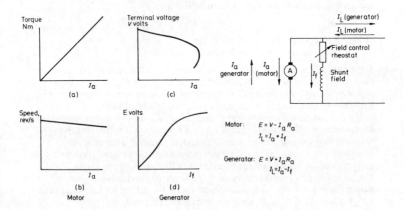

Fig 8

From the torque equation we see that $T \propto \phi$ and I_a. Now since ϕ is constant, $T \propto I_a$. This is a straight line relationship (*Fig 8 (a)*).

In the torque equation $E = V - I_a R_a$ so that as I_a increases with load, E falls. From the e.m.f. equation we have

$$E = \frac{2P\phi Zn}{c} \text{volts}$$

Since ϕ is constant together with 2, P, Z and c: $E \propto n$. As E falls, n falls at the same rate (*Fig 8 (b)*).

Consider the generator condition. In the self-excited generator part of the armature output current is used to excite its own field so that $I_L = I_a - I_f$. An increase in load current causes $I_a R_a$ to increase and the terminal voltage V will fall.

The field current $I_f = V/R_f$ so that a reduction in terminal voltage results in a reduction in the field current and hence the field flux. Since E is proportional to that flux ϕ, a reduction in flux causes a reduction in generated e.m.f. and a further fall in V. The terminal voltage therefore falls quite rapidly as the load current increases (*Fig 8 (c)*). When driven at a constant speed with no load connected, the relationship between field current and generated e.m.f. is the same as that between flux density B and magnetising force H for any iron cored coil. With zero field current there is a small output voltage which is produced by the residual magnetism in the pole pieces without which the generator cannot commence generation. The characteristic is shown in *Fig 8 (d)*.

8 **The series connection**

Fig 9 shows the series connection. The field winding comprises a few turns of very heavy gauge copper wire or strip. It is connected in series with the armature

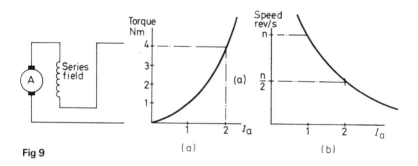

Fig 9

and so carries the same current. For this reason it must have a very low resistance or the power loss will be excessive.

As a motor:

Since $T \propto \phi$ and I_a and ϕ is itself proportional to I_a, doubling the armature current also doubles the flux produced and this results in a quadrupling of the torque (*Fig 9 (a)*).

Again, $E = \dfrac{2P\phi Zn}{c} \text{volts}$

In this case ϕ is proportional to the armature current. Hence doubling the load current doubles the flux. Considering E as very nearly constant, doubling ϕ must cause n to fall to one half of its former value if the e.m.f. equation is to balance (*Fig 9 (b)*).

The series connection is rarely if ever used in a generator since with no load on the machine there is no current in the field winding and the output voltage is near zero. When a current flows, the flux and voltage increase. The terminal voltage is thus a function of the load current.

9 **The compound connection**

Fig 10 shows machines with some shunt and some series field. Both shunt and series coils are wound on the same pole pieces and the series field may either assist (cumulative winding) or oppose (differential winding) the shunt field. Both motors and generators are compounded to give particular characteristics as shown in *Fig 11* suited to special applications.

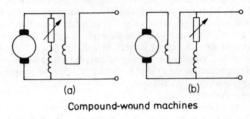

Compound-wound machines

Fig 10

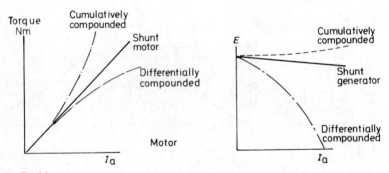

Fig 11

10 **Further work on commutation**

Fig 12 shows one coil of a lap winding. The negative brush is resting on segment 4 of the commutator. As viewed, the current direction in the coil 3,3′ is anti-clockwise.

In *Fig 12(b)* the conductors have moved a distance equivalent to one half of a commutator segment to the right. Both coil sides are now between poles and there is no induced e.m.f. in the coil. The brush now shorts out the coil since it

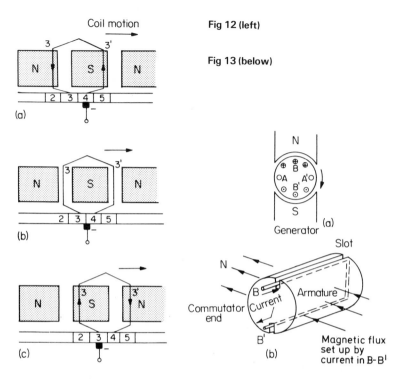

Fig 12 (left)

Fig 13 (below)

Coil motion

(a)

(b)

(c)

N   S   N

N   S   N

N   S   N

N
Generator (a)
S

Slot

N

B   Armature
Commutator Current
end

B'

Magnetic flux
set up by
current in B-B'

spans segments 3 and 4. In *Fig 12(c)* both coil sides are again under poles and the direction of the current is clockwise. This means that in the time taken for the armature to move from position (a) to position (c) the current in the coil must reverse in direction. When the current changes in an inductive circuit a voltage is induced. This is given by the expression

$$e = L\frac{\mathrm{d}i}{\mathrm{d}t} \text{ volts}$$

where L = inductance of the circuit in henrys;

$\dfrac{\mathrm{d}i}{\mathrm{d}t}$ = the rate of change of current in amperes per second.

In a d.c. machine this voltage is known as **reactance voltage.** It opposes the current reversal. If this reversal is not complete by the time the commutator segment moves from under the brush, sparking will result.

11 **Armature reaction**

In *Fig 13* a simple armature is shown revolving between two magnetic poles. The current directions are as shown. The coil A,A′ which lies horizontally has no e.m.f. induced in it and its current is undergoing commutation. The coil B,B′ which is in the vertical plane at this instant is shown separately in *Fig 13(b)*. The current in this coil produces a magnetic north pole on the left-hand side of the

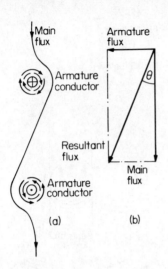

Main flux

Armature conductor

Armature conductor

(a)

Armature flux

Resultant flux

θ

Main flux

(b)

Fig 14 (left)

Fig 15 (below)

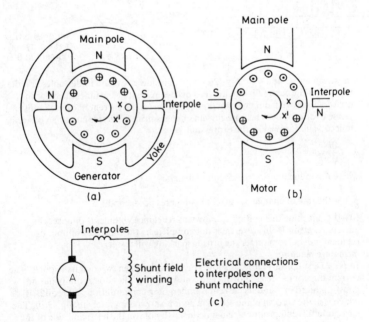

Main pole

N

N

S

Interpole

S

Yoke

Generator

(a)

Main pole

N

S

Interpole

N

S

Motor

(b)

Interpoles

A

Shunt field winding

Electrical connections to interpoles on a shunt machine

(c)

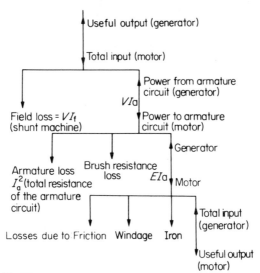

Fig 16

armature. The effect is increased by the other two current carrying coils. The strength of this cross magnetic field will depend on the number of turns and the value of armature current. The effect of the armature flux on the main flux is called armature reaction. It causes the flux crossing the armature to be turned through an angle marked θ in *Fig 14*.

Coils which, on 'no-load', are in the correct position for commutation to take place will find themselves in the magnetic field when this has been twisted around. Thus one of the effects of armature reaction is to cause severe sparking as the brushes short out coils in which an e.m.f. is being generated. (See also *Problem 10*).

12 Interpoles

Many d.c. machines are fitted with interpoles. These are very thin poles with windings carrying armature current situated between the main poles. They are wound to give a polarity which anticipates the action of the next main pole. They assist the reversal of the current in the armature coil undergoing commutation. The interpole not only neutralises the effect of armature reaction local to the conductors undergoing commutation but overcomes the effects of reactance voltage. As the conductor moves from X to X' in *Fig 15(a)* and *(b)*, in both cases the interpole acts in a generating mode establishing the current direction required by the south pole at the bottom.

13 The power flow diagram (see *Fig 16*).

B WORKED PROBLEMS ON D.C. MACHINES

Problem 1   Describe with the aid of suitable sketches the development of d.c. machines having: (a) the lap winding; (b) the wave winding.

(a)   *The lap winding*
   Fig 17 shows a lap coil comprising two turns. It is coil number 1 and its two sides are labelled 1 and 1′ respectively. Its two ends are connected to adjacent segments on a commutator and coil number 1 starts on segment number 1. The other end of the coil is connected to segment number 2. In

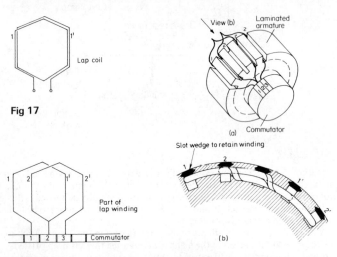

Fig 17

Fig 18

Fig 19

Fig 18 coil number 2 is added and this starts on segment number 2 of the commutator. Only one turn per coil is shown here making the diagram easier to follow. There may in fact be many turns in each coil.
   The coils are situated in slots in a laminated iron armature and part of the winding is shown in *Fig 19(a)*. *Fig 19(b)* shows how the windings overlap. The complete winding is made up in this manner until all the slots in the armature contain two coil sides, one on top which starts at the commutator segment and which carries its number, 1,2,3 etc and the other at the bottom which is the return coil side numbered 1′, 2′, 3′, etc.
   With the lap winding there are always the same number of brushes as poles, the brushes under like poles being connected in parallel. For a four-pole machine there are 4 brushes and the arrangement is shown in *Fig 20*. There are therefore 4 parallel paths through the armature. It is possible to find a route from a positive to a negative brush from A to B, from C to B, from C to D and A to D.

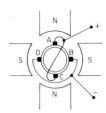

Fig 20

Wave coil

Fig 21

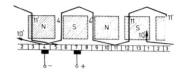

Fig 22

For a lap winding:
The number of parallel paths = number of brushes = number of poles.

(b) *The wave winding*
An alternative to the lap winding where a higher voltage is employed is the wave winding. *Fig 21* shows a coil for a wave winding. The ends of the coil are not connected to adjacent segments on the commutator but to segments some distance apart. Again using a four-pole machine as an example, the winding is shown in part in *Fig 22*. It will be seen that the commutator segments 2 and 3 are repeated at each end of the commutator so that it may be envisaged in its circular form. There is an additional commutator segment, number 13, which causes the winding to progress in waves. Starting with the negative brush presently on segment 4 follow conductors 4 and 4′ to segment 11 and then conductors 11 and 11′ to segment 5. Four conductors are involved in progressing one segment along the commutator. The process may be continued following four more conductors (not shown) so returning to segment 6. A further 4 conductors, making 12 in all allows us to progress to segment 7 upon which the positive brush rests.

With this winding two parallel paths through the armature exist. One of them is as described above and the other could be traced from segment 4 progressing in the other direction starting with conductor 10′ which passes under the south pole on the right of the diagram, eventually returning again to segment 7.

Problem 2 Describe typical applications for d.c. machines which are: (a) shunt connected; (b) series connected; (c) compound connected.

Shunt motors are used where virtually constant speed is required on such drives as machine tools and fans.

Series motors produce very high torques at low speeds and so they are suitable for starting very heavy loads. The main uses are in traction. Series motors are used extensively in trains, electric buses, trams and milk delivery vehicles.

Compound motors with a differential winding can be arranged to have almost exactly constant speed and are used for coal feeders on boilers and oil pumps. The cumulative winding is used where a high starting torque is required together with a safe maximum speed, for example, in conveyor systems, hoists and cranes.

Cumulatively compounded generators are used where a slightly rising terminal voltage is required to counter voltage drops in lines so that the load terminal voltage at the far end of the line remains constant (closely). Differential compound is used in welding sets where 110 V is required to strike the arc but only 20–25 V to maintain it thereafter.

Problem 3 Explain why it is necessary to employ a starter to start a d.c. motor. Draw a sketch and explain the action of a simple faceplate starter.

Since

$$E = \frac{2P\phi Zn}{c} \text{ volts,}$$

it follows that when a motor is at rest, since $n =$ zero, whatever the value of flux, the back e.m.f. is zero.

But $E = V - I_a R_a$. Therefore $O = V - I_a R_a$

Transposing gives

$$I_a = \frac{V}{R_a} \text{ amperes.}$$

The resistance of the armature is kept as small as possible to keep the losses to a minimum. It follows that the armature current under these conditions will be extremely large and damage due to heating or mechanical forces may result. To prevent these excessive currents flowing, the resistance of the armature circuit is increased during the starting period. However it is essential to have the maximum possible field strength in the motor at this time since both torque and back e.m.f. E are proportional to flux.

Fig 23 shows a suitable faceplate starter for a shunt motor. The handle is moved manually from the off position to make contact with the first resistance stud. This puts resistances R_1, R_2, R_3 and R_4 in series with the armature. Full voltage is applied to the field through the copper strip. On the way to the field the current flows through the hold-on coil, H. As the speed of the motor increases the handle is moved slowly across the studs until stud number 5 is reached. The armature is now connected directly across the supply. In this position the handle is in contact with the faces of the electromagnet H. Either the whole handle or a small pad fixed to it is made of a magnetic material so that provided a suitable current is flowing in the field winding, the handle will be held in the running position.

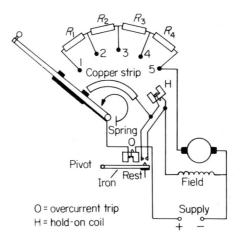

Fig 23

All the current being supplied to the motor flows through the small coil on the horseshoe shaped piece of iron of the overcurrent trip 0. A beam beneath the coil will be attracted upwards if excessive current flows thus shorting out the hold-on coil. The handle will be released when it will be carried back to the off position by the return spring.

Problem 4   List and briefly discuss the losses which occur in d.c. machines.

Field loss
In the shunt machine the field loss $= VI_f$ watts.
In the series machine, since the field winding carries armature current,
loss $= I_a^2 R_{sf}$ watts.

The field loss is a function of the number of ampere turns necessary to magnetise the pole pieces and so is dependent on the grade of steel used.

Armature loss
(a) $I_a^2 R_a$ watts loss in the armature coils.
(b)   *Iron losses.* Since the armature is subject to alternating magnetisation as it passes under north and south poles there will be hysteresis and eddy current losses in the steel. Both are dependent on the speed of rotation, the grade of steel used and the maximum working flux density. Eddy currents are limited by using laminations to make up the armature.

Commutator losses.
(a)   *Resistance loss.* There is resistance between the brush surface and the commutator and the loss depends on the grade and quality of the brushes used.
(b)   *Friction loss.* There is rubbing friction between the brush and commutator surface and the power loss depends on the coefficient of ffriction and the rubbing speed.

Bearing friction

The armature is supported in bearings which may be of the ball, roller or sleeve types according to motor application. The frictional loss is a function of the type of bearing and the rotational speed.

Windage   There will be friction between the surface of the armature and the air in the casing. In addition, power will usually be required to drive a cooling fan.

Problem 5   Using as an example, a single turn coil rotating in a constant magnetic field, describe the action of a commutator.

The action of the commutator is shown in *Fig 24*. The brushes are shown inside the commutator for clarity. Assume that there is an external load connected so that current flows in the coil. The left-hand coil side connected to segment 1

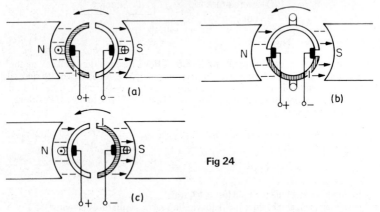

Fig 24

(shaded) has the current direction shown. This is deduced using Fleming's right-hand rule.

Current is flowing towards the left-hand brush which delivers current to the load. This brush therefore has positive polarity. Current returns from the external circuit to the right hand brush and flows in the coil away from the commutator segment.

In *Fig 24(b)* we see the coil turned through 90°. The coil sides are outside the field so that the generated e.m.f. is zero. The brushes are shorting out the coil since they are touching both halves of the commutator at once. In *Fig 24(c)* the coil has turned through a further 90° and commutator segment 1 is now on the right. The current direction in the coil side connected to it has reversed being now away from the commutator. However since a commutator is being used the left hand brush is now connected to the other side of the coil and so still has the same polarity.

The e.m.f. generated in the coil is alternating but by using a mechanical reversing switch or commutator the current flowing in the external circuit is a series of uni-directional pulses.

Problem 6 An 8-pole, d.c. lap-wound generator has 36 slots on the armature. Each slot contains 10 conductors. When the speed of the armature is 600 rev/min, the induced e.m.f. in each conductor is 3.5 V.

Calculate: (a) the total number of conductors on the armature; (b) the total number of turns on the armature; (c) the number of conductors in series in each parallel group; (d) the total generated e.m.f.; (e) the rating of the generator if each conductor can carry 10 A before overheating.

(a) Total number of conductors = number of slots × number of conductors in each slot

$$= 36 \times 10 = \mathbf{360}$$

(b) Two conductors joined across the back of the armature comprise one turn. Hence:

Number of turns $= \dfrac{360}{2} = \mathbf{180}$

(c) Since it is a lap wound machine and there are eight poles, there will be eight brushes and eight parallel paths through the armature. Therefore

Number of conductors in series in each group $= \dfrac{360}{8} = \mathbf{45}$

(d) Generated e.m.f. = e.m.f. per conductor × number of conductors connected in series

$$= 3.5 \times 45 = \mathbf{157.5\ V}$$

(e) Each conductor can carry 10 A and there are eight parallel paths.

Total current from the armature $= 8 \times 10 = 80$ A.

Rating $= V \times I = 157.5 \times 80 = 126000$ W $= \mathbf{12.6\ kW.}$

Problem 7 A d.c. shunt motor has an armature circuit resistance of 0.6 Ω and a shunt field resistance of 250 Ω. It is connected to a 250 V supply. On no-load the input current is 2.5 A and the speed is 1500 rev/min. When fully loaded the input current is 10 A. Calculate the value of back e.m.f. generated and the speed of the motor on full load.

From *Figure 25*, $I = I_a + I_f$. Therefore

$I_a = 2.5 - \dfrac{250}{250} = 1.5$ A on no load.

Using suffix 1 to indicate original no-load conditions:

$E_1 = V - I_{a(1)}R_a = 250 - (1.5 \times 0.6) = 249.1$ V

Now

$E = \dfrac{2P\phi Zn}{c} = k\phi n \quad$ where $k = \dfrac{2PZ}{c}$

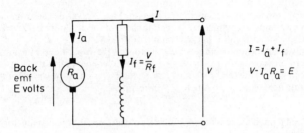

$I = I_a + I_f$

$V - I_a R_a = E$

R_a = Resistance of the armature

R_f = Resistance of shunt field circuit (including rheostat)

Fig 25

Thus $E_a = k\phi n_1$ and on no load, $n_1 = \dfrac{1500}{60} = 25$ rev/s

Therefore

$$k\phi = \frac{E_1}{n_1} = \frac{249.1}{25} = 9.964$$

When the total current = 10 A, $I_a = 9$ A since the field current remains unchanged in a shunt machine.

Using suffix 2 to denote the new conditions:

Hence back e.m.f. generated

$$E_2 = 250 - 9 \times 0.6 = \textbf{244.6 V}$$

Since the flux is unchanged, $k\phi$ is unchanged at 9.964

$$E_2 = k\phi n_2$$

Transposing gives

$$n_2 = \frac{E_2}{k\phi} = \frac{244.6}{9.964} = \textbf{24.55 rev/s (1473 rev/min)}$$

As an alternative, we can argue that since $E_1 \propto n_1$, and $E_2 \propto n_2$

$$\frac{E_1}{E_2} = \frac{n_1}{n_2}$$

Hence

$$n_2 = n_1 \times \frac{E_2}{E_1} = 25 \times \frac{244.6}{249.1} = \textbf{24.55 rev/s}$$

Problem 8 A series motor has an armature resistance of 0.15 Ω and a series field resistance of 0.25 Ω. It is connected to a 250 V supply and at a particular load runs at 30 rev/s when drawing 10 A from the supply. Calculate the speed of the motor when the load is changed such that the armature current is increased to 20 A.

Using suffix 1 to denote original conditions:

$E_1 = V - I_a(R_a + R_{sf})$

where R_{sf} = resistance of the series field.

$= 250 - 10(0.15 + 0.25) = 246$ V

Now $E_1 = k\phi n_1$ so that

$k\phi_1 = \dfrac{E_1}{n_1} = \dfrac{246}{30} = 8.2$ (see also *Problem 7*)

Using suffix 2 to denote new conditions:

When $I_a = 20$ A, $E_2 = 250 - 20(0.15 + 0.25) = 242$ V

Now since the armature current has doubled, the current in the series field has doubled which, if saturation can be ignored, will result in double the magnetic flux being produced. Let the new flux be ϕ_2 so that $\phi_2 = 2\phi_1$
Therefore, since $k\phi_1 = 8.2$, $k\phi_2 = 2 \times k\phi_1 = 16.4$

$E_2 = k\phi_2 n_2$

Transposing gives

$n_2 = \dfrac{E_2}{k\phi_2} = \dfrac{242}{16.4} = \mathbf{14.76\ rev/s}$

Problem 9   A resistance starter as shown in *Fig 23* is used to limit the current input to the armature of a d.c. shunt motor at standstill to 50 A when connected to a 200 V supply. The armature resistance = 0.3 Ω.
  Calculate: (a) the resistance connected in series with the armature at starting; (b) the value of the armature current when the speed has risen to a value such that the back e.m.f. is 50 V, all the resistances remaining connected; (c) the new value of armature current at the speed in (b) above if the starting resistance is reduced by 0.7 Ω.

(a)   Let the resistance of the starter be R_s Ω.
      At start, the total resistance in circuit = $(R_a + R_s)$ Ω.
      Now $V - I_a(R_a + R_s) = E = 0$ at standstill.
      Therefore $V = I_a(R_a + R_s)$

$\dfrac{V}{I_a} = (R_a + R_s) = \dfrac{200}{50} = 4\ \Omega$

      Since $R_a = 0.3$ Ω, $R_s = 3.7$ Ω.
(b)   When $E = 50$ V, $200 - I_a \times 4 = 50$
                        $200 - 50 = 4I_a$

$I_a = \dfrac{150}{4} = 37.5$ A

(c)   With the starting resistance decreased by 0.7 Ω, the total resistance in circuit = 3.3 Ω.

Therefore $200 - 3.3I_a = 50$ (Note that since the speed is unchanged, E is unchanged)

$$I_a = \frac{150}{3.3}$$

$$= 45.5 \text{ A}.$$

Problem 10 The effect of armature reaction in a d.c. machine is to twist the magnetic field around the armature (see *Fig 14*). Explain how this may result in an overall reduction of magnetic flux from the main poles. How will such a reduction affect the performance of (i) a shunt motor (ii) a shunt generator.

Twisting the flux round has the effect of concentrating all the flux into one side of each pole piece which may be driven into saturation as a result. Since the top limit to flux density in iron is in the region of 1.6 to 1.8 tesla (T) this may result in a reduction in total flux.

Let us assume that the normal flux density in the poles of a d.c. machine is 1.1 T and that each pole has a cross-sectional area of 0.05 m². Let us also assume that the effect of armature reaction at a particular load is to concentrate the flux into one half of the pole face.

The total flux per pole = flux density × area = $1.1 \times 0.05 = 0.055$ Wb.

Half the pole face has an area of $0.05/2 = 0.025$ m²

Concentrating the flux into this area should result in a flux density of

$$\frac{0.055}{0.025} = 2.2 \text{ T}$$

This is above saturation. The flux density cannot rise about 1.8 T.

At 1.8 T and an area of 0.025 m² the flux per pole = $1.8 \times 0.025 = 0.045$ Wb.

This is approximately a 20% reduction (from 0.055 Wb).

In a shunt motor, such a reduction in flux will result in an increase in speed since

$$E = \frac{2P\phi Z_n}{C} \text{ volts}.$$

The increase in speed will result in increased armature current to drive the load. In a generator, a reduction in flux will cause a reduction in output voltage.

C FURTHER PROBLEMS ON D.C. MACHINES

(a) SHORT ANSWER PROBLEMS

1   Draw a sketch of a d.c. machine showing:
(i) main poles; (ii) armature; (iii) commutator; (iv) interpoles

2   How is the magnetic field in a d.c. machine generally produced?

3   Why has commutation to take place when the coil in question is outside the magnetic field of the main poles?

4   What is the basic action of a commutator in a d.c. generator?

5 How many parallel paths are there through a lap wound armature fitted in a 6-pole d.c. motor?

6 Write down a formula connecting E, V, I_a and R_a for a d.c. generator. What change in the formula is required for motor operation?

7 A self-excited d.c. shunt machine runs as a motor at 1430 rev/min on no load when drawing 3 A from a constant-voltage 400 V d.c. supply. By engaging a clutch the machine is driven by a diesel engine at 1540 rev/min when the power input to the d.c. machine is 25 kW. What change(s) occur(s) in:
(i) the armature current; (ii) the field current, considering magnitude and direction?
(e.g. larger, smaller, unchanged etc.)

8 The torque developed by the armature of a d.c. shunt motor is 95 Nm when the armature current is 50 A. What torque would be developed when the armature current is 25 A assuming (a) constant field current; (b) an increase in field current of 20%?

9 Draw schematic arrangements showing a d.c. machine (a) shunt connected; (b) series connected; (c) compound connected.

10 Draw a sketch showing the general arrangement of a coil to be fiteed in a wave-wound d.c. armature.

11 What is armature reaction?

12 What is the effect of armature reaction on commutation in a d.c. generator?

13 Why is it necessary to employ a starter to start a d.c. motor?

14 A d.c. motor has a total input power of 25 kW. The field loss is 400 W. The armature losses total 1.3 kW. The efficiency of the motor is 0.892 p.u. Determine the value of the output power and the combined friction, windage and iron loss.

15 The gross torque developed by a d.c. series motor is 50 Nm when the armature current is 25 A. What value of gross torque would be developed when the armature current was 50 A? (Ignore saturation)

(b) MULTI-CHOICE PROBLEMS (answers on page 213)

1 In a d.c. shunt motor the total input current $= I_L$ amperes and the field current $= I_f$ amperes.
The relationship between terminal voltage V and back e.m.f. E volts is:
(i) $V - (I_L - I_f)R_a = E$;   (ii) $V + (I_L - I_f)R_a = E$;
(iii) $V - (I_L + I_f)R_a = E$;   (iv) $E - (I_L - I_f)R_a = V$.

2 The armature resistance of a d.c. shunt generator is 0.5 Ω. It delivers 15 A to a load at terminal voltage 250 V. The field current = 1 A. The value of the generated e.m.f. E is:
(i) 257 V; (ii) 242 V; (iii) 258 V; (iv) 243 V.

3 The two ends of a coil in a lap winding are connected to segments on the commutator
(i) one pole pitch apart; (ii) which are adjacent; (iii) on opposite sides of the armature.

4   Through a wave connected armature there are:
    (i)   as many parallel current paths as there are poles;
    (ii) four parallel paths;
    (iii) two parallel paths.

5   A lap wound armature and a wave wound armature both have the same number
    of conductors. Each is fitted in a 6-pole d.c. generator and both are driven at the
    same speed. The terminal voltage on no load at the lap wound machine's
    terminals is 200 V. The no-load terminal voltage of the wave machine would be
    (closely)
    (i) 200 V; (ii) 66 V; (iii) 1200 V; (iv) 600 V.

6   A d.c. series motor develops a torque of 60 Nm with an armature current of
    10 A. Increasing the load on the machine such that the torque is 120 Nm would
    cause the armature current to change to approximately:
    (i) 20 A; (ii) 14.2 A; (iii) 40 A.

7   Armature reaction in a d.c. machine is:
    (i)   the torque produced on the field poles by the rotating armature;
    (ii) the induced voltage in the armature coils as the current reverses;
    (iii) the effect of the magnetic field set up by the armature currents on the main
          field;
    (iv) the induced voltage in the armature coils created by the interpoles.

8   The effect of armature reaction in a d.c. motor is to:
    (i)   reduce the no-load speed;
    (ii) increase the no-load speed;
    (iii) cause the reduction in speed which occurs as the motor is loaded to be less
          than expected especially at high loading;
    (iv) cause the speed to reduce dramatically as full load is marginally exceeded.

9   Commutating or interpoles are fitted to d.c. motors in order to:
    (i)   control the speed;
    (ii) overcome the effect of reactance voltage;
    (iii) allow the machine to carry momentary overloads since being series
          connected an increase in current will increase the available field;
    (iv) allow the motor to be reversed without undue sparking at the commutator.

10 The hysteresis loss in the armature of a d.c. machine is a function of
    (i)   the maximum working flux density;
    (ii) the thickness of the laminations used;
    (iii) the resistivity of the steel;
    (iv) the speed of rotation.
    Select *two* of the factors given.

11 Eddy current losses in the armature of a d.c. machine are reduced by:
    (i)   reducing the resistance of the steel used;
    (ii) using thin strips or laminations;
    (iii) using grain oriented steel;
    (iv) increasing the working flux density.

(c) CONVENTIONAL PROBLEMS

1   A four-pole, wave wound d.c. generator has the following details:

Number of slots on the armature 64;   Induced e.m.f. per conductor 1.8 V;
Number of conductors per slot 15;   Maximum current per conductor 15 A.
Determine (a) the output voltage; (b) the maximum current which the machine
can safely deliver.   [864 V; 30 A]

2   A d.c. generator has 4 poles and 72 conductors on the armature. The e.m.f.
    generated per armature conductor is 10 V at a particular speed. The current
    carrying capacity of each conductor is 20 A. Calculate the output voltage and
    maximum power rating for (a) lap connection; (b) wave connection.
                                              [(a) 180 V; (b) 360 V; 14400 W]

3   A wave wound armature of a six-pole d.c. generator has 30 slots and in each slot
    there are 8 conductors. The flux per pole is 0.0174 Wb. Calculate the value of the
    e.m.f. generated when the speed of the armature is 1200 rev/min.   [250.6 V]

4   A lap-wound d.c. generator is to have an output voltage of 500 V at 26 rev/s.
    The armature has 28 slots each containing 12 conductors. Calculate the required
    value of flux per pole.   [0.057 Wb]

5   A lap-wound armature for a four-pole d.c. machine has 56 slots each containing
    10 conductors. For a flux per pole of 36 mWb calculate: (a) the generated voltage
    E at a speed of 25 rev/s; (b) the speed at which the machine will run as a motor
    when drawing an armature current of 25 A from a 600 V supply given that the
    armature resistance is 0.5 Ω.   [(a) 504 V; (b) 29.14 rev/s]

6   Repeat *Problem 5* assuming that the armature is wave wound, all other
    conditions remaining unchanged.   [(a) 1008 V; (b) 14.57 rev/s]

7   Calculate the value of generated e.m.f. developed by the following 6-pole, d.c.
    generators:
    (a)   lap wound, flux per pole = 20 mWb, number of slots on the armature = 86,
          conductors per slot = 5, speed 15 rev/s;
    (b)   wave wound, flux per pole = 25 mWb, number of slots = 24, conductors per
          slot = 10, speed 20 rev/s.   [(a) 129 V; (b) 360 V]

8   A d.c. machine has an armature resistance of 0.5 Ω. It is connected to 500 V
    mains. When drawing 20 A from the supply it runs at 25 rev/s. At what speed
    must it run as a generator in order to deliver 20 A to the electrical system? The
    flux remains constant. The field current is ignored.   [26 rev/s; $E = 510$ V]

9   The armature of a six-pole lap wound d.c. motor has 54 slots and 8 conductors in
    each slot. The total flux per pole is 0.05 Wb. The resistance of the armature is
    0.3 Ω. When connected to a 240 V supply, at a particular load the armature
    current is 20 A. Calculate: (a) the speed under these conditions; (b) the value of
    flux per pole required in order to increase the speed to 15 rev(s all other
    conditions remaining unchanged.   [(a) 10.83 rev/s; (b) 0.036 Wb]

10 Sketch speed/armature current and torque/armature current characteristics for
    (a) a shunt connected motor; (b) a series connected motor.

11 A d.c. motor has an armature resistance of 0.3 Ω. It is to be started using a
    resistance type starter. The supply voltage is 250 V. Determine the value of
    starting resistance required to be connected in series with the armature so that the
    current at standstill does not exceed 25 A.
        If at a particular speed the back e.m.f. has risen to 125 V to what value should
    the starting resistance be adjusted to restore the current to its original value?
                                              [Add 9.7 Ω, Add 4.7 Ω]

12 What relationship must exist between armature coils and field poles at the instant of commutation if excessive sparking is to be avoided? What design features are incorporated in many machines to assist commutation? Illustrate your answer with simple sketches.

13 Construct a power flow diagram for a d.c. motor showing the input, the general losses and useful output. How may the diagram be modified to illustrate generator operation?

14 A d.c. shunt machine has the following parameters:
$R_a = 0.5\ \Omega$; $R_f = 220\ \Omega$; Brush resistance loss = 100 W,
Friction, windage and iron losses total 1500 W; Supply voltage = 440 V.
Determine the output power and efficiency of the machine when operating as a motor with an armature current of 50 A. [Output 19 150 W; eff. 0.837 p.u]

15 For the machine in *Problem 14*, operating as a generator and supplying 50 A to the electrical system, determine the total mechanical power input and its efficiency. [Input 25 832 W; eff. 0.852 p.u]

16 (a) A d.c. shunt motor armature has a resistance of 0.6 Ω and carries a current of 30 A at a particular load when the speed is 30 rev/s. The supply voltage is 500 V. The friction and windage losses total 1.2 kW. Determine: (i) the value of gross torque; (ii) the value of net torque.
(b) If the gross torque is to be increased to 100 Nm, to what value would the armature current rise assuming that the flux remains unchanged?
[(a) (i) 76.7 Nm; (ii) 70.3 Nm; (b) 39.1 A]

7 Measuring Instruments

A SUMMARY OF FORMULAE AND DEFINITIONS ASSOCIATED WITH MEASURING INSTRUMENTS

1 *Fig 1* shows the correct method of connecting a **voltmeter** and an **ammeter** into a circuit in order to measure the load **potential difference** and **current** respectively.

2 The basic instrument for many electrical measurements is the **permanent-magnet moving-coil ammeter.** The movement is constructed using very fine wire so that it can only pass a very small current without overheating. By the addition of an external bypass resistor, or shunt, it may be used to measure larger currents. *Fig 2* shows the connection of a shunt to a moving-coil ammeter.

3 Where a moving-coil instrument is to be used as a voltmeter it is necessary to limit the current flowing through it to that value required to give full-scale deflection. This is done by connecting a resistance, or multiplier, in series with it as shown in *Fig 3*.

4 **The ohmmeter**

The ohmmeter comprises an ammeter with its face calibrated in ohms, a battery and calibration resistances. As an example let us assume a battery voltage of 4 V and an ammeter which gives full-scale deflection when 0.05 A flows in it. In *Fig 4*, R_y is adjusted to such a value that with the external leads connected together, i.e. $R_x = 0$, the ammeter is fully deflected. The scale is marked 0 Ω at $I = 0.05$ A.

Hence, $R_z + R_y = \dfrac{4}{0.05} = 80 \ \Omega$.

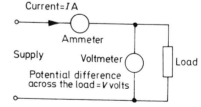

Fig 1

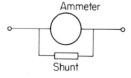

Fig 2

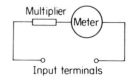

Fig 3

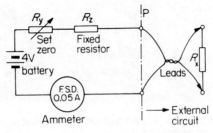

Fig 4

With the external leads disconnected, R_x is infinity ($\infty\,\Omega$) and the meter current falls to zero.

When $I = 0.03$ A, the total resistance in circuit $= \dfrac{4}{0.03} = 133.3\ \Omega$.

R_x must therefore be $133.3 - 80 = 53.3\ \Omega$. For any other current there is a

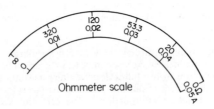

Ohmmeter scale

Fig 5

corresponding value of external resistance and the scale can be calibrated as in *Fig 5*.

Having set the zero ohms position correctly using the resistor R_y, the meter will read directly the resistance of any external resistor connected to the leads.

5 **Rectifier instruments**

The deflection of the permanent-magnet moving-coil instrument is proportional to the average current flowing in the movement. In a d.c. circuit, connecting the meter terminals correctly causes the pointer to move up the scale whilst reversing the connections results in the pointer being forced back on the zero stop.

If the meter is connected into a circuit carrying alternating current the meter indicates zero since the average value over a complete cycle of a symmetrical alternating current is zero. In order to employ a moving-coil meter in an a.c. circuit it is necessary to connect it in series with a rectifier.

Fig 6 shows the use of a single-phase bridge rectifier in a voltmeter circuit. The series resistor is used in exactly the same manner as in the direct-current circuit to limit the current. *Fig 7* shows the connections for a rectifier ammeter. A current transformer is generally used to reduce the current to a suitably low value for the meter. An alternative would be to use a meter shunt whilst the rectifier passes the total current.

Fig 6 (below)

Fig 7 (right)

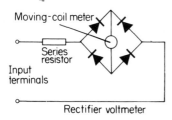

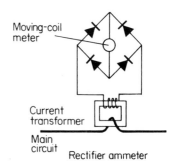

Moving-coil meter

Input terminals

Series resistor

Rectifier voltmeter

Moving-coil meter

Current transformer

Main circuit

Rectifier ammeter

6 Errors

(a) *Waveform errors* For a pure sine wave the r.m.s. value of the wave = 1.11 × the average value. The value 1.11 is known as the form factor of the wave. The deflection of a moving coil meter is a function of the average current in the coil. The meter must however indicate the effective or r.m.s. value so that it is necessary to re-scale the meter face, increasing the values by a factor of 1.11. The scale markings are therefore only correct if the input to the meter is of sinusoidal form.

When rectifier instruments are used in circuits containing iron, i.e. transformers, chokes etc the voltage and current waveforms may not be sinusoidal resulting in the indication being in error.

(b) *Frequency errors* The anode and cathode of any rectifying device make up a small capacitor since they are sections of conducting material separated by an insulator.

Considering the half-wave rectifier and meter shown in *Fig 8*, during the

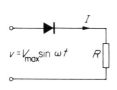

$v = V_{max} \sin \omega t$

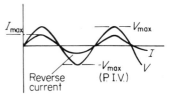

Reverse current

$(P.I.V.)$

Fig 8

positive half cycles of voltage the rectifier conducts and the potential difference across it is small.

$V_{max} = I_{max} \times R$ (closely)

During the negative half cycles, ideally the current is zero. However the reverse potential difference across the rectifier causes charge to move round the circuit in the opposite direction to that during the positive half cycle, charging the capacitance of the device. Charge moving in the opposite direction will reduce the meter reading.

103

The amount of charge in the opposite direction and hence the reduction in meter reading is a function of the capacitance of the device and the number of such movements per second (that is, the frequency of the supply, f Hz). *Note: current in amperes = charge moved in a circuit measured in coulombs during a period of 1 second.)*

7 Use of the multimeter

There are many different makes of multimeter so that it is only possible to give general guidance as to their use. Generally the meter has two selection knobs and the meter face has at least two different scales covering typical ranges as shown in *Fig 9*.

If an alternating voltage of unknown value is to be measured, the left-hand knob is turned to the a.c. position. The right hand knob is turned to the 1000 V

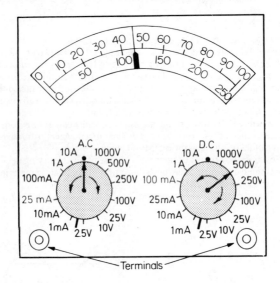

Fig 9

range. With this range, the scale to be observed is that from 0–100 and each of the scale values must be multiplied by 10. As the supply to be measured is connected to the meter terminals the pointer will move up the scale. If it moves to a position of less than 50 on the scale (less than 500 V applied) the right hand knob should be turned one position clockwise so that the 500 V range is selected. Either scale is now suitable. The top scale is multiplied by 5 or the bottom scale is multiplied by 2.

The voltage knob is turned through one position at a time until the pointer is deflected to near full scale. Care must be taken not to cause the pointer to deflect past the end of the scale or damage may result.

As a further example, where direct current is to be measured, the right hand knob is turned to d.c. whilst the left hand knob selects first the 10 A range then

TABLE 1

	Moving-coil meter	*Moving-iron meter*
Deflection or driving torque	Current flowing in a coil of fine wire suspended between the poles of a permanent magnet	Usually repulsion between a fixed and moving iron. The current is carried by a stationary coil which surrounds the irons
Restraining torque	Hair springs	Hair springs
Damping torque	Electrodynamic. The coil is wound on a conducting former. As the coil moves, the former is driven through the magnetic field so acting as a generator. Current flowing in the former produces a retarding torque which ceases when the coil comes to rest	Vane or fane moving through air in a cylinder or dash pot
Other comments	D.C. only, the movement carries at least part of the current being measured. Very sensitive, full scale deflection for only a few micro-amperes is possible. High precision type, expensive to manufacture. Uniform scale. Little effect on the meter by external magnetic fields	D.C. and a.c. of power frequencies. (100 Hz unless manufactured specially for a particular frequency.) Reads true r.m.s. Needs larger currents for full-scale deflection, possibly 100 mA. Non-linear scale, often a section near zero which is uncalibrated. Cheap and robust

moving progressively down if the current value permits, in order to obtain a large deflection.

8 Comparison between moving-coil and moving-iron meters (see *Table 1*).

9 **Use of the wattmeter**

The power in a single-phase circuit = $VI \cos \phi$ watts. The wattmeter therefore needs both a current and a voltage element to measure power. In the dynamometer wattmeter, the circuit current flows in a pair of fixed coils so setting up a magnetic field. A moving coil carrying a current proportional to the circuit voltage is situated in this field. The deflection of the moving coil is a

Representing current coils

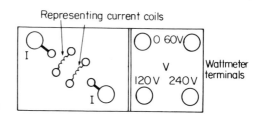

Fig 10

function of the magnetic field strength, the current in the voltage coil and the phase angle between them.

The terminal arrangement of a typical laboratory wattmeter is shown in *Fig 10*. There are two current coils shown but in many instruments these are further sub-divided into two making four coils in all. Each coil is capable of carrying 5 A typically. In *Fig 10*, for currents up to 5 A the coils are connected in series, whilst for currents between 5 A and 10 A they are connected in parallel. Different voltage ranges are provided, typically from zero to 60 V, 120 V, and 240 V. As with a voltmeter these are obtained by using different series resistors.

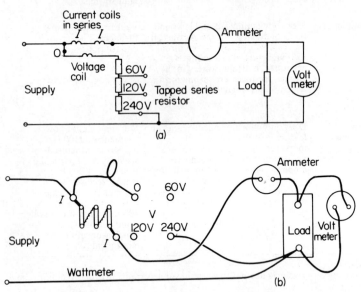

(a)

(b)

Fig 11

Voltage range	Current	Power
60 V	5 A	Face value
120 V	5 A	X 2
240 V	5 A	X 4
60 V	10 A	X 2
120 V	10 A	X 4
240 V	10 A	X 8

Fig 12

For a circuit taking less than 5 A at a voltage between 120 V and 240 V, the schematic and actual arrangements are shown in *Fig 11*. On every wattmeter there should be a plate giving the scale factors. Since the wattmeter has only one scale, adjustment of the current and voltage ranges alters the range of the instrument, as in the case of the multimeter. A typical plate is shown in *Fig 12*.

B WORKED PROBLEMS ON MEASURING INSTRUMENTS

Problem 1 A moving coil ammeter has a coil resistance of 5 Ω and is fully deflected when a current of 2.5 mA flows through it (see *Fig 13*).
(a) Calculate the value of a shunt required in order that the meter will be fully deflected when it is connected into a circuit carrying 1 A.
(b) Calculate the value of a multiplier to be fitted to enable it to be used as a voltmeter with a range 0–50 V.

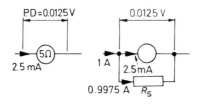

(a)

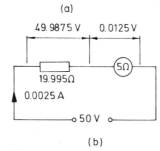

(b)

Fig 13

(a) When fully deflected the potential difference across the meter coil $= IR$ volts.

p.d. $= 2.5 \times 10^{-3} \times 5 = 0.0125$ V

This voltage must never be exceeded or damage to the meter will occur. Total circuit current $= 1$ A. Therefore the shunt must carry $1 - 2.5 \times 10^{-3} = 0.9975$ A. The potential difference across meter and shunt are the same since they are connected in parallel. Hence,

$$\frac{\text{Potential difference}}{\text{Current in shunt}} = R_{\text{shunt}} = \frac{0.0125}{0.9975} = \textbf{0.0125 } \Omega$$

(b) The current through the coil must not exceed 2.5×10^{-3} A with 50 V applied.
The total resistance of the circuit must be therefore

$$\frac{50}{2.5 \times 10^{-3}} = 20 \times 10^3 \, \Omega$$

The resistance of the movement itself = 5 Ω
The value of the multiplier = $20 \times 10^3 - 5 = \textbf{19 995 } \Omega$

Problem 2 With reference to moving-coil and moving-iron meters, explain the terms: (a) Deflecting or driving torque; (b) Restraining torque; (c) Damping torque.
  How are these torques produced in each of these meters?

(a) *Deflecting or driving torque* This is the torque which causes the meter movement to be deflected so driving the pointer up the scale. In the moving-coil meter this torque is produced by current flowing in a coil of fine wire suspended between the poles of a permanent magnet. In the moving-iron meter, repulsion between a fixed and moving iron, both magnetised by a current flowing in a stationary coil which surrounds the irons, provides the force required. The coil being stationary can be constructed of heavy gauge wire and will thus be able to carry large currents.

(b) *Restraining torque* This torque operates in opposition to the deflecting torque. Without it, the smallest current in the meter coil would cause full-scale deflection of the pointer and when the current ceased it would not return to the zero position. In both types of meter this torque is provided by hair springs which are wound up as the movement is deflected. The restraining torque is proportional to the angle of deflection, thus a greater current is necessary to provide a greater torque to give a greater deflection. The pointer comes to rest on the scale when the driving or deflecting torque is equal to the restraining torque.

(c) *Damping torque* This is necessary to prevent undue oscillation of the pointer about the true reading. Damping torque is only present whilst the pointer is moving. Ideally, the meter should be 'dead-beat' which means that when the supply is connected to the meter the pointer moves steadily up the scale coming to rest at the correct reading. With slightly less damping the pointer passses the correct point on the scale once and then comes to rest on its return. Without damping the pointer would first over-swing and then under-swing. It would only settle down gradually at the correct reading.

  In the moving coil meter the damping is electrodynamic. The coil is wound on a conducting former of light gauge aluminium. As the coil moves, the former is driven through the magnetic field, so acting as a generator. Current flowing in the former as a result produces a retarding torque which ceases when the coil comes to rest. An alternative way of considering this is to realise that energy is required to drive a generator and this energy comes from the moving coil which will be retarded as a result.

In the moving-iron meter a vane or fan moving through air in a cylinder or a dashpot damps the movement this is a similar effect to the hydraulic dampers on a motor vehicle.

Problem 3 Explain with the aid of an example why it is that errors occur in rectifier-type meters due to waveform variation.

In order to employ a moving-coil meter in an a.c. circuit it is necessary to connect it in series with a rectifier. Assuming full-wave rectification the ideal wave shape of the current in the meter is as shown in *Fig 14(a)*.

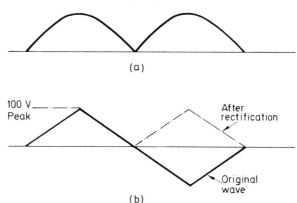

(a)

100 V Peak

After rectification

Original wave

Fig 14   (b)

The meter deflection is proportional to the average current.
For a sine wave the average value of current $= 0.637 I_{max}$ (see *Fig 5,* Chap. 10). However, in a.c. circuits it is the r.m.s. value which is important since we have the expression

Power $= I^2R$ watts, where $I =$ the r.m.s. value of current

It can be shown that the r.m.s. value or direct current equivalent $= 0.707 I_{max}$. Therefore, for a sine wave

$$\frac{\text{r.m.s. value}}{\text{average value}} = \frac{0.707 I_{max}}{0.637 I_{max}} = 1.11.$$

This value is known as the form factor of the wave.

It follows that although the deflection is due to average current, the scale ought to be calibrated in r.m.s. values. The scale markings are increased by a factor 1.11 on the assumption that the input will be of sine form. Consider the effect of the input being of triangular form and with 100 V peak value

(*Fig 14(b)*). The average value of a triangle is half its vertical height, i.e. 50 V in this case. Allowing for the scale adjustment the indication will be $1.11 \times 50 = 55.5$ V. The r.m.s. value of a triangular wave is in fact 57.73 V. (Obtainable mathematically or by using a true r.m.s. indicating instrument.)

The meter indication is therefore $57.73 - 55.5 = 2.23$ V low. (3.86% error)
Now since r.m.s. value = form factor × average value

$$\text{Form factor} = \frac{57.73}{50} = 1.155$$

From the above it follows that waves with form factors greater than 1.11 will result in low meter indication.

Problem 4   A wattmeter with a scale plate as shown in *Fig 12* is used to measure the power in an a.c. circuit. The current is 8.6 A and the voltage 225 V. Assuming that the correct connections have been made to the wattmeter determine:
(i) the power in the circuit; (ii) the operating power factor, when the indication on the wattmeter is 205.6 W.

The current of 8.6 A is greater than 5 A so that the current coils must be connected in parallel allowing for a maximum current of 10 A. The voltage is 225 V so that the potential coil must be connected to allow for 240 V. Under these conditions, from the scale plate we see that the indication must be multiplied by 8.
(i)   Power in circuit $= 8 \times 205.6 = 1644.8$ W

(ii)   Power factor $= \dfrac{W}{VI} = \dfrac{1644.8}{225 \times 8.6} = 0.85$

C   FURTHER PROBLEMS ON MEASURING INSTRUMENTS

(a) SHORT ANSWER PROBLEMS

1   A moving-coil ammeter has a resistance of 1.5 Ω and is fully deflected when a current of 1 mA flows through it. Calculate the value of shunt required in order that the meter will be fully deflected when it is connected in a circuit carrying 25 mA. Draw a sketch showing the meter and shunt correctly connected.

2   A moving-coil ammeter has a resistance of 0.5 Ω and is fully deflected by a current of 10 mA. What value of multiplier is required to convert the meter to a voltmeter with full scale deflection of 5 V?

3   Under what circumstances is it necessary to connect a rectifier in series with a moving-coil meter?

4   Why is the indication of a rectifier-type moving-coil instrument affected by the supply waveform?

5   What effect has increasing frequency on the performance of a rectifier-type moving-coil instrument?

110

6   What is there about the design of a moving iron ammeter that makes it capable of handling directly far larger currents than the moving-coil type?

7   How is it that the moving iron meter can measure both d.c. and a.c. quantities without having to employ a rectifier?

8   Draw a circuit diagram showing a voltmeter, an ammeter and a wattmeter correctly connected to measure voltage, current and power respectively in a single-phase circuit.

9   What features are incorporated in a dynamometer wattmeter to enable it to handle (a) a range of different currents, (b) a range of different voltages?

(b) MULTI-CHOICE PROBLEMS (answers on page 213)

1   A moving coil meter with a resistance of 2 Ω suffers full-scale deflection with 5 mA flowing. It is now fitted with a shunt which has a resistance of 0.01 Ω. The meter will be fully deflected when connected into a circuit carrying:
(i) 0.5 A; (ii) 1 A; (iii) 10 A; (iv) 5 A.

2   The deflection of a moving-coil meter is proportional to: (i) the average current (ii) the r.m.s. value of current. When such a meter is connected into a circuit carrying alternating current with sinusoidal waveform the indication will be
(a)   true r.m.s.;   (c)   zero;
(b)   r.m.s. value÷1.11   (d)   peak of the a.c. wave.
Select *one* from (i) and (ii) and *one* from (a) to (d) to form a correct statement.

3   A moving-coil meter employing a full-wave rectifier is connected into a circuit carrying a pure sine wave current of 1 A peak value. Assuming that the meter is correctly calibrated for use in this manner, it will indicate:
(i) 1 A; (ii) 1.414 A; (iii) 1.11 A; (iv) 0.707 A.

4   A rectifier moving-coil voltmeter is calibrated so as to indicate r.m.s. values when the input is a pure sine wave. It is installed in a circuit carrying current with a form factor of 1.3.

The form factor = $\dfrac{\text{r.m.s. value}}{\text{average value.}}$

The indication on the meter will be:
(i) correct; (ii) high; (iii) low.

5   When operated at high frequencies a rectifier moving-coil meter tends to read (i) high; (ii) low, due to the effect of (iii) the rectifier inductance; (iv) the rectifier capacitance; (v) changing rectifier conductance.
Select *one* from (i) and (ii) together with *one* from (iii), (iv) and (v) to make a correct statement.

6   The damping torque in a moving-iron meter is produced by:
(i)   hair springs;   (iii) a vane or fan moving through air;
(ii) the use of a conducting former for   (iv) repulsion between fixed and
      the coil;   moving irons.

7   A wattmeter has two current coils, the connections to which may be altered to suit different currents. The wattmeter is connected to indicate the power in a single-phase circuit. With the current coils in series the indication is 100 W. If the

current coils are re-connected in parallel, the circuit conditions remaining unchanged, the indication will be:
(i) 100 W; (ii) 50 W; (iii) 200 W.

CONVENTIONAL PROBLEMS

1 (a) What is the function of a shunt when used in association with a moving-coil ammeter? Draw a simple sketch showing the correct arrangement of meter and shunt.

   (b) Calculate the value of shunt to be used in order that a moving-coil ammeter with coil resistance 5 Ω and which is fully deflected by a current of 15 μA can be connected in a circuit which carries a maximum current of 150 mA.
   $[5 \times 10^{-4} \, \Omega]$

2 (a) What is the function of a multiplier when used in association with a moving-coil ammeter?

   (b) Calculate the value of multiplier required to enable the meter in *Problem 1* (without its shunt) to be used as a voltmeter with full-scale deflection at 15 V.
   $[999\,995 \, \Omega]$

3 A moving-coil meter has a coil resistance of 1 Ω and is fully deflected by a current of 1 mA. Three shunts are available for use with this meter and these have values of (i) $1.001 \times 10^{-3} \, \Omega$; (ii) $2.004 \times 10^{-3} \, \Omega$; (iii) 0.010101 Ω respectively.
   Determine the maximum values of circuit current which could be measured using each of these shunts in turn correctly connected to the meter.
   [(i) 1 A; (ii) 0.5 A; (iii) 0.1 A]

4 A moving-coil meter is fully deflected by a current of 5 mA in its movement. In order to use this meter as a voltmeter with full-scale deflection at 100 V it is connected in series with a multiplier.
   Calculate (a) the total resistance of meter and multiplier, (b) the value of an additional resistance necessary to enable full-scale deflection to be obtained for 500 V applied.
   $[(a)\,20\,000\,\Omega; (b)\,80\,000\,\Omega]$

5 Why is a rectifier necessary when a moving-coil instrument is to be used in an a.c. circuit? Draw circuit diagrams showing a moving-coil meter and bridge rectifier being used as (a) an ammeter; (b) a voltmeter.

6 A moving-coil rectifier instrument is used in a circuit in which the current is non-sinusoidal. Explain why the meter indication cannot be trusted. Under what circumstances would the meter indicate (a) high; (b) low?
   $\left[\begin{array}{l} \text{(a) Form factor less than 1.11} \\ \text{(b) Form factor greater than 1.11} \end{array} \right]$

7 Why is damping necessary in a voltmeter? Explain how damping is achieved in (a) a moving-coil meter; (b) a moving-iron meter.

8 The hair springs in a moving-coil meter have two functions. What are they?

9 A wattmeter has a scale plate as shown in *Figure 12*. It is used to measure the power in an a.c. circuit. It has two current coils each rated at 5 A. The indication is 53 W when these are connected in parallel and the voltage range is 0–240 V. What is the value of power in the circuit?
   [424 W]

8 Planned maintenance

A SUMMARY OF FORMULAE AND DEFINITIONS ASSOCIATED WITH PLANNED MAINTENANCE

1 There are two approaches to the maintenance of plant:
   (a) to allow it to run until it breaks down and then carry out repairs. This is known as breakdown maintenance.
   (b) to regularly test and inspect it, replacing worn parts, oiling and greasing, revarnishing windings, etc to attempt to prevent breakdowns as far as possible. This is known as preventive maintenance.
   Preventive maintenance does not generally prevent breakdowns altogether but minimises their incidence. Such work can often be carried out during periods of light loading on the factory or during holidays of the production staff rather than at the most inconvenient time, which is when breakdowns always seem to occur. Routine maintenance allows the work force to be employed evenly over the year instead of through day and night occasionally during periods of breakdown.

2 The frequency of testing and inspection will depend on one or more of the following factors:
   (a) the type of equipment and the environment in which it works;
   (b) previous plant history;
   (c) plant running hours;
   (d) the availability of the plant for testing.

3 **The 'Megger' insulation tester**   Manufactured by Evershed and Vignoles Ltd. For cable, switchgear and motor insulation resistance testing a device which can measure millions of ohms while stressing the material with hundreds or even thousands of volts is required. Such a device is the 'Megger'; this comprises a hand-cranked d.c. generator and an ohmmeter-type movement. Models are available working at 250 V, 500 V, 1000 V and 2500 V.

Fig 1 shows the 'Megger' tester being used to measure the insulation resistance between the core and sheath of a concentric cable. The handle is turned at an increasingly rapid rate until it appears to turn more easily. This occurs at the speed required to generate the voltage of the particular test set. After a short interval the pointer comes to rest on the scale, when the insulation resistance may be read.

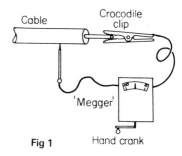

Fig 1

113

4 **Cable testing** The cable must first be disconnected from the supply by opening the associated switch or circuit breaker. If the cable feeds a piece of equipment and it is desired to test the cable alone, the equipment must be disconnected. Electrical tests are then carried out using the 'Megger'. For circuits operating normally at 415/240 V, a 500 V 'Megger' is generally used. Higher voltage test sets are used at higher voltages.

On single-phase circuits, insulation resistance tests are carried out between the two cores and from each core to earth. On three-phase circuits the tests are carried out between each pair of conductors, Red to Yellow, Yellow to Blue, Blue to Red; and from each of the cores to the earthed sheath. No absolute figures can be quoted for the insulation resistance since this will depend on the length and type of cable but the readings should generally be hundreds of megohms. (1 megohm (1 MΩ) = 1 million ohms.)

At the same time visual checks should be made of the cable ends. Lead-covered paper insulated cables have their ends terminated in compound-filled boxes. There should be no oil seeping from the box and all cable ends should appear clean and in good order. Plastic-insulated cables are terminated in a screwed gland and it is necessary to check for cleanliness and appearance.

5 **Motor tests** The supply is isolated and the motor disconnected from its supply cable. On a single-phase motor, the insulation resistance between one of the terminals and earth is checked. In the case of a 3-phase motor the windings are separated by removing the links in the terminal box. The insulation tests are then as for the three-phase cable.

On a d.c. motor the armature and field windings are separated and the insulation resistance of each part to earth tested. Visual checks should be made of the following: the coupling between the motor and its load; the windings (by removing either or both end covers); and the bearing grease or oil. A darkened grease with a bad smell often indicates trouble which could necessitate taking the motor to the workshop to change the bearings.

6 **Transformer tests** The input and output cables are isolated by opening the appropriate circuit breakers and locking them in this position. The cable ends are disconnected from the windings at the terminal boxes and the windings separated if there are available links. The insulation tests are then as for a motor on both the primary and secondary windings separately.

Where a tap-changer is fitted, a visual check of the mechanism and contacts is advisable if possible. On oil-filled transformers, the cold oil level is checked and a sample of oil taken for checks on electrical breakdown value, moisture content and acidity.

Due to the inherent reliability of transformers the full range of insulation tests is not often carried out unless trouble is suspected.

7 **Switchgear tests** The switch is isolated from the supply and a visual check made of the linkages, contacts and any operating coils, after removing the oil tank on oil-filled gear. The switch is closed manually to check contact movement and alignment. Any operating coils are isolated electrically and the 'Megger' used to check the insulation resistance between the windings and the chassis of the switch. With the switch open the insulation tests are as for the 3-phase cable on both the input and output sides.

With oil-filled switchgear a visual check for blackening of the oil is carried out. Similar tests can be carried out on the oil as for the transformer but colour and smell are usually good enough indications of condition.

8 **Isolation and earthing** When work is to be carried out on high and extra-high voltage equipment, isolation from all sources of danger must be carried out. To prevent the potential of that equipment rising above that of earth, due to accidental contact with live metal or inductive or capacitive effects, it is solidly connected to earth. At low and medium voltages, isolation from the supply is sufficient without earthing.

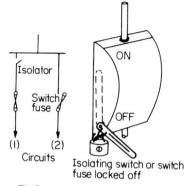

Fig 2

For isolation at 415/240 V an isolator or switch fuse is often used as shown in *Fig 2*. On h.v. or e.h.v. circuits up to 33 kV, isolation is often achieved using withdrawable-type switchgear.

Fig 3 shows two views of a bulk oil circuit breaker for use up to 33 kV, with horizontal isolation. The circuit breaker is mounted on wheels which run on tracks. In order to energise the circuit, the circuit breaker truck is pushed into its cubicle. The shutters are lifted at the last possible moment by small wheels on the

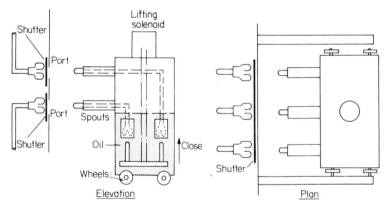

Fig 3

side of the breaker engaging lifting levers attached to them. The male spouts enter the ports to make contact with the female rose contacts. The truck is locked in position. The circuit breaker may now be operated normally. To isolate the circuit, the circuit breaker is opened and withdrawn from its cubicle. The shutters are locked closed.

If work is to be done on the cable an extension piece is fitted to each of the

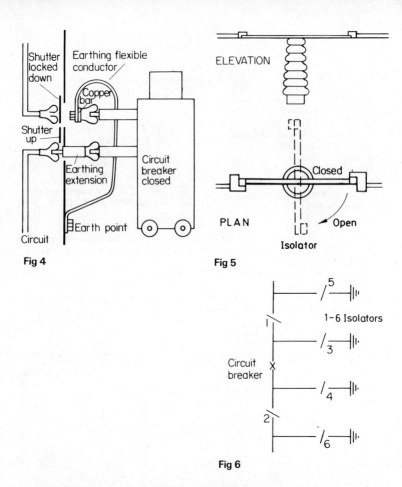

Fig 4

ELEVATION

PLAN

Isolator

Fig 5

Circuit breaker

1-6 Isolators

Fig 6

circuit spouts as shown in *Fig 4*. A copper bar is screwed to the top spouts and this is solidly earthed. The circuit breaker is pushed into the cubicle, only the bottom shutters opening to allow the earthing extension pieces to make contact with the circuit roses. The circuit breaker is closed so connecting the circuit to earth.

In open air substations at 132 kV and 400 kV, isolators are used as shown in *Fig 5*. To work on the circuit breaker, it is first opened. Isolators 1 and 2 are opened. Isolators 3 and 4 are closed connecting the conductors to earth. Isolators 5 and 6 are used to earth the line if the associated circuit breakers are open at the far ends of the lines.

9 **Dangers** The main danger concerned with switchgear is that a live circuit may be directly connected to earth resulting in a severe explosion. On withdrawable gear this may be brought about by connecting the extension pieces and earthing

bar to the wrong sets of spouts due to a misunderstanding or carelessness. Where fixed isolators are used as in *Fig 6* an incorrect sequence of operations, closing the earthing isolators 3 and 4 before opening isolators 1 and 2 connects the live line directly to earth.

Accidents can occur due to incompetence or forgetfulness but where a proper system of safe working has been instituted and is enforced, these should be rare. Accidents occur at medium voltage in the main where electricians are allowed to perform their own isolations. A few examples will illustrate the point.

(i)   A fitter decides to make a small adjustment to a contactor without isolating the circuit. A flashover occurs when a screwdriver touches two live terminals.

(ii) Fuses are withdrawn from a fuseboard which constitutes an isolation. Another person restores the supply unexpectedly by borrowing fuses from another way in the fuseboard.

(iii) Painters decide to work in the path of a travelling crane without first locking it off.

(iv) Work is carried out on electric heaters which happen to be cold and are therefore thought to be switched off. They are in fact controlled by a thermostat which operates whilst the work is going on.

10 **Locks and warning notices**   When a circuit has been isolated and earthed, locks prevent anyone from tampering with the isolation or removing earths by oversight or in order to do unauthorised testing. Warning notices quoting any 'Permit-to-work' number and possibly the name of the responsible person are placed at all control positions, at the circuit breaker and at the equipment upon which it is safe to work. If the surrounding area is dangerous, the safe area may be roped off and warning notices, coloured flags, etc, attached to the rope.

B   WORKED PROBLEMS ON PLANNED MAINTENANCE

Problem 1   Explain the difference between preventive and breakdown maintenance. What are the advantages of the former?

There are two approaches to the maintenance of plant:
1. Allow it to run until it breaks down and then carry out repairs.
2. Regularly test and inspect it in an attempt to prevent breakdowns as far as possible.
Case 1 is known as breakdown maintenance whilst case 2 is preventive maintenance.

The approach depends in part on the process being carried out. A breakdown may result in a period of non-production with a loss of revenue and it may also cause considerable damage to associated plant. The breakdown of an oil pump providing lubrication for a gearbox on a large piece of equipment could cause the gearbox to be wrecked. The failure of a circuit breaker attemping to open to clear a fault could cause severe burning and disruption of the system. On the other hand the failure of a vacuum cleaner in the works canteen would probably be merely inconvenient.

Preventive maintenance does not generally prevent breakdowns altogeth, but minimises their incidence. Regular inspections to check on wear and general deterioration can be carried out either during periods of light loading or during holidays of the production staff, rather than waiting for a breakdown to occur. Spares can be ordered well in advance and plans drawn up for known necessary work during the next few years. Preventive maintenance enables the workforce to be employed steadily for periods of the year instead of days and nights occasionally during periods of breakdown.

Problem 2   Describe a safe system of working for maintenance on a 415 V, 3-phase motor and its associated contactor. The main supply is via 100 A switch fuse located in the main factory substation.

The person authorised to carry out isolations of plant will check to see whether the machine being driven by the motor in question may safely be shut down and will inform interested parties that this is to be done. The motor is stopped in the normal manner using its main contactor and any local isolating switch opened.

The substation is visited and the controlling switch fuse opened and locked in the open position (see *Fig 2*). A warning notice is securely fixed to the switch. This will generally state the name of the person doing the isolation or a document number relating to the work to be carried out. The isolation is checked at the motor starter using a voltmeter or test lamp. This will ascertain that the supply is indeed off. A warning notice will be posted here. The key to the lock on the main switch fuse is locked away in a lockout box which has several different locks on it.

A written authorisation is prepared detailing the work to be carried out and the limits of the isolation. This is signed for by the person who is to carry out the work and he is given one key to the lockout box. Any other interested parties are issued with keys so ensuring that the motor cannot be started without the consent of all these persons. Upon completion of the work the keys are returned and the isolation removed. The authorisation is cancelled. In some cases the authorisation may be verbal but it is unsafe to proceed without a locking off system.

C FURTHER PROBLEMS ON PLANNED MAINTENANCE

(a) SHORT ANSWER PROBLEMS

1   What is the difference between preventive and breakdown maintenance?

2   What is the function of a 'Megger'?

3   List three factors which help to determine the intervals between plant inspections in a programme of preventive maintenance.

4   What routine tests may be carried out on an underground cable?

5   What visual checks may be made on an electric motor to help determine its state of health?

6   Before work can commence on extra-high-voltage equipment, what safety measures are required?

7   Briefly describe two methods of isolating e.h.v. switchgear.

8   What is the function of a lockout box?

(b) MULTI-CHOICE PROBLEMS (answers on page 213)

1   When testing the insulation resistance of an electric motor
    (i) a high voltage test set; or
    (ii) an ohmmeter;
    is used since
    (iii) an ohmmeter is able to measure resistance with great accuracy;
    (iv) a high voltage is necessary to overcome possible high contact resistance of a fault;
    (v) an ohmmeter is much smaller and therefore more portable than the high voltage test set;
    (vi) the high voltage test set has a much higher ohms range necessary when measuring resistances in the metagohm range.
       Select (i) or (ii) together with one from (iii) to (vi) to make a correct statement.

2   Transformer oil is tested periodically to determine its fitness for further use. Tests made include those for
    (i)   electrical breakdown value;   (v)   de-mulsification value;
    (ii)   specific gravity;   (vi)   acid content;
    (iii) viscosity;   (vii) alkali content.
    (iv)   moisture content;
    Select *three* tests.

3   Work is to be carried out on the circuit breaker shown in *Fig 6*. Starting from isolators 1 and 2 closed, the circuit breaker closed, all other isolators open and the circuit alive, the correct procedure for isolating and making the circuit breaker safe to work on is:
    (i)   Open 1, open 2, close 4, close 5;
    (ii)   Close 4, close 5, open circuit breaker, open 1, open 2;
    (iii) Open circuit breaker, open 1, open 2, close 4, close 3;
    (iv)   Open circuit breaker, close 4, close 5, open 1, open 2.

4   When testing a large 3-phase motor to establish its electrical fitness for service, the windings are isolated electrically by removing the connecting links. Measurements of resistance are taken:
    (i)   between each winding and its neighbour;
    (ii)   from end to end of each winding;
    (iii) from each winding to earth.
    (a)   For which of these tests would a result in excess of 100 Ω indicate that the motor is unserviceable?
    (b)   For which of these tests would a result of less than 100 kΩ indicate that the motor is unserviceable? Select (a), (i); (b), (ii) etc.

(c) CONVENTIONAL PROBLEMS

1   Consider a piece of equipment with which you are familiar. (This may be in a factory, college or home). Discuss the financial and other effects that a

breakdown of this equipment would have on (i) personnel; (ii) production; (iii) other equipment.

If, to avoid a recurrence, a programme of preventive inspections and maintenance were to be undertaken, discuss what this would involve and state with reasons the period between inspections.

2   Why is a battery-driven ohmmeter inadequate for cable insulation testing?

3   A 3-phase motor has just been overhauled and it is to be returned to service. Describe the tests and procedures which you would carry out to determine its fitness for further service.

4   Describe the essential features and the operation of a 'Megger' high-voltage tester. How does one know when the correct output voltage from such a tester has been attained?

5   Describe the routine tests which should be carried out on paper insulated lead-sheathed cables to determine their capability of continuing to function correctly

6   Why is the cold-oil level checked on oil-filled transformers during routine checks? What reasons could there be for low level?

7   Describe the process of isolation and methods of ensuring safe working on one piece of equipment with which you are familiar.

8   Describe one situation concerning electrical apparatus which could lead to an accident.

9   What is the function of a Warning Notice when posted in conjunction with a Permit-to Work?

9 Passive and active components in electric circuits

A SUMMARY OF FORMULAE AND DEFINITIONS ASSOCIATED WITH PASSIVE AND ACTIVE COMPONENTS

1 **Resistors** Several different types of resistor are available for use in electrical and electronic circuits. They vary in rating between a fraction of a watt to several kilowatts (see *Problem 1*).

2 **Resistor characteristics**

(i) *Temperature coefficient of resistance* When a resistor experiences a temperature change its resistance will also change. This change is expressed in ohms change per ohm per degree centigrade starting generally at zero degrees centigrade (symbol α_0):

e.g. $\alpha_0 = \Omega/\Omega/°C$

Since ohms divided by ohms (Ω/Ω) is simply a ratio, α_0 is sometimes expressed in the form '/°C' e.g. $\alpha_0 = 0.0042/°C$
The approximate formula connecting the resistance at $t°C$ (R_t); the resistance at $0°C$ (R_0); the operating temperature (t) is:

$R_t = R_0(1 + \alpha_0 t)\ \Omega$

Typical values of α_0 are:
Carbon between -0.001 and $+0.001$.
Nickel–chromium $+0.00007$.
Copper–nickel $+0.00002$.
Metal film between $+0.0002$ and $+0.0006$ according to material.
Oxide coating between -0.0005 and $+0.0005$.

(ii) *Frequency response* Carbon resistors up to about $10\,000\ \Omega$ in value act as pure resistors at all frequencies up to the megaherz range. At extremely high frequencies they develop some capacitive effect. When using the cracked carbon and wirewound types which are constructed of turns of conducting material, inductance must be considered.

(iii) *Power dissipation* The carbon and metal film types are available with ratings from 0.25–5 W. Oxide film construction allows up to 6 W dissipation. Wirewound resistors may be constructed to give almost any power dissipation, even in kW.

(iv) *Temperature limits* Damage to a component will occur if the temperature is allowed to rise too high. For resistors, the following limits in °C are generally adopted: Carbon 110, cracked carbon 150, wire 300 (except where high precision is required when 100 is recommended), oxide film 300.

3 *The resistor colour code* Resistors are generally colour coded with the exception of wirewound types which often have the actual values marked (see *Fig*

121

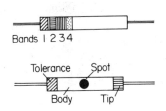

Bands 1 2 3 4

Tolerance Spot

Body Tip

Fig 1

10(e), (f) and (g)). The colour code splits the value into four parts (see *Fig 1*), i.e.

Band 1 or the body colour indicates the first figure.

Band 2 or the tip indicates the second figure.

Band 3 or the spot indicates the number of zeros to be added (the multiplier).

Band 4 or the left hand tip when viewing the spot indicates the tolerance.

4 **Capacitors** *Fig 2* shows some arrangements of conducting surfaces and dielectrics in capacitors. The paper-insulated capacitor comprises two aluminium foils separated by very thin paper soaked in paraffin wax; the mica capacitor, foils separated by mica sheets and the ceramic capacitor, layers of silver plating with a ceramic tube as dielectric. All these are suitable for a.c. or d.c. working.

In the electrolytic capacitor a very thin layer of aluminium oxide forms the dielectric. This type of capacitor is so called because the electrical contact with the oxide is made through a conducting fluid, the electrolyte. Electrolytic capacitors are very much smaller than the paper or mica types, for a given capacitance, and can only be used in circuits with permanent d.c. bias since the action of alternating voltages is to destroy the oxide coating. They are marked for polarity, working voltage and capacitance.

5 **Cores for chokes and transformers** In a transformer or choke the winding is on an iron core. When an alternating current flows in the coil an alternating magnetic field is set up which induces an alternating voltage in the core. This

TABLE 1. COLOUR CODE

Colour	First band or body (First figure)	Second band or tip (Second figure)	Third band or spot (Times)	Fourth band or left hand tip (Tolerance)
Black	0	0	1	—
Brown	1	1	10	1%
Red	1	2	100	2%
Orange	3	3	1000	3%
Yellow	4	4	10000	4%
Green	5	5	100000	—
Blue	6	6	1 million	—
Violet	7	7	10 million	—
Grey	8	8	—	—
White	9	9	—	—
Gold			0.1	5%
Silver			0.01	10%
No colour				20%

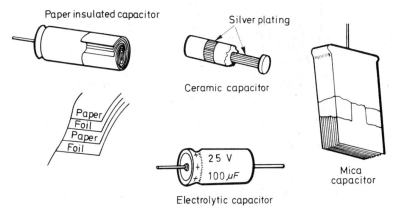

Paper insulated capacitor

Silver plating

Ceramic capacitor

Paper
Foil
Paper
Foil

25 V
100 μF

Electrolytic capacitor

Mica
capacitor

Fig 2

voltage drives what are known as eddy currents through the core material, so
producing heat (see *Fig 3*). In addition there is a hysteresis loss which is due to
the reversal of the magnetic field in the core material. Energy is required to
orientate very small groups of atoms called 'Domains' so as to create a magnetic
field in one direction during a positive going half cycle and then to re-orientate
them with opposite polarity during the negative going half cycle. In electrical
machines working at frequencies up to a few kilohertz, high fluxes are required
and consequently steel with its high working flux density is used to minimise the
cross sectional area required.

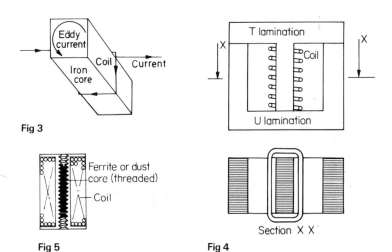

Eddy
current

Iron
core

Coil

Current

Fig 3

T lamination

X

X

Coil

U lamination

Ferrite or dust
core (threaded)

Coil

Fig 5

Section X X

Fig 4

123

The eddy currents are reduced by increasing its resistance to current flow. This is achieved by laminating the core. A lamination is a sheet of steel, typically 0.3–0.4 mm thick, which is carefully cleaned and varnished or anodised on one side. A large number of laminations are pressed together to form the core (*Fig 4*). Adding between 0.5 and 4% of silicon to the steel further increases the resistance but at the expense of the magnetic properties.

Laminations of nickel iron at thicknesses less than 0.1 mm may be used at frequencies up to about 10 MHz. Because eddy current losses are proportional to the frequency squared, these losses at higher frequencies may be considerable with even the thinnest laminations. For this reason dust or ferrite cores as shown in *Fig 5* are used at frequencies up to about 150 MHz in communications equipment. Dust cores comprise iron, nickel-iron or molybdenum particles individually covered with an insulating material and then held together in a resinous binder. Ferrites have very high resistivity and are free from eddy current losses at all but the very highest frequencies. However, since they saturate at low flux densities a larger cross-sectional area is required than when using steel. In ultra-high frequency applications air cores may have to be used since air suffers no hysteresis or eddy current losses.

Hysteresis losses in power equipment are minimised by using cold-rolled grain-oriented steel which is very much easier to magnetise in the direction of rolling than the non-oriented variety.

6 Failure of passive components

(i) *Resistors* The resistance is measured using either an ohmmeter or the voltmeter and ammeter method. The value of resistance obtained will indicate:

 (a) that the resistor is sound, the value measured being within the tolerance band.

 (b) an open circuit (partial or complete) the value being much higher than nominal.

 (c) a short circuit (partial or complete) the value being much lower than nominal.

(ii) *Capacitors* A d.c. voltage slightly in excess of normal rated value is applied to the capacitor through a low-range series-connected ammeter. Care must be taken to see that the correct polarity is used on electrolytic capacitors. After a short initial charging period there should be virtually no current in the circuit. Current flowing indicates leakage possibly due to a failure of the dielectric.

 Substituting an a.c. supply and a.c. ammeter it should be possible to measure current flow, e.g.

$$I = V \times 2\pi f C \text{ amperes}$$

from which C can be calculated.

Zero current or a value yielding a very low value of capacitance from the calculation indicates an open circuit within the capacitor.

(*Note:* electrolytic capacitors must be tested using a low voltage applied for only a few seconds or they may break down during the test.)

(ii) **Inductors** The resistance is measured using the same method as for resistors. Using an a.c. supply:

$$V/I = Z \ \Omega \text{ and } Z^2 - R^2 = X_L^2 \text{ from which } X_L \text{ is calculated.}$$
 Then: $X_L = 2\pi f L \ \Omega.$

The value of inductance so obtained is compared with the nominal value. A *high* value of *resistance* indicates an open circuit. A *low* value of *inductance* indicates short-circuited turns within the coil.

7 **Terminal locations of active devices**   These may generally be determined using an ohmmeter with a low internal voltage (1.4 V typically). It should be noted that when using a commercial multi-purpose meter, the negative (black) terminal

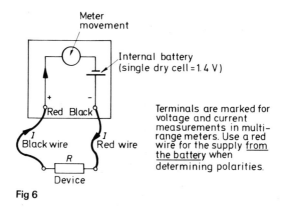

Fig 6

when used for measuring voltages and currents becomes the positive terminal for resistance measurements so that the correct current direction in the meter movement is maintained. This should be clear from *Fig 6*. A separate battery and milliammeter may be used, a high current indicating a low resistance.

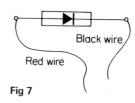

Fig 7

(i) *The diode*   The ohmmeter will indicate a low value of resistance when connected as shown in *Fig 7*. Reversing the connections will yield a near-infinity reading.

(ii) *Bipolar junction transistors.*
   (a) *p-n-p transistors*   Easy current flow from *p* to *n*. In *Fig 8(a)* Red on e and black on b gives low resistance. Red on c and black on b gives low resistance.
   (b) *n-p-n. transistors*   In *Fig 8(b)* Red on b and black on c gives low resistance. Red on b and black on e gives low resistance.
   For either transistor, any other combination of connections gives a near-infinity resistance.

(iii) *JFET transistors*   From gate to source or from gate to drain the resistance will be very nearly infinity. All that can be done here is to find a pair of terminals between which a lower resistance can be measured. These two terminals must be source and drain. The third terminal must be the gate.

125

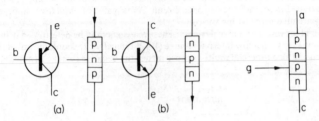

Fig 8   Fig 9

(iv) *Thyristor* From cathode to anode with either polarity connected, a near-infinity resistance reading is obtained (see *Fig 9*).

With red on g and black on c a low resistance reading is obtained. With black on g and red on c a higher resistance value is obtained. This may vary between only slightly greater and considerably greater than the previous reading according to the devices tested.

B WORKED PROBLEMS ON PASSIVE AND ACTIVE COMPONENTS

Problem 1 Describe with the aid of suitable sketches the construction of the following types of resistor:

(i)   Moulded carbon;   (iv) Wirewound;
(ii) Carbon film;   (v)   Metal film;
(iii) Cracked carbon;   (vi) Oxide film;
                                     (vii) Variable resistors

(i)   *Moulded carbon resistors* These are made from carbon dust, refractory material and resin, compressed to the correct shape and then heat cured.

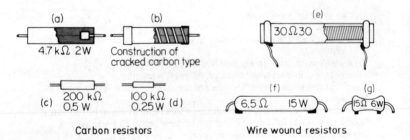

Carbon resistors   Wire wound resistors

Fig 10

The connections are made by either spraying each end with metal and then soldering tags to this metal or by using inserted ends as shown in *Fig 10(a)*.

(ii) *Carbon film resistors*   A glass tube is coated with a thin film of carbon which is then heated to fix the material and stabilise the value of resistance.

(iii) *Cracked carbon resistors*   Carbon is deposited at high temperature on ceramic rod. Spiral grooves are cut in the carbon to give the final resistance value (*Fig 10(b)*.) *Figs 10(c)* and *(d)* show the relative sizes of carbon resistors with different power ratings.

(iv) *Wirewound resistors*   These are made by winding nickel-chromium or copper-nickel wire on a ceramic former. The resistor so formed may be coated in vitreous enamel and fired to give protection, see *Figs 10(e), (f)* and *(g)*.

(v) *Metal film resistors*   Nickel-chromium or gold-platinum is evaporated and deposited inside a ceramic tube. The connections are made by silver plating the ends.

(vi) *Oxide film resistors*   Tin-antimony oxides are deposited on a ceramic tube forming a glass-like surface.

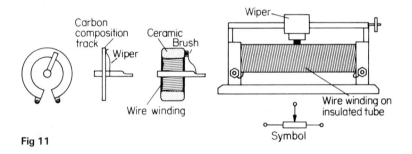

Fig 11

(vii) *Variable resistors*   *Fig 11* shows the arrangement of carbon track and wirewound variable resistors. The carbon type is almost invariably used as a low-rated potentiometer whereas the wirewound types may be used both as potentiometers and as series resistors.

Problem 2   Explain why the physical size of a carbon resistor is generally no indication of its resistance value.

When current flows in a resistor heat is produced which has to be dissipated to the surrounding environment, often into the air. The heat dissipation is a function of the surface area and of the difference between resistor and ambient temperatures. The upper temperature of the resistor is limited to minimise the change in resistance due to the temperature coefficient of resistance and the effect on surrounding equipment such as the circuit board etc. At extremely high temperatures, the resistor itself could fail due to melting, for example.

It is therefore necessary that the surface area of the resistor be related to the power rating and not to the resistance value. As an example consider two resistors, one of 5 Ω and the other of 5000 Ω. Each is connected to a 20 V supply.

Power loss in the 5 Ω resistor = $\dfrac{V^2}{R} = \dfrac{20^2}{5} = \textbf{80 W}$

Power loss in the 5000 Ω resistor = $\dfrac{20^2}{5000} = \textbf{0.08 W}$

The 5 Ω resistor would need to have a considerably greater surface area than the 5000 Ω resistor and therefore would be physically larger.

Resistors are made with ratings of (typically) $\frac{1}{4}$ W, $\frac{1}{2}$ W, 2 W and 5 W; each size with a large number of standard and non-standard resistance values.

Problem 3 A factory production line is producing inductors for use in power supply units. The design parameters are: $R = 50$ Ω, $L = 0.2$ H when measured at 100 Hz. Three coils were selected for testing and the following results obtained:

	Fed from a 5 V, d.c. supply	Fed from a 5 V, 100 Hz supply
Coil 1	$I = 98$ mA	$I = 64$ mA
Coil 2	$I = 100$ mA	$I = 37$ mA
Coil 3	$I = 1.5$ mA	No test

Comment on the suitability of the three coils for use as specified.

Coil 1   On d.c., $R = \dfrac{V}{I} = \dfrac{5}{98 \times 10^{-3}} = 51.02$ Ω

On a.c., $Z = \dfrac{V}{I} = \dfrac{5}{64 \times 10^{-3}} = 78.13$ Ω

$X_L = \sqrt{(Z^2 - R^2)} = \sqrt{(78.13^2 - 51^2)} = 59.16$ Ω

$X_L = 2\pi f L.$

Hence

$$L = \dfrac{59.16}{2\pi \times 100} = 0.094\ H$$

This coil seems to have the correct number of turns since the d.c. resistance is correct (closely) but some of the turns are short circuited giving a low value of inductance.

Coil 2   *On d.c.*, $R = \dfrac{5}{100 \times 10^{-3}} = 50$ Ω

On a.c., $Z = \dfrac{5}{37 \times 10^{-3}} = 135.14$ Ω

$X_L = \sqrt{(135.14^2 - 50^2)} = 125.5$ Ω

$$L = \frac{125.5}{2\pi \times 100} = 0.2 \text{ H}$$

This coil is on specification.

Coil 3   *On d.c.,* $R = \frac{5}{1.5 \times 10^{-3}} = 3300 \ \Omega.$

This coil is virtually open circuit, possibly poor soldering at the terminals. There is no point in performing the a.c. test. Therefore the coil is not suitable for use.

Problem 4   A resistor has a value of 15 000 Ω at 25°C. It has a temperature coefficient of resistance of −0.001 $\Omega/\Omega/°C$. Determine the value of its resistance at: (i) 0°C; (ii) 100°C.

(i) $R_t = R_0(1 + \alpha_0 t) \ \Omega$ and at 25°C, $R_t = 15 \, 000 \ \Omega$

Substituting values in the formula:

$15 \, 000 = R_0(1 + (-0.001) \times 25) = R_0(1 - 0.025)$

Transposing gives:

$R_0 = \frac{15 \, 000}{0.975} = \mathbf{15 \, 384.6} \ \Omega.$

(ii)   At 100°C

$R_t = R_0(1 + (-0.001) \times 100)$

$= 15 \, 384.6 \times 0.9 = \mathbf{13 \, 846.1} \ \Omega.$

Problem 5   A capacitor draws 1.26 mA from a 20 V, 100 Hz supply. When connected to a d.c. supply the current supplied is zero.
(i)   Determine the value of the capacitor;
(ii)   If the same value of current had been drawn from both supplies, what would this mean?

When connected to the d.c. supply the current is zero. This indicates that either the capacitor is in working order or that the connection are open circuited. Since current is taken from the a.c. supply, the latter possibility is discounted.

(i) $X_C = \frac{V}{I} = \frac{20}{1.26 \times 10^{-3}} = 15873 \ \Omega.$

$X_C = \frac{1}{2\pi f C} \ \Omega$

Transposing gives

$C = \frac{1}{2\pi f X_C} = \frac{1}{2\pi \times 100 \times 15873} = \mathbf{0.1} \ \mu\mathbf{F}$

(ii)   If the same value of current had been taken from both supplies, a short circuit within the capacitor would have been concluded.

C FURTHER PROBLEMS ON PASSIVE AND ACTIVE COMPONENTS

(a) SHORT ANSWER PROBLEMS

1 Name three types of resistor used in electrical circuits.

2 What is the effect on its electrical properties of increasing temperature of (a) a carbon resistor; (b) a wire-wound resistor?

3 What is the basic difference between a 10 Ω, 0.5 W carbon resistor and a 10 Ω, 2 W carbon resistor?

4 Why is the upper temperature of a resistor during operation limited?

5 What values of resistance and tolerance, where relevant, are indicated by the following colours?

Band 1	Band 2	Band 3	Band 4
White	Brown	Yellow	Brown
Orange	White	Yellow	Yellow
Brown	Black	Brown	—
Yellow	Violet	Red	Gold
Yellow	Violet	Silver	Red

6 What colour markings would indicate the following values of resistance?
(a) 25 Ω; (b) 57 Ω; (c) 150 Ω; (d) 58 000 Ω?

7 Why is an electrolytic capacitor not suitable for use in a.c. circuits?

8 How is the capacitance of an electrolytic capacitor made much greater than that of a paper insulated capacitor of the same physical size?

9 What are eddy current losses? How may these be minimised in the core of a choke operating at 100 MHz.

10 Why would a ferrite core not be used in a power transformer?

11 An inductor which has been in service for some time is tested and found to have a substantially lower inductance than when new. What could cause a low value? Suggest a way in which this might have come about.

(b) MULTI-CHOICE PROBLEMS (answers on page 213)

1 Three resistors are colour coded as follows:

	Band 1	Band 2	Band 3
Resistor (i)	Yellow	Violet	Black
Resistor (ii)	Yellow	Violet	Brown
Resistor (iii)	Yellow	Violet	Green

The values are (a) 470 Ω; (b) 4700 Ω; (c) 47 Ω; (d) 470 000 Ω; (e) 4.7×10^6 Ω. Allocate one value from (a) to (e) to each of the resistors (i), (ii) and (iii).

2 The dielectric in an electrolytic capacitor is: (i) paper; (ii) a conducting fluid; (iii) aluminium oxide; (iv) a thin sheet of aluminium.

3 Complete the following sentences 1 and 2 using, in each case, *one* of the following statements (i) to (iii)

Sentence 1   Non-electrolytic capacitors are suitable for use in situations where the potential at its terminals . . . .

Sentence 2   Electrolytic capacitors are suitable for use in situations where the potential at its terminals . . . .

Select from (i) is uni-directional; (ii) is alternating; (iii) may be steady, varying or alternating.

4   Dust cores may be used in transformers and coils for operation at frequencies between 100 MHz and 150 MHz. They are used to:
(i)   minimise the hysteresis losses;
(ii) increase the maximum working flux
(iii) make fabrication of various core shapes easier than when using laminations;
(iv) reduce eddy current losses.

5   An air-cored coil has a nominal inductance of 20 mH and a resistance of 60 Ω when measured at 400 Hz. On test a particular coil gave the following results: 10 V at 400 Hz applied to the coil, $I = 0.14$ A. On d.c. the results showed that the resistance was substantially correct. It may therefore be deduced that:

(i)   the coil is suitable for use, i.e. the value of the inductance L is correct;
(ii) the inductance is higher than the design value;
(iii) the coil is partially open circuited;
(iv) the coil has short-circuited turns;
(v)   the coil has been wound with a larger diameter wire than design so reducing the number of turns in the given volume hence reducing the inductance.

6   Which of the following pairs of conditions is true for an *n-p-n* bipolar junction transistor? (b = base, e = emitter, c = collector)
(i)   Low resistance between b and c and between e and c
(ii) Low resistance between b and c and between b and e
(iii) High resistance between b and c and between b and e
(iv) Low resistance between b and e, high resistance between b and e

7   A resistor with $\alpha_0 = +0.005$ $\Omega/\Omega/°C$ has a resistance of 5.3 Ω at 20°C. Its resistance at 65°C will be:
(i) 4.326 Ω; (ii) 6.493 Ω; (iii) 6.384 Ω.

(c) CONVENTIONAL PROBLEMS

1   A moulded carbon resistor and a wirewound nickel chromium resistor both have a resistance of 1 Ω at 0°C. What will their respective resistances be at 50°C? The temperature coefficient of resistance of carbon = -0.001 $\Omega/\Omega/°C$ and that of nickel-chromium = $+0.00007$ $\Omega/\Omega/°C$.

[Carbon, 0.95 Ω; Nickel-chromium 1.0035 Ω]

2   Draw graphs to scale on the same axes showing how the resistance of a resistor with value 50 Ω at 20°C varies as the temperature is changed from 0°C to 100°C if:
(i) $\alpha_0 = +0.0005$ $\Omega/\Omega/°C$; (ii) $\alpha_0 = -0.0005$ $\Omega/\Omega/°C$.

$$\left[\begin{array}{l} \text{(i) } R_0 = 49.5 \ \Omega; \ R_{100} = 51.98 \ \Omega; \\ \text{(ii) } R_0 = 50.5 \ \Omega; \ R_{100} = 47.98 \ \Omega \end{array} \right]$$

3 Explain why wirewound resistors are not suitable for use in circuits operating at very high frequencies. Write down the colour coding for the following resistors: (a) 150 Ω, 4%; (b) 58 Ω, 2%; (c) 0.58 Ω, 10%

> [(a) Brown green brown yellow;
> (b) Green grey black red;
> (c) Green grey silver silver.]

4 What values of resistance are indicated by the following colour banding?

	Band 1	Band 2	Band 3	Band 4
Resistor (a)	Grey	Brown	Green	Gold
Resistor (b)	Violet	Orange	Red	Silver
Resistor (c)	Brown	Yellow	Blue	Orange

> [8.1 MΩ 5%;
> 7300 Ω 10%;
> 14 MΩ 3%;]

5 The capacitance of a capacitor increases as the plate area is increased. What methods are employed by the capacitor manufacturer to contain a large plate area within a small volume?

6 What is a lamination as employed in transformer manufacture? Why are laminations used in preference to a solid core?

7 A capacitor with a nominal value of $10\,\mu\text{F}$ is connected to a 100 V, 50 Hz supply when a current of 0.05 A is indicated on a series connected ammeter. What may be deduced from these results?
[Correct current for $10\,\mu\text{F} = 0.314$ A. Capacitor open circuited]

8 A coil is tested on d.c. and the resistance is found to be 2 Ω. When connected to a 50 V, 50 Hz supply a current of 10 A flows in the coil. What is the inductance of the coil? [$X_L = 4.58\,\Omega; L = 14.58\,\text{mH}$]

9 (a) A resistor has a value of 470 Ω at 17°C. It has a temperature coefficient of resistance of $-0.0008\ \Omega/\Omega/°C$. Determine its value at 100°C.
(b) A second resistor has a temperature coefficient of resistance of $+0.0005\ \Omega/\Omega/°C$.
Determine the required value of resistance for this resistor at 0°C in order that it shall have the same resistance as that in (a) above at 100°C
Both resistors at 100°C = 438.36 Ω
$R_0(\text{b}) = 417.49$ Ω

10 A coil has a resistance of 50 Ω at 15°C. It has a temperature coefficient of resistance $+0.0042\ \Omega/\Omega/°C$. It operates at a power factor of 0.707. What will its operating power factor be at 105°C? Assume that temperature has no effect on inductance.
(*Hint:* What is the value of X_L at 15°C to give a phase angle of 45°: power factor of 0.707?)
[$R_{105} = 67.77\ \Omega; \phi = 36.4°$; power factor $= 0.805$]

11 Three, 3-terminal devices are tested using an ohmmeter connected as shown in *Fig 6*. The red wire is connected to the positive of the internal battery. The following readings were noted:

Device (a)

Red wire on terminal 1, black wire on terminal 3, $R = 1$ MΩ

Red wire on terminal 1, black wire on terminal 2, $R = 1$ MΩ

Red wire on terminal 2, black wire on terminal 3, $R = 10\ \Omega$

Red wire on terminal 3, black wire on terminal 2, $R = 500\ \Omega$

Device (b)

Red wire on terminal 2, black wire on terminal 1, $R = 100,000\ \Omega$

Red wire on terminal 2, black wire on terminal 3, $R = 10\ \Omega$

Red wire on terminal 3, black wire on terminal 2, $R = 10\ \Omega$

Device (c)

Red wire on terminal 1, black wire on terminal 2, $R = 50\ \Omega$

Red wire on terminal 3, black wire on terminal 2, $R = 50\ \Omega$

Red wire on terminal 1, black wire on terminal 3, $R = 1000\ \Omega$ and the same value of resistance is obtained if the polarity is reversed.

Draw a circuit diagram of each of the devices naming them and marking the terminals.

(a) Thyristor 1 = anode; 2 = gate; 3 = cathode

(b) JFET 1 = gate; 2 and 3 = source and drain

(c) *p-n-p* Bipolar junction transistor

1 = emitter; 2 = base; 3 = Collector.

10 Simple power supplies

A SUMMARY OF FORMULAE AND DEFINITIONS ASSOCIATED WITH SIMPLE POWER SUPPLIES FOR ELECTRONIC APPARATUS

1 Rectifier circuits

(a) *Half wave*   The simplest rectifier circuit employs a single diode connected as shown in *Fig 1(a)*. An isolating transformer is used to obtain the correct voltage for the load circuit. The diode conducts for only one direction of applied voltage so that the current in a resistive load is unidirectional as shown in *Fig 1(b)*.

(b) *Full wave*   Using two diodes, current may be caused to flow in the load during both half cycles. In *Fig 2* during positive half cycles diode D1 conducts whilst diode D2 blocks current flow so that current flows in the load through D1. During negative half cycles diode D2 conducts whilst diode D1 blocks the current. Current flows in the load through D2. Only one half of the transformer winding conducts during each half cycle and this rectifier is in effect two, half-wave rectifiers back to back. An improvement in transformer usage is obtained by employing the bridge circuit shown in *Fig 3*. The whole of the transformer secondary winding carries current during each half cycle. The waveforms for both full wave rectifiers are shown in *Fig 4*.

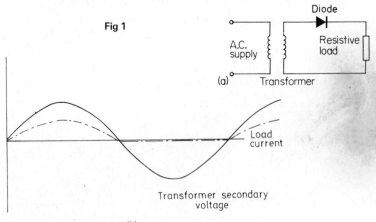

Fig 1

Diode

A.C. supply

Resistive load

(a)   Transformer

Load current

Transformer secondary voltage

(b)

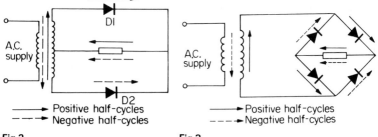

Fig 2

→ Positive half-cycles
--→ Negative half-cycles

Fig 3

→ Positive half-cycles
--→ Negative half-cycles

2 **Ripple**   With the half wave rectifier, the load current and voltage change from zero to a peak value and back to zero again during one half cycle of the a.c. supply, whilst with the full wave rectifiers the changes occur twice per cycle. The magnitude of the voltage changes is known as the **ripple voltage** and the number of times that it occurs per second is the **ripple frequency.** The ripple may be

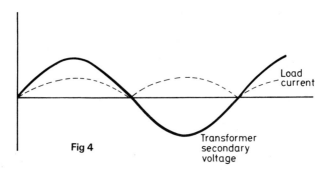

Fig 4

Load current

Transformer secondary voltage

observed by using an oscilloscope with the input leads connected directly across the load where this is resistive. Alternatively a small standard resistor may be connected into the circuit and the oscilloscope leads connected to the ends of this.

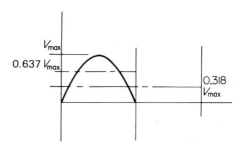

Fig 5

V_{max}
$0.637 V_{max}$
$0.318 V_{max}$

3 **Average values** The average value of a sinusoidal voltage wave over one half cycle is 0.637 times the maximum value (*Fig 5*). Similarly for current:

$$I_{av} = 0.637\, I_{max}.$$

For the half wave connection,
the average over the conducting half cycle = $0.637\, I_{max}$.
Since there is no conduction during the next half cycle this value must be divided by 2 to give the average over the complete cycle, i.e.

$$I_{av} = 0.318\, I_{max}.$$

For the full-wave rectifier,

$$I_{av} = 0.637\, I_{max}.$$

The average values of voltage and current are measured using moving-coil meters connected as in *Fig 1* (chapter 7).

4 **Smoothing** For many applications a supply with a large amount of ripple is not acceptable. A simple method of reducing this is to connect a capacitor having a large value of capacitance in parallel with the load.

Consider the diode and capacitor shown in *Fig 6*, initially with the load not

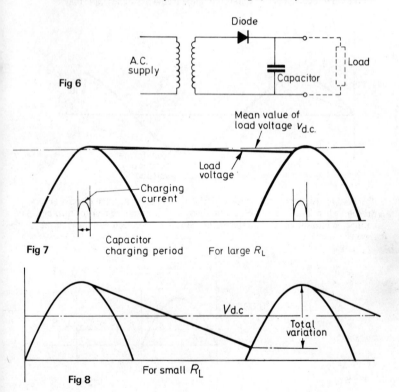

Fig 6

Fig 7

Fig 8

connected. During the positive half cycle of voltage the diode conducts, charging the capacitor to the peak value of the a.c. voltage. As the supply voltage falls from the peak value the capacitor voltage is greater than that of the supply. It cannot discharge back into the supply however, since the diode blocks reverse current flow. The capacitor voltage remains constant at the peak value.

Now consider the effect of connecting the load. At the peak of the voltage wave the load is fed directly from the supply. As the supply voltage falls below its maximum value the capacitor supplies current to the load and whilst losing charge, its voltage falls (*Fig 7*). If the load resistance is high the current will be low and the voltage will fall only slowly. The capacitor is charged each time the supply voltage exceeds that remaining on it.

The effect of lowering the load resistance and so increasing the load current is to increase the ripple and so lower the value of $V_{\text{d.c.}}$. Using a full-wave rectifier reduces ripple since the intervals between charging the capacitor are shorter (*Fig 8*).

5 **Approximate value of smoothing capacitor** (*Fig 9*)   With *n* pulses per second, the time interval between voltage peaks is $1/n$ seconds. This is very nearly equal to the capacitor discharge time for small values of ripple. Let the mean d.c. current $= I_{\text{d.c.}}$ amperes

For a capacitor, Q = Capacitance in farads × voltage change, where Q = charge in coulombs

In symbols: $Q = C\Delta V$ coulombs.

Also $Q = It$, where I = current in amperes and t = time in seconds.

Now, charge given to load = charge lost by capacitor between charging pulses

Hence $I_{\text{d.c.}} \times \dfrac{1}{n} = C\Delta V$

Transposing: $C = \dfrac{I_{\text{d.c.}}}{n} \times \dfrac{1}{\Delta V}$

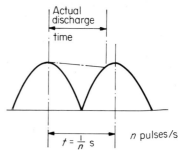

Fig 9

6 **Improved smoothing methods**   Even when a capacitor having a very large value of capacitance is used, the ripple can still be excessive for many applications. An extremely smooth output can be achieved by using either of the arrangements shown in *Fig 10*.

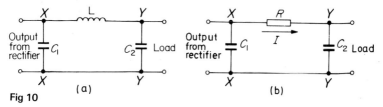

Fig 10

137

In *Fig 10(a)* voltages are induced in the inductor which oppose those causing the current changes (Lenz's law). As current tends to increase, the induced voltage opposes the increase and as current tends to decrease, the induced voltage helps to maintain the flow. In *Fig 10(b)*, as the ripple voltage increases on C_1 the current in the resistor R increases.

Now $V_{YY} = V_{XX} - IR$. V_{YY} is somewhat lower than V_{XX}.

As the ripple voltage falls to its minimum value it approaches that held on C_2, i.e. V_{YY}, so that the current I falls to a very low value and the voltage drop IR is small. Hence the ripple voltage is taken up by increasing and decreasing the volt drop in R.

7 **Voltage stabilisation**   The change in voltage which occurs due to a change in load can have undesirable effects. Consider as an example a simple cassette tape player. The speed of the drive motor is a function of the voltage applied to its terminals. When playing a tape, increasing the output volume causes more current to be drawn from the supply, which can reduce the output voltage. It clearly would be most unsatisfactory if every time a loud passage were played, the voltage fell and the tape travel slowed. Voltage stabilisation is therefore desirable for many applications.

8 **The zener diode**   A device with a characteristic as shown in *Fig 11(a)* is known as a zener diode. It is non-conducting up to a precisely known reverse voltage, 6.8 V in this case, when it suddenly becomes conducting. The result of trying to further increase the voltage is to cause it to conduct whatever current is necessary to produce voltage drops in circuit components and connections to maintain 6.8 V at its terminals, even if in so doing, it destroys itself by overheating. The voltage at which conduction commences in a particular diode is specified in

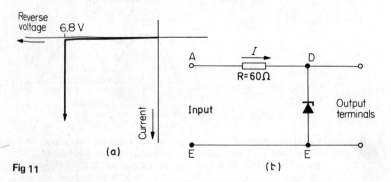

Fig 11

maker's catalogues and devices are purchased for particular applications.

Simple voltage stabilisation is achieved using the circuit shown in *Fig 11(b)*. The voltage V_{DE} is to be 6.8 V whilst the input voltage V_{AE} is (say) 8 V.

$$V_{AE} - V_{DE} = 8 - 6.8 = 1.2 \text{ V}$$

This must be dropped across R which is 60 Ω in this case.

$$I = \frac{1.2}{60} = 20 \text{ mA}.$$

138

This current is constant for the voltage levels specified.

With a load of 680 Ω connected, $I_{load} = \dfrac{6.8}{680} = 10$ mA.

Thus 10 mA flows in the load and, 10 mA flows in the zener diode making 20 mA in all in the stabilising resistor.

This sharing continues up to the point where $I_{load} = 20$ mA when the zener diode ceases conduction. For load currents in excess of this value the volt drop across R is too great and the output voltage falls below 6.8 V.

Generally: $\dfrac{V_{AE} - V_{DE}}{R} =$ maximum value of load current at constant voltage.

B WORKED PROBLEMS ON SIMPLE POWER SUPPLIES

Problem 1   An unsmoothed uni-directional supply with average value 50 V is to be obtained using a full-wave rectifier fed from a single-phase, 240 V a.c. supply through an isolating transformer. What would be the required turns ratio of the isolating transformer:
(i) a bi-phase (2 diode) rectifier; (ii) a bridge rectifier.
The volt drops in the diodes may be ignored.

For full-wave rectification, $V_{av} = 0.637\,V_{max}$

Therefore for $V_{av} = 50$ V, $V_{max} = \dfrac{50}{0.637} = 78.5$ V

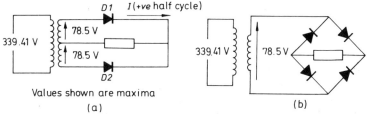

Values shown are maxima

(a)   (b)

Fig 12

(i)   *Bi-phase connection*   Only one half of the winding is conducting at any one time. The maximum voltage of 78.5 V must therefore appear across one half of the winding as shown in *Fig 12(a)*.

The total secondary voltage = 2×78.5 V = 157 V (max)

Note that during the positive half cycle there is 78.5 V (max) induced in the bottom half of the winding but this has no effect on the load since diode D2 is blocking. The input to the transformer is at 240 V (r.m.s.) so to compare ke with like it is necessary to express this as a peak value also.

240 V r.m.s. = $\sqrt{2} \times 240 = 339.41$ V (max)

The transformer ratio = 339.41 : 157 = **2.16 : 1**

Bridge connection With the bridge connection the total secondary voltage of the transformer is applied to the load.

The transformer ratio = 339.41 : 78.5 = **4.32 : 1**

Problem 2 (a) Why is it often necessary to smooth the output from a rectifier circuit?
(b) Draw a circuit diagram showing a single-phase bridge rectifier with a single capacitor for smoothing feeding a simple voltage stabilising circuit. Why would the stabilising circuit of itself decrease te ripple in the output voltage?

For many applications, e.g. audio equipment, a supply with a large amount of ripple is not acceptable since it produces a hum in the output. For applications where counting is being done excessive ripple may cause the device to count the half cycles of its power input rather than or in addition to what it is supposed to be counting.

The zener diode in the stabilising circuit will maintain constant voltage at its terminals. With ripple on the output voltage from the rectifier the voltage V_{XX} in

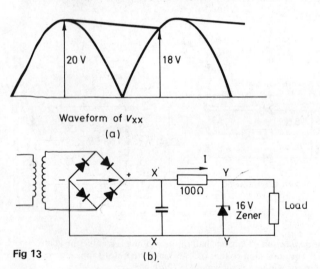

Waveform of V_{XX}

(a)

Fig 13

(b)

Fig 13(b) will rise and fall. Consider an example where the waveform is as shown in *Fig 13(a)*:

When V_{XX} is at its peak value of 20 V, $I = \dfrac{20 - 16}{100} = 40$ mA

140

When V_{XX} is at its minimum value of 18 V, $I = \dfrac{18-16}{100} = 20$ mA

The current in the stabilising resistor varies between 40 mA and 20 mA whilst maintaining V_{YY} constant. For load currents up to 20 mA the load voltage would be constant (closely). For load currents above this, during the periods of low input voltage, the load voltage would be less than the required 16 V.

Problem 3   A load is supplied with 50 mA at a mean voltage of 285 V using a full-wave rectifier. The peak value of the a.c. supply is 300 V and the frequency 50 Hz. Calculate the approximate size of a suitable smoothing capacitor.

At 50 Hz, with a full-wave rectifier, the time interval between successive peaks

$$= \frac{1}{2f}s = \frac{1}{100} = 0.01 \text{ s (see para 5)}.$$

Discharge during this time $= I_{d.c.} \times$ time

$$= 50 \times 10^{-3} \times 0.01 = 0.5 \times 10^{-3} \text{ C}$$

Mean d.c. voltage $= V_{d.c.} = 285$ V. Peak voltage $= 300$ V
Change in voltage from mean to maximum $= 15$ V. By symmetry, the change from mean to minimum voltage will also be 15 V.
Total voltage variation $= 30$ V (see *Fig 8*).
Therefore, since $C\Delta V =$ charge in coulombs

$$C \times 30 = 0.5 \times 10^{-3}$$

$$C = \frac{0.5 \times 10^{-3}}{30} = 16.67 \times 10^{-6} = \mathbf{16.67\,\mu F}$$

Problem 4   A 50 μF capacitor is used for smoothing the output from a full-wave rectifier connected to a 50 Hz supply. If $V_{d.c.} = 150$ V, estimate the total voltage variation and the ripple expressed as a percentage of $V_{d.c.}$ for a load resistor of 3000 Ω.

$$I_{d.c.} = \frac{V_{d.c.}}{R_{load}} = \frac{150}{3000} = 0.05 \text{ A}$$

and from para 5
$I_{d.c.} \times$ time between pulses $= C\Delta V$

The time between the peaks of the pulses $= 0.01$ s(see *Problem 3*)
Therefore $0.05 \times 0.01 = 50 \times 10^{-6} \times \Delta V$

$$\Delta V = \frac{0.05 \times 0.01}{50 \times 10^{-6}} = 10 \text{ V}$$

For a total variation in voltage of 10 V, it must vary between $150 + 5 = 155$ V and $150 - 5 = 145$ V.

The change in voltage from $V_{d.c.}$ to the maximum value or from $V_{d.c.}$ down to the minimum value, expressed as a percentage of the mean value $V_{d.c.}$ is known as the percentage ripple, as called for in the question.

Percentage ripple $= \frac{5}{150} \times 100 = \textbf{3.33\%}$

Problem 5   A 10 V zener diode is used to stabilise a d.c. supply at 10 V for load currents between zero and 0.5 A. The input voltage is 15 V.
Determine: (a) the value of a suitable stabilising resistor and (b) the current and power dissipation in the zener diode when the load current is 0.2 A.

Volt drop across the stabilising resistor $= 15 - 10 = 5$ V

From para 7, $\frac{5}{R} = 0.5$ A

Transposing: $R = \frac{5}{0.5} = 10\,\Omega$

With 0.2 A flowing in the load, the zener diode current $= 0.5 - 0.2 = 0.3$ A
Power dissipation in the zener diode $=$ voltage $\times$ current
$$= 10 \times 0.3 = \textbf{3 W}$$

Problem 6   What is the value of the total voltage variation and the ripple frequency delivered from the output terminals of a full-wave rectifier which is fed from a 9 V, 50 Hz supply? There is no smoothing. Ignore forward voltage drops in the diodes.

---

9 V is the r.m.s. value of voltage
$\therefore$ The peak value $= \sqrt{2} \times 9 = 12.73$ V
The rectified output voltage will rise from zero to a peak of 12.73 V and return to zero twice per cycle of the alternating voltage input.
The total voltage variation is thus **12.73 V**
The frequency = **100 times per second.**

C   FURTHER PROBLEMS ON SIMPLE POWER SUPPLIES

(a) SHORT ANSWER PROBLEMS

1   What is a diode?

2   Sketch the voltage waveform developed across a resistor connected in series with a single diode to an alternating supply.

3   A full-wave rectifier is used in conjunction with a 50 V, 100 Hz a.c. supply to deliver unsmoothed, uni-directional current to a load. What is the value of (a) the ripple frequency; (b) the total voltage variation?

4   A half-wave rectifier connected to a 100 V a.c. system is used to supply a load. Ignoring the forward voltage drop in the diode, determine the mean value of the voltage developed across the load.

5   An a.c., single-phase supply and a bridge rectifier are used to supply a resistive load with direct current. The load voltage waveform is observed using a cathode-ray oscilloscope. What change in the CRO trace would become apparent if a capacitor having a large value of capitance were connected in parallel with the load?

6   What would be the effect of using an unsmoothed supply derived from a rectifier to drive an amplifier connected to a record player?

7   Draw a circuit diagram showing a smoothing circuit employing two capacitors and an inductor.

8   Explain why voltage stabilisation is required for some applications.

9   A 12 V zener diode is used in conjunction with a 5 Ω stabilising resistor to stabilise the voltage from a 14 V source. What power will be dissipated in the zener diode when there is no load connected to the circuit?

(b) MULTI-CHOICE PROBLEMS (answers on page 213)

1   The ripple frequency of the voltage output from a bi-phase, full wave rectifier connected to 50 Hz mains is:
(i) 25 Hz; (ii) 100 Hz; (iii) 50 Hz; (iv) 200 Hz.

2   The average value of direct voltage output from a half-wave rectifier connected to 240 V a.c. mains is:
(i) 76.3 V; (ii) 152.6 V; (iii) 108 V; (iv) 215.8 V.

3   A half-wave rectifier fed from a 60 V a.c. supply has its output smoothed by the addition of a 200 μF capacitor. The maximum possible reverse voltage across the diode is:
(i) 169.7 V; (ii) 84.8 V; (iii) 120 V; (iv) 60 V.

4   The ripple voltage in the smoothed output from a rectifier is reduced when
(i)   the value of the load resistance is reduced;
(ii) the size of the smoothing capacitor is reduced;
(iii) the operating frequency is reduced;
(iv) the current drawn by the load is reduced.

5   The output from a full-wave rectifier and smoothing circuit has a maximum voltage of 205 V and a minimum value of 195 V during each half cycle of the mains input voltage. The ripple expressed as a percentage of the mean direct voltage $V_{d.c.}$ is
(i) 5%; (ii) $2\frac{1}{2}$%; (iii) 10%; (iv) 1.25%.

6   The output from a full-wave rectifier connected to a 400 Hz supply is smoothed using a single 5 μF capacitor. The load current $I_{d.c.}$ has a value of 10 mA. The mean load voltage = 100 V. The ripple expressed as a percentage of $V_{d.c.}$ is:
(i) 5%; (ii) 1.25%; (iii) 3%; (iv) 2.5%.

7   When using a zener diode for voltage stabilisation, as in *Fig 11*, the maximum power dissipation in the zener diode occurs when:
(i)   the external load draws its maximum current;
(ii) the external load is disconnected;
(iii) the external load resistance is equal to that of the stabilising resistor.

8   The smoothed output voltage from a rectifier is at 20 V. A 12 V zener diode is to be used to stabilise the voltage to a piece of equipment over load currents ranging from zero to 0.25 A. The power dissipation in (a) the stabilising resistor and (b) the zener diode when the load current is 0.1 A is:
(i) 2 W; (ii) 1.2 W; (iii) 3 W; (iv) 1.8 W; (v) 1.5 W.
Select an answer from (i)–(v) for (a) and another for (b); e.g. (a) & (ii).

(c) CONVENTIONAL PROBLEMS

1   Determine the average value of d.c. output voltage from (a) a half-wave rectifier
    and (b) a full-wave rectifier, when fed from a 20 V a.c. supply.
                                                    [(a) 8.99 V; (b) 17.98 V]

2   A smoothed rectified voltage has a mean value of 120 V and 5% ripple expressed
    in terms of $V_{d.c.}$. What are the minimum and maximum values of the output
    voltage?   [126 V; 114 V]

3   Estimate the size of a smoothing capacitor to give a mean value of d.c. voltage of
    50 V when the peak supply voltage is 52 V using a full-wave rectifier connected to
    (a) 50 Hz and (b) 400 Hz mains. The load resistance is 500 Ω.
                                                    [(a) 250 μF; (b) 31.25 μF]

4   Determine the value of ripple expressed as a percentage of $V_{d.c.}$ when a 100 μF
    capacitor is used for smoothing the output from a full-wave rectifier connected
    to a 400 Hz supply, when $V_{d.c.}$ is 12 V and the load current is 10 mA.   [0.52%]

5   Under what conditions is a zener diode connected in a stabilising circuit most
    likely to fail due to overheating? How may the heat produced be dissipated?

6   A constant voltage of 12 V is to be maintained across a load using a zener diode
    and a stabilising resistor. Determine (a) the required input voltage for a load
    current of 0.1 A when using a 5 Ω stabilising resistor and (b) the maximum
    current which can be delivered to the load at 12 V, if the input is at 18 V and the
    stabilising resistor has a value of 24 Ω. For both cases determine the maximum
    power dissipation in the zener diode.
                                          [(a) 12.5 V, 1.2 W; (b) 0.25 A, 3 W]

7   Estimate the size of a suitable smoothing capacitor for the following duty when a
    full-wave rectifier is used.

    $V_{d.c.}$ = 400 V. Ripple = 3% of $V_{d.c.}$. Load resistance = 5000 Ω.
    Frequency = 50 Hz.   [33.3 μF]

8   Estimate the size of a smoothing capacitor to give a mean value of d.c. voltage of
    240 V. (a) with a load current of 5 mA and (b) with a load current of 100 mA.
    The peak supply voltage is 250 V using a half-wave rectifier connected to a 50 Hz
    supply.   [(a) 5 μF; (b) 100 μF]

9   A 22 V supply is to be used to supply a load at a constant voltage of 18 V. An
    18 V zener diode and a 10 Ω stabilising resistor are used. Calculate the range of
    current over which the stabilisation is effective.   [Zero to 0.4 A]

10 A 37 V zener diode is to be used to stabilise the voltage across a load, the
    minimum value of which is 20 Ω. A 5 Ω stabilising resistor is to be used. What
    value of output voltage is required from the rectifier?
          [I_L = 1.85 A; Volt drop 9.25 V; Rectifier output voltage = 46.25 V]

11 Basic transistor amplifiers

A SUMMARY OF FORMULAE AND DEFINITIONS ASSOCIATED WITH BASIC TRANSISTOR AMPLIFIERS

1 **The Junction Field Effect Transistor (JFET)** The JFET transistor is made up from p- and n-type semiconducting materials in the form of a sandwich, either a layer of n-type material between two layers of p-type material (n-channel) or a layer of p-type material between two layers of n-type material (p-channel).

In both types, current flows through the channel from the source to the drain. The two outer layers are connected electrically and form a gate through which current must flow. *Figs 1(a)* and *(b)* shows the arrangement of channels in n- and p-channel devices together with circuit symbols and typical terminal configurations.

2 **Operation** When a p-n junction is forward biased, electrons pass easily from n to p material. (Conventional current flow is from p to n). When reverse biased, a

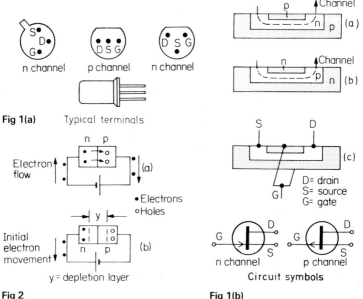

Fig 1(a) Typical terminals

Fig 2

Fig 1(b)

barrier or depletion layer is formed between the *n* and *p* materials and the junction becomes a good insulator (see *Fig 2*).

In *Fig 3* both layers of *p*-type material are connected to the negative terminal of the gate supply. The *n*-type material of the channel is connected to the positive terminal of both supplies. The *p-n* junctions formed on both sides of the device are therefore reverse biased so that depletion layers are formed as shown in *Fig 3(c)*. The area of *n*-type material in the channel through which current can flow is restricted. The thickness of the barrier layers is a function of the gate/source voltage V_{GS}. The greater is V_{GS} the thicker is the depletion layer. Reducing the

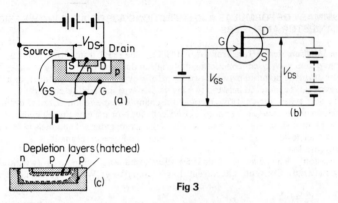

Fig 3

area of the channel increases its resistance. The relationship between the drain current flowing through the channel, I_D, and the voltage V_{GS} whilst maintaining V_{DS} constant is shown for a typical device in *Fig 4*.

Using the circuit shown in *Fig 3(a)* with two voltmeters and an ammeter, a set

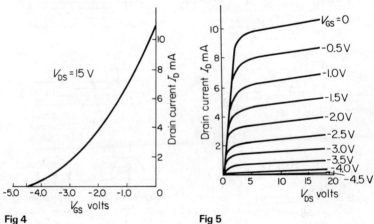

Fig 4

Fig 5

146

of readings may be obtained from which the characteristics shown in *Fig 5* have been plotted. For V_{GS} at zero, V_{DS} is varied in steps over a range from zero to the maximum value specified for the particular device by the manufacturer. At each step the drain current I_D is noted. Further readings of V_{DS} and I_D are taken for values of V_{GS} up to that which results in zero drain current, i.e. what is known as the pinch-off value. *Figs 4* and *5* are typical in shape but are not for any particular device.

3 **The bipolar junction transistor (BJT)** *Fig 6* shows a schematic diagram of a bipolar junction transistor in common-base configuration together with its circuit symbol; it is made up of two diodes. One diode is the junction between n_1 and p and the other the junction between p and n_2. The junction between n_1 and p is forward biased by battery B_1 so that electrons can flow readily from n_1 to p.

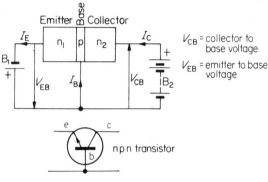

Fig 6   Circuit symbol

The n_1 layer is termed the emitter. The input resistance is very low so that a very small voltage here can cause a large emitter current to flow. The junction diode formed between n_2 and p is reverse biased so that with battery B_1 disconnected, this junction is non-conducting.

With battery B_1 connected, electrons flow from n_1 to p and would complete the circuit back to the battery through the base were it not made very difficult for this to happen. The base layer is made extremely thin and so has a high resistance. Also any electrons in the base layer are extremely close to the strong positive potential of battery B_2 in the n_2 layer of the transistor. Most of the electrons are attracted to this layer and complete the circuit back to battery B_1 through battery B_2.

Although it is usual to explain the action of the transistor in terms of electron flow, circuit symbols show the directions of conventional currents which are in the opposite direction. The positive terminal of battery B_2 is at the top so that the collector current I_C flows into the device and emitter current I_E away from the device. The base current is a very small proportion of the emitter current, in a silicon transistor being typically $0.005I_E$.

4 **Circuit configurations**   Referring to the bipolar junction transistor, if an input signal is applied between emitter and base terminals and the output taken from collector and base terminals so that the base connection is common to both input and output circuits, the transistor is said to be in common (or grounded) base

configuration. The equivalent configuration for the JFET is shown in *Fig 7(b)*. The gate connection is common to both input and output circuits.

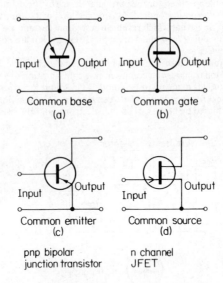

Common base
(a)

Common gate
(b)

Common emitter
(c)

Common source
(d)

pnp bipolar junction transistor

n channel JFET

Fig 7

Both these circuits have limited application however and *Figs 7(c)* and *(d)* show the more usually adopted configurations in which the emitter/source is the common terminal. In this configuration, using the bipolar junction transistor, varying a small base current causes the collector current to vary over a much wider range. This current flowing in a resistance of several thousand ohms produces a large voltage variation. There is thus both current and voltage gain. With the JFET, a small gate voltage controls the drain current which, in driving through a large resistance gives voltage amplification.

5 **Simple single-stage transistor amplifier circuits** *Fig 8* shows a single *n-p-n* transistor connected in the common emitter configuration. The current in the base of a bipolar junction transistor must always flow in the same direction. In the case of the *n-p-n* transistor this direction is towards the base region. Should

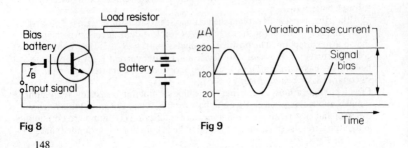

Fig 8

Fig 9

the base current become zero or attempt to reverse the transistor shuts off and there is no collector or emitter current. When an alternating signal is to be amplified it is necessary to provide a steady bias current in the base circuit, in the correct direction, of such a size that when the signal polarity reverses the base current continues to flow in the correct direction.

In *Fig 8* consider, for example, that the input signal e.m.f. has a magnitude sufficient to drive a sinusoidal current with a peak value of $100 \mu A$. A bias voltage must be introduced of sufficient magnitude to drive a steady current in excess of $100 \mu A$ towards the base of the transistor. In *Fig 9* the bias current is shown with a value of $120 \mu A$. When the signal voltage drives towards the base the base current will rise to $120 + 100 = 220 \mu A$ and when the signal voltage reverses the base current will fall to $120 - 100 = 20 \mu A$.

With no signal applied, the bias current in the base causes a much larger current to flow in the collector and this current flowing in the load resistor creates a steady potential difference across it. With the signal applied, the base current varies between $220 \mu A$ and $20 \mu A$ causing changes of considerably greater magnitude in the collector current with corresponding changes in voltage across the load resistor. Thus an alternating input signal superimposed on a bias gives rise to an alternating output current and load voltage both superimposed on steady values. With both current and voltage gain a considerable power gain is achieved.

Fig 10 shows a similar circuit employing an *n*-channel JFET. In this case since the voltage on the gate must always be negative with respect to the source, it is necessary to provide a negative voltage bias slightly greater in magnitude than the peak value of the signal voltage. The addition of an alternating voltage signal to the steady bias causes the drain current to alternate about its mean value and to develop a large voltage across its load resistor as with the bipolar junction transistor. We

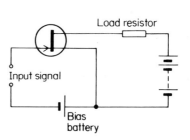

Fig 10

cannot consider power gain since there is virtually no current in the input.

6 **A.C. input resistance** This is the resistance offered to an alternating current by the input side of a device with specified conditions on the output side. For a bipolar junction transistor the input resistance is different for different levels of input current. In the case of the JFET in common source configuration, the input resistance is in the region of 1 MΩ so that the gate current is virtually zero as already mentioned.

7 **Load line for the bipolar junction transistor** *Fig 5* illustrated the characteristics of the JFET in common source configuration. *Fig 11(a)* shows the characteristics for a typical bipolar junction transistor and it can be seen that these are very similar in form to those for the JFET. Collector current is plotted against collector/emitter voltage V_{CE} for a range of base currents.

A graphical method to determine the output conditions from the input conditions involves the use of the 'load line' which is drawn on these characteristics. The load line intersects the characteristics enabling the collector current and the collector/emitter voltage to be obtained for any level of base current. This enables current and voltage gains to be determined.

Consider the simple amplifier stage shown in *Fig 11*. When $I_C = 0$ the voltage drop across the 1000 Ω load resistor = 0. Therefore under these conditions $V_{CE} = 10$ V (the full supply voltage.)
When $I_C = 10$ mA, the voltage drop across the load resistor = $10 \times 10^{-3} \times 1000 = 10$ V.
$V_{CE} = 10 - 10 = 0$ volts.
For $I_C = 5$ mA, the volt drop across the load resistor = 5 V
Therefore $V_{CE} = 10 - 5 = 5$ V, etc.

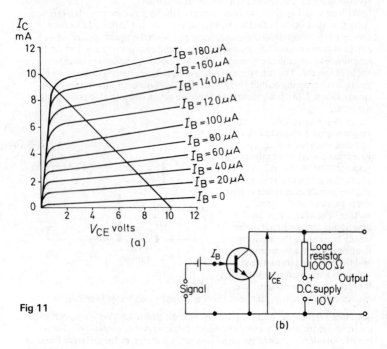

Fig 11

The load line is drawn on the characteristics in *Fig 11(a)*. It passes through the points:

$V_{CE} = 10$ V when $I_C = 0$
$V_{CE} = 5$ V when $I_C = 5$ mA
$V_{CE} = 0$ V when $I_C = 10$ mA

In practice it is necessary only to fix the two end points where V_{CE} is equal to the full supply voltage and zero respectively.
For a full calculation involving the use of the load line see *Problems 2 and 3*.

150

8   **Load line for the JFET**   The characteristics of the JFET and the bipolar
    junction transistor are similar in form and the load line for the JFET is
    constructed in exactly the same manner as in para. 7 above (see *Problem 4*).

9   **Incorrect bias conditions**   In para. 5 we considered a signal with peak value
    $100 \, \mu A$ and saw that a bias current of $120 \, \mu A$ would be suitable, see *Fig 9*. If the
    bias current had been only $80 \, \mu A$ the input to the base of the transistor would
    have had a maximum value of $180 \, \mu A$. During the negative half cycle of the
    signal, as soon as it reached a value of $-80 \, \mu A$ the base current would be zero
    and it would remain so until the signal became less than $-80 \, \mu A$ once again since
    the base current cannot reverse (see *Fig 12*).

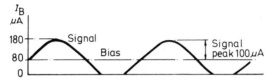

Fig 12

The waveform of I_C and hence of the voltage across the load resistor will be
similarly distorted and it this type of distortion which gives small radio sets the
characteristic 'out-of-a-box' sound.

10 **High and low frequency effects**   The voltages applied to transistors create
    barrier layers at reverse biased junctions (see para. 2). Each of these layers is a
    good insulator and a capacitor is formed with the depletion layer as dielectric
    and the adjacent conducting layers as plates. The width of the depletion layer
    and hence the value of capacitance depends on the applied voltage as seen
    particularly in the case of the JFET. The effect of the capacitance is to allow the
    a.c. components of current to take paths other than those intended, so shunting
    part of the input signal and output current.

    As the frequency increases the value of capacitive reactance falls. At a
    particular frequency dependent on the design of the circuit and its component
    parts, a frequency is reached at which no amplification takes place. Where
    capacitors are used to couple stages of an amplifier together there will be a low-
    frequency cut off since at low frequencies the capacitive reactance of these
    capacitors will be large.

B   WORKED PROBLEMS ON BASIC TRANSISTOR AMPLIFIERS

Problem 1   (a) Explain what is meant by 'A.C. input resistance' with particular
reference to the *n-p-n* bipolar junction transistor as shown in *Fig 13*. Why is the
value of resistance different at different current levels. (b) The transistor in *Fig
13* yielded the following test results:
(i)   With initial conditions set so that $I_B = 10 \, \mu A$, increasing V_{BE} by $20 \, mV$
       caused I_B to rise to $15 \, \mu A$.
(ii)   With initial conditions set so that $I_B = 50 \, \mu A$, increasing V_{BE} by $10 \, mV$
       caused I_B to rise to $60 \, \mu A$.
For each condition determine the value of input resistance.

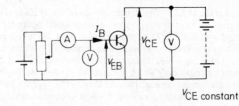

Fig 13

V_{CE} constant

(a) The a.c. input resistance of a device is the resistance offered to an alternating current by the input side of the device with specified conditions on the output side. In this case there is no load resistor and we are maintaining the voltage V_{CE} at a value of 10 V. The base current I_B is set to a value suitable as bias for a particular input signal. It is increased and decreased from the bias value over a range, corresponding to the peak to peak value of the signal to be handled. This is achieved by adjusting the emitter/base voltage V_{EB}, using in this case, the potentiometer on the left of the diagram.

$$\text{The a.c. resistance} = \frac{\text{Total change in } V_{EB}}{\text{Corresponding change in } I_B}$$

For a pure resistor the value is the same whatever range is used. The transistor, in common with the junction diode, has a non-linear relationship between current and voltage so that a.c. resistance has different values for different ranges and for different bias conditions. It also changes slightly as V_{CE} is changed.

It can be seen from *Fig 14* that small changes in V_{BE} near the origin of the graph cause less change in I_B than a corresponding change at high values of I_B. For the pure resistor, a change in V of (say) 20 mV at any point on the graph causes the same change in current. In common base configuration, V_{CB} is maintained constant whilst varying V_{EB} and noting the corresponding changes in I_E.

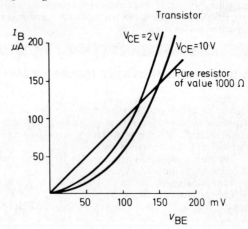

Fig 14

(b) (i)

$$R = \frac{\Delta V_{BE}}{\Delta I_B} = \frac{20\,\text{mV}}{(15-10)\,\mu\text{A}} = \frac{20 \times 10^{-3}}{5 \times 10^{-6}} = 4000\,\Omega$$

(ii)

$$R = \frac{10\,\text{mV}}{10\,\mu\text{A}} = 1000\,\Omega$$

Problem 2   Plot a family of I_C/V_{CE} curves for a common emitter amplifier using the following data.

V_{CE} volts	1.0	2.0	4.0	8.0	12.0	
I_C mA	2.4	2.5	2.75	3.1	3.4	$(I_B = 50\,\mu\text{A})$
	5.0	5.2	5.4	5.8	6.1	$(I_B = 100\,\mu\text{A})$
	7.6	7.75	8.1	8.5	8.8	$(I_B = 150\,\mu\text{A})$
	9.7	10.2	10.5	11.0	11.4	$(I_B = 200\,\mu\text{A})$
	11.6	12.2	12.6	13.4	14.0	$(I_B = 250\,\mu\text{A})$

The input resistance = 1000 Ω at the centre of the characteristics.

(a)   For a common emitter amplifier stage as shown in *Fig 8* with a load resistor of 800 Ω and a d.c. supply at 12 V, draw a load line on the characteristics and decide on a suitable operating bias for a sinusoidal input signal of peak value 100 μA.

(b)   Using the information given and the load line, determine:
 (i)   the r.m.s. value of the signal current;
 (ii)   the r.m.s. value of the potential developed across the load;
 (iii)   the r.m.s. value of the collector current;
 (iv)   the r.m.s. value of the signal voltage;
 (v)   the current gain;
 (vi)   the voltage gain; and
 (vii)   the power gain.

(a)   Having plotted the characteristics as shown in *Fig 15* the load line is added by considering two points.
 Point 1   When $I_C = 0$ the volt drop across the 800 Ω load resistor is zero. Therefore, under these conditions $V_{CE} = 12$ V, the full battery voltage.
 Point 2   When $I_C = 12/800 = 0.015$ A the voltage dropped across the load resistor = $0.015 \times 800 = 12$ V. Therefore $V_{CE} = 0$. The load line is drawn across the characteristics through the points:

$V_{CE} = 12\ \text{V}\quad I_C = 0$
$V_{CE} = \ \ 0\text{V}\quad I_C = 0.015\ \text{A}.$

Since the signal has a peak value of 100 μA a bias current of at least this value is required to prevent the transistor shutting off during part of the cycle. The range of characteristics given covers base currents from 250 μA to 50 μA so that a suitable bias current is $I_B = 150$ μA. Where the load line crosses this characteristic, point Q is marked. Q is for quiescent, the starting point. At this point $V_{CE} = 5.4$ V and $I_C = 8.2$ mA. These are the steady values described in para. 5.

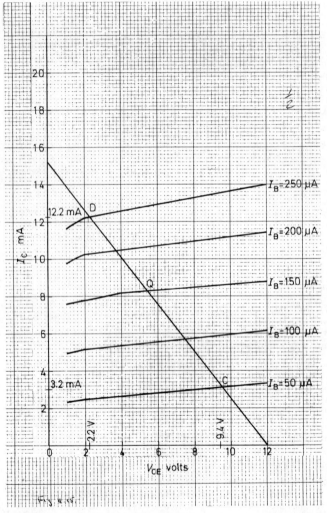

Fig 15

As the signal rises to its maximum possible positive value the base current will rise to $150 + 100 = 250\,\mu A$.

As the signal drives negative, at its maximum value of $100\,\mu A$, the base current will be $150 - 100 = 50\,\mu A$.

When $I_B = 50\,\mu A$, $I_C = 3.2$ mA and $V_{CE} = 9.4$ V (point C on the characteristics)

When $I_B = 250\,\mu A$, $I_C = 12.2$ mA and $V_{CE} = 2.2$ V (point D on the characteristics)

Note that we are only concerned with changes in voltage and current which occur as a result of the signal input (see *Problem 4*).

(b) (i) *r.m.s. value of the signal current* The peak value of the signal $= 100\,\mu A$. A sine wave has an r.m.s. value of

$$\frac{\text{peak value}}{\sqrt{2}} \quad = \frac{100}{\sqrt{2}} = 70.71\,\mu A$$

(ii) *r.m.s. value of load potential*

When $I_B = 50\,\mu A$, $V_{CE} = 9.4$ V, hence the voltage drop across the load resistor

$= 12 - 9.4 = 2.6$ V

When $I_B = 250\,\mu A$, $V_{CE} = 2.2$ V, hence voltage drop across the load resistor

$= 12 - 2.2 = 9.8$ V

The voltage change across the load is therefore $9.8 - 2.6 = 7.2$ V peak to peak, i.e. from maximum positive to maximum negative.

   Once this method is understood, this result is best achieved by simply considering the change in V_{CE}. From part (a), this is $9.4 - 2.2 = 7.2$ V.

From voltage zero to positive peak $= \dfrac{7.2}{2} = 3.6$ V

r.m.s. value $= \qquad \dfrac{3.6}{\sqrt{2}} = \mathbf{2.545\ V}$

(iii) *r.m.s. value of collector current*

The collector current changes from 12.2 mA (point D) to 3.2 mA (point C)

Peak to peak change $= 12.2 - 3.2 = 9$ mA

r.m.s. value $= \dfrac{9}{2\sqrt{2}} = \mathbf{3.18\ mA}$

(iv) *r.m.s. value of signal voltage*

r.m.s. value of signal voltage $=$ r.m.s. value of signal current $\times$ input resistance

$= 70.71 \times 10^{-6} \times 1000 = 0.0707$, i.e. **70.7 mV**

(v) *Current gain*

Current gain $= \dfrac{\text{load current}}{\text{signal current}} = \dfrac{3.18 \times 10^{-3}}{70.71 \times 10^{-6}} = \mathbf{44.97}$

(vi) *Voltage gain*

Voltage gain $= \dfrac{\text{load voltage}}{\text{signal voltage}} = \dfrac{2.545}{0.0707} = \mathbf{36}$

(vii) *Power gain*

Power gain = current gain × voltage gain = 44.97 × 36 = **1619**

or $\dfrac{V \times I \text{ (load)}}{V \times I \text{ (signal)}} = \dfrac{2.545 \times 3.18 \times 10^{-3}}{0.0707 \times 70.71 \times 10^{-6}} = \mathbf{1619}$

Problem 3 Draw the load line for the JFET in the circuit shown in *Fig 16(a)* on the characteristics shown in *Fig 16(b)*. Use the load line to determine the value of voltage gain and load power for an input signal of 0.4 V peak.

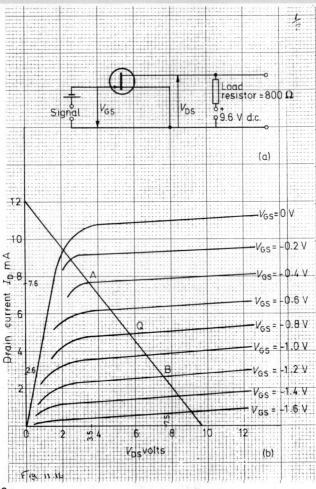

Fig 16

Using the principles introduced in *Problem 2:*

When $I_D = 0$, $V_{DS} = 9.6$ V (the full supply voltage)

When $I_D = \dfrac{9.6}{800} = 0.012$ A, $V_{DS} = 0$

The load line is drawn through these two points.

A Q-point is chosen on the line in such a position that V_{GS} remains negative at all times and at a point where the greatest linearity of response to changes in V_{GS} is to be found. A suitable point for Q is where the load line crosses the $V_{GS} = -0.8$ V characteristic.

As the signal swings ± 0.4 V, the limits of V_{GS} are $-0.8 + 0.4 = -0.4$ V and $-0.8 - 0.4 = -1.2$ V

At $V_{GS} = -0.4$ V, $V_{DS} = 3.5$ V, $I_D = 7.6$ mA (point A on the characteristics)

At $V_{GS} = -1.2$ V, $V_{DS} = 7.5$ V, $I_D = 2.6$ mA (point B on the characteristics)

The r.m.s. value of the signal voltage $= \dfrac{0.4}{\sqrt{2}} = 0.283$ V

The r.m.s. value of the output voltage $= \dfrac{7.5 - 3.5}{2\sqrt{2}} = 1.41$ V

The r.m.s. value of the drain current $= \dfrac{7.6 - 2.6}{2\sqrt{2}} = 1.77$ mA

Voltage gain $= \dfrac{\text{load voltage}}{\text{signal voltage}} = \dfrac{1.41}{0.283} = 5$

Load power $= V_{load} \times I_{load} = 1.41 \times 1.77 \times 10^{-3} = 2.5$ mW

The power input is virtually zero since the input resistance is extremely large so that power gain is not relevant.

Problem 4 Draw a simple common emitter amplifier circuit which employs capacitors to isolate the signal source and the load from the direct battery voltage. Briefly explain the need for and the action of such capacitors.

In the circuit shown in *Fig 8* the bias current provided by the bias battery must flow through the signal source since they are are connected in series. This may be avoided by using a decoupling capacitor. In *Fig 17* the required value of bias current is obtained by the adjustment of V_{BB} and R_B. The alternating voltage signal causes a displacement of charge on the capacitor C_1 with a corresponding current flow in the emitter/base circuit and this is superimposed on the bias current.

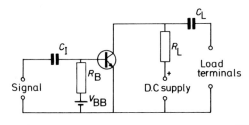

Fig 17

In audio equipment, only the changes in voltage and current output are useful since these cause a movement of a loudspeaker cone. The steady current in the output circuit, of whatever size gives no audible output except perhaps a click as the circuit is energised and the loudspeaker cone moves into a position determined by the steady current. Adding a further capacitor C_L allows only alternating current to reach the output terminals. The changes in voltage across the load resistor cause the capacitor to charge and discharge and this charge displacement is passed through the load or where several stages of amplification are used, into the next stage input. At the same time the load circuit is isolated from the main d.c. supply.

C FURTHER PROBLEMS ON BASIC TRANSISTOR AMPLIFIERS

(a) SHORT ANSWER PROBLEMS

1 Draw the circuit symbol for (a) an n-p-n bipolar junction transistor and (b) an n-channel JFET.

2 Draw a simple diagram showing the position of the n and p materials within a p-channel JFET.

3 What is a barrier or depletion layer? Where are they found?

4 With reference to a JFET, what is meant by 'pinch-off' voltage?

5 Draw a circuit diagram showing an n-p-n bipolar junction transistor with batteries connected to give correct biasing in the common emitter configuration.

6 Draw a circuit diagram showing an n-p-n bipolar junction transistor with batteries connected to give correct biasing in the common base configuration.

7 Repeat questions 5 and 6 above for p-n-p transistors.

8 For a particular bipolar junction transistor $I_C/I_E = 0.99$. What is the corresponding value of I_C/I_B? (Hint: $I_B + I_C = I_E$).

9 Why is it that in a bipolar junction transistor connected in common-base configuration almost all the emitter current crosses a reverse biased junction to appear at the collector?

10 Why do most audio-frequency amplifiers employing BJTs or JFETs use them in the common emitter or common source configurations respectively?

11 Why is 'power gain' not a meaningful quantity when referring to JFETs?

12 What is the effect of insufficient bias in a common-emitter amplifier stage?

13 When testing a bipolar junction transistor in common emitter configuration, V_{CE} was held constant at 12 V whilst V_{EB} was varied between 0.1 and 0.15 V. The corresponding change in I_B was 62.5 μA. What is the input resistance of the transistor under these conditions?

14 A single-stage amplifier has a power gain of 2000. Its output is fed to the input of a further stage which has a power gain of 1500. What ideally will be the power gain of the two stages combined?

15 A BJT in common emitter configuration is used as an amplifier with a 1500 Ω load resistor. The d.c. supply voltage = 10 V. What will be the value of I_C when $V_{CE} = 0$?

1 In normal operation the junctions of an *n-p-n* bipolar junction transistor are:
   (i)   both reverse biased;   (ii) both forward biased;
   (iii) base/emitter forward and   (iv) base/emitter reverse and
         base/collector reverse biased;   base/collector forward biased.

2 *p-n-p* bipolar junction transistor has a forward current gain in common base
   configuration of 0.985 ($= I_C/I_E$). Given that the base current = 0.015 mA, the
   value of the collector current will be:
   (i) 1 mA; (ii) 0.985 mA; (iii) 1.015 mA.

3 The base current in a bipolar junction transistor connected in common emitter
   configuration is largely dependent on:
   (i)   the value of V_{CE};   (iii) the value of the load resistor;
   (ii) the value of V_{BE};   (iv) the value of the input de-coupling
                                                    capacitor.

4 The input signal to an *n*-channel JFET has an r.m.s. value of 0.1 V. A suitable
   value of bias on the gate would be:
   (i) + 0.1 V; (ii) + 0.2 V; (iii) –0.1 V; (iv) –0.15 V.

5 The resistance between the gate and channel in a JFET is typically:
   (i) between 500 and 750 Ω; (ii) several hundred kΩ or even 1 MΩ; (iii) very low,
   below 100 Ω.

6 A load line is to be drawn on a set of JFET characteristics showing I_D against
   V_{DS}. The supply voltage = 10 V and the load resistor = 1000 Ω. Three points on
   the load line are to be located:
   (a) When $V_{DS} = $ 0; $I_D = $ x mA,
   (b) When $V_{DS} = $ 10 V; $I_D = $ y mA.
   (c) When $V_{DS} = $ 5 V; $I_D = $ z mA.
   Select correct answers for conditions (a), (b) and (c) from:
   (i) 10 mA; (ii) 15 mA; (iii) zero; (iv) 5 mA; (v) 100 mA; (vi) 1 mA.

7 A de-coupling capacitor is used in the output side of a transistor amplifier to:
   (i)   improve its high frequency   (iii) block the direct voltage of the
         response;   supply from the load;
   (ii) improve its low frequency   (iv) isolate the signal from the load.
         response;

8 During the operation of a BJT amplifier in common emitter configuration, in
   response to signal changes the collector current alternates between 2.4 mA and
   12.6 mA. The load resistance is 900 Ω. Assuming sinusoidal variation, the power
   developed in the load will be:
   (i) 0.012 W; (ii) 0.023 W; (iii) 0.047 W; (iv) 0.036 W.

9 At (a) very low frequencies and (b) very high frequencies the output from a
   transistor amplifier falls off because:
   (i)   the inductive reactances of the circuit components change;
   (ii) the reactances of the coupling capacitors become significant;
   (iii) the operating point (Q) moves so that the output voltage waveform
         becomes 'clipped';
   (iv) the capacitive reactances of the barrier layers become significant;
   (v)   electrons cannot travel faster than the speed of light.
   Select *one* reason from the list for (a) and *one* for (b).

10 The current gain of an *n-p-n* bipolar junction transistor amplifier in common emitter configuration is 50 and the voltage gain is 70. The power gain is:
(i) 120; (ii) 3500; (iii) 1.4; (iv) 0.714; (v) 2500; (vi) 4900.

11 The *n-p-n* transistor in question 10 is reconnected in common base configuration. The current gain would:
(i)   increase;   (iii) decrease considerably;
(ii)   decrease slightly;   (iv)   remain unchanged.

(c) CONVENTIONAL PROBLEMS

1 A bipolar junction transistor with the characteristics shown in *Fig 18* is used as an amplifier in the common emitter configuration.
The d.c. supply voltage = 10 V
The load resistance = 1000 Ω
The input resistance at the centre of the characteristics = 600 Ω
The signal to be amplified is of sinusoidal form has a peak value of 60 μA
Draw a suitable load line on the characteristics and choose an operating point
Deduce: (i) the current gain; (ii) the voltage gain; and (iii) the power gain; for the amplifier stage.   [(i) 45; (ii) 76; (iii) 3438]

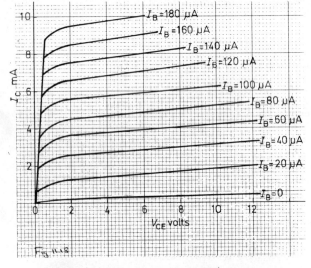

Fig 18

2 Using the characteristic *Fig 18* deduce the power gain of a common emitter stage employing this transistor when the d.c. supply voltage is at 9.6 V, the load resistance is 800 Ω and the sinusoidal input signal has a peak value of 40 μA.
[Current gain 46; voltage gain 60; power gain 2794]

3 A bipolar junction transistor operating in the common emitter configuration carries a steady collector current of 5 mA. The quantity I_C/I_B is 150. Calculate the values of (a) the emitter current and (b) the base current.
[(a) 5.033 mA; (b) 33.3 μA]

4 Explain with the aid of a numerical example why it is necessary to provide a bias voltage or current when using a transistor to amplify alternating signals.

5 Explain how a bipolar junction transistor may be used as an on/off switch.

6 When testing a simple amplifier stage employing a bipolar junction transistor in common emitter configuration the following results were obtained:
Input resistance = 850 Ω.
Bias current = 25 μA
Peak base current = 40 μA. Minimum base current = 10 μA
Minimum value of $V_{CE} = 6.8$ V. Maximum value of $V_{CE} = 8$ V
Minimum value of $I_C = 1.3$ mA. Maximum value of $I_C = 4$ mA
Determine (a) the current gain, (b) the voltage gain and (c) the power gain of the stage.   [(a) 90; (b) 47; (c) 4235]

7 When testing a bipolar junction transistor in common emitter configuration, with V_{CE} held constant, a change in V_{BE} from 0.06 V to 0.17 V caused the base current to change from 100 μA to 220 μA. What is the value of the a.c. input resistance under these conditions? Why might a different value of resistance be obtained for different changes in V_{BE}?   [917 Ω]

8 What is the effect on the output current and voltage waveforms from a transistor amplifier of (a) insufficient bias and (b) too large an input signal? Illustrate your answers with suitable sketches.

9 The data in the table refers to a bipolar junction transistor in common emitter configuration.

Collector current, I_C mA

Collector/emitter voltage, V_{CE} volts	For $I_B = 20$ μA	For $I_B = 70$ μA	For $I_B = 120$ μA
1	0.8	3.3	5.8
3	1.2	3.8	6.4
5	1.6	4.4	7.1
7	2	4.9	7.7
9	2.4	5.4	8.35

Draw a load line on these characteristics for a d.c. supply voltage of 8 V and a load resistance of 800 Ω. The input resistance at the centre of the characteristics = 1000 Ω.
Determine for a sinusoidal signal with 50 μA peak value:

(a)	the r.m.s. value of the signal current;	(a) 35.35 μA
(b)	the r.m.s. value of the load current;	(b) 1.59 mA
(c)	the r.m.s. value of the load voltage;	(c) 1.27 V
(d)	the current gain;	(d) 45
(e)	the voltage gain, and	(e) 36
(f)	the power gain.	(f) 1620

12 High-power electronics (the S.C.R.)

A SUMMARY OF FORMULAE AND DEFINITIONS ASSOCIATED WITH HIGH POWER ELECTRONICS

1 **The silicon controlled rectifier** The silicon controlled rectifier or thyristor is a four layer *p-n-p-n* semiconductor device as shown in *Fig 1*. Its action may be explained in terms of the two transistor model (see *Problem 1*).

This rectifier is used to control large currents using a small controlling (gate) current. A small voltage at the gate of positive polarity with respect to the cathode drives a gate current which causes the device to become conducting between anode and cathode if the anode voltage is positive at that instant. Once the gate current has been supplied and the through current is flowing, no variation in the gate current or its polarity will cause the device to shut off. This can only be achieved by reducing the applied voltage V_A to zero, or driving it negative, for a short period.

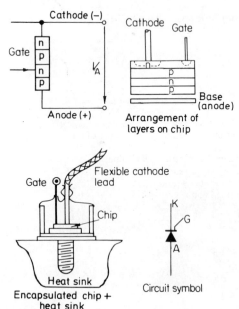

Fig 1(a)

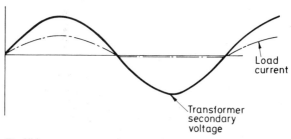

Load
current

Transformer
secondary
voltage

Fig 1(b)

2 **Thyristor characteristics** The thyristor will break down and become conducting in either direction if sufficient voltage is applied. *Fig 2* shows the forward and reverse characteristics with no gate current. Steadily increasing the anode voltage in the forward direction causes little current to flow until the forward breakover voltage is reached when the anode current suddenly increases and the voltage drop across the device falls to a very low value.

The current flowing immediately after breakdown is called the holding current which is a value of anode current below which the thyristor may turn off. This condition is determined by the resistance of the external circuit. With large resistance the holding current may not be reached when the forward voltage drop across the device remains large. With small external resistance this value of current is exceeded and the forward voltage drop across the device falls to about 1 volt. For each ampere flowing there is therefore 1 watt of power loss. $(1 \text{ V} \times 1 \text{ A} = 1 \text{ W})$

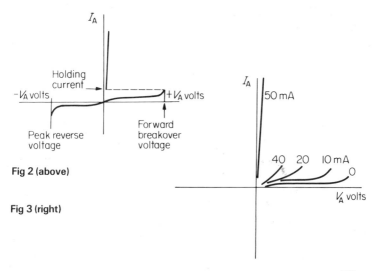

Fig 2 (above)

Fig 3 (right)

For all but the very smallest ratings a heat sink must be provided to dissipate the heat produced (see *Fig 12,* Chap 4). If the anode voltage polarity is reversed the thyristor becomes conducting when the peak reverse or peak inverse voltage is reached. *Fig 3* shows the effect on the forward characteristic of increasing the gate current. If a gate current in excess of 50 mA is used for this particular device, the forward voltage drop is extremely small and the device becomes conducting almost immediately. Smaller gate currents cause uncertain operation and are to be avoided.

The desired shape of a current pulse to trigger a thyristor is one which has a rapid rate of rise to the required value to cause conduction.

3 **Simple control circuits for single-phase operation**   A method which produces steep-fronted pulses and so triggers the thyristor at a precise instant is shown in *Fig 4*. A peaking transformer is used which has a ferrite core which saturates suddenly at a fairly low level of flux density.

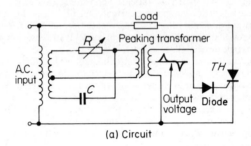

(a) Circuit

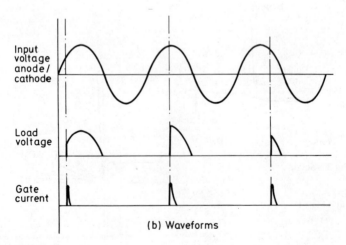

(b) Waveforms

Fig 4

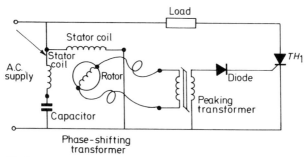

Fig 5

Considering a sinusoidal input voltage to the transformer: as the magnetising current increases and the core flux increases, a voltage is induced in the secondary. The core quickly saturates and for much of the half cycle there is no further change in core flux. Whilst the flux is constant there is no voltage induced in the secondary. Voltage will be induced in the secondary at the end of the positive half cycle and beginning of the negative half cycle as the flux is reduced and then reversed followed by a further period of zero voltage. A spiky voltage waveform is produced as shown in *Fig 4*.

The phase of the input voltage to the peaking transformer is varied through very nearly 180° by varying R between zero and a very large value thus a triggering pulse may be provided at any instant during the positive going half cycle. *Fig 5* shows a phase-shifting transformer providing the required phase shift at the primary of the peaking transformer. The phase of the output voltage is changed through 360° by turning the rotor with respect to two stator coils which carry currents mutually displaced by 90°.

4 **Full wave operation (a.c. in load)**   Load current is obtained during both positive and negative half cycles of the supply voltage by using two thyristors. In *Fig 6(a)* positive going pulse causes current to flow towards the gate of TH_1 which becomes conducting and current flows in the load from the supply, through TH_1 and D_2. At the end of the positive half cycle conduction ceases. A pulse in the opposite direction will cause current to flow towards the gate of TH_2 which becomes conducting and current flows in the load through TH_2 and D_1 during the negative half cycle.

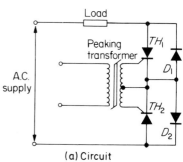

Fig 6(a) circuit. The waveforms are shown in Fig 6(b)

(a) Circuit

165

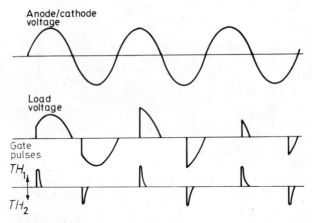

Fig 6(b) waveforms

5 **The cathode ray oscilloscope (CRO)**   The waveforms (*Figs 4* and *6*) may be viewed using a CRO, connecting the input leads to the relevant terminals in the circuit. When doing this, however, care must be taken to ensure that parts of the circuit are not inadvertently earthed. If one of the CRO terminals is earthed, connecting it across the load terminals for example, to view the load voltage waveform, will cause either the main input or the anode of the thyristor to become earthed. The danger may be avoided by using an earth-free oscilloscope or an isolating transformer either to feed the main circuit or the oscilloscope.

6 **Full-wave controlled rectification**   Where the load is to be provided with a controlled level of d.c. the circuit shown in *Fig 6* is modified to form the bridge circuit shown in *Fig 7* which gives full wave rectification. The load voltage waveshapes are then as in *Fig 4* with the addition of a conducting period during each negative half cycle.

7 **The chopper**   *Fig 8* shows a simple circuit of a chopper which enables the power being supplied to a load from a d.c. supply to be varied without the use of series resistors. Consider both thyristors to be off. TH_1 receives a trigger pulse and current flows in the load, TH_1 and one half of the centre-tapped inductor. The sudden increase in current gives rise to induced voltages in both halves of the inductor since all of the turns are linked with the changing flux. The direction of

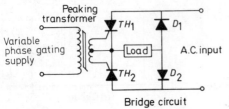

Bridge circuit   **Fig 7**

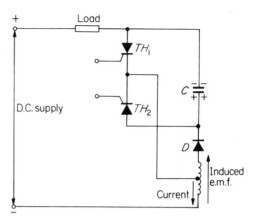

Fig 8

the e.m.f. together with the resulting charge on the capacitor *C* are shown in *Fig 8*. If now TH_2 is triggered, the cathode of TH_1 is connected directly to the positively charged plate of the capacitor and is thereby switched off. Load current ceases and may be re-established by triggering TH_1 again. The triggering pulses are generated by an oscillator and the power in the load is controlled by varying the 'on' time.

8 **The invertor**   The invertor is used to produce alternating voltages and currents using a direct source of power. The mode of operation is similar to that of the chopper. In *Fig 9*, starting with both thyristors off; TH_1 is triggered and current flows from the supply through half of the transformer primary winding and back to the supply negative. The increasing flux produced by the rising current induces voltages in both the primary and secondary windings of the transformer. The direction of this e.m.f. and the resulting charge on capacitor C is shown in the diagram. Triggering TH_2 effectively connects the positive plate of the capacitor to the cathode of TH_1 which switches off. Current now flows from the supply through the second half of the transformer winding so that the polarity of the induced e.m.f. and charge on the capacitor are reversed. Triggering TH_1 and

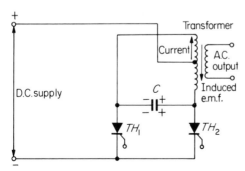

Fig 9

TH_2 in a regular sequence, again using an oscillator, causes a periodically
varying voltage to be induced in the transformer secondary winding.

9 **The convertor**   A.C. of one frequency is rectified and the resulting d.c. fed to
an invertor which operates at the required frequency. Thus two systems of
different frequencies may be interconnected or a.c. of one frequency may be
produced using an a.c. source of a different frequency.

B   WORKED PROBLEMS ON THE SILICON CONTROLLED RECTIFIER

Problem 1   Describe with the aid of diagrams the operation of a silicon
controlled rectifier using the two bipolar junction transistor model.

Consider the two transistors shown in *Fig 10(a)*. T_1 is a *p-n-p* type whilst T_2 is an
n-p-n type. They have current gains in the common emitter configuration of β_1
and β_2 respectively. T_2 needs a current towards its base to become conducting
and T_1 a current outwards from its base.

If a current I_G is injected into the base of T_2 whilst its collector is at a positive
potential with respect to its emitter, the collector current will rise to $\beta_2 I_G$. Again

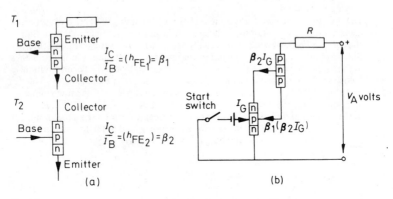

Fig 10

provided that the polarity of the supply is correct, this current flowing in the base
of T_1, *Fig 10(b)*, will cause the collector current to rise to $\beta_1(\beta_2 I_G)$. This will be
many hundreds of times greater than I_G. This current is fed back to the base of
T_2 where it will cause a further increase in the collector current and hence in the
base current of T_1. In a very short time the device becomes a short circuit, and
since the forward volt drop is very small the current flowing is limited only by the
external circuit resistance. R in *Figure 10(b)*.

Problem 2 Explain with the aid of diagrams how two thyristors together with any auxiliary equipment necessary may be used to control:
(a)   the speed of a d.c. shunt motor;
(b)   the speed of an a.c. series connected motor, the supply in each case being single-phase a.c.

(a)   *Fig 11* shows a bi-phase full wave rectifier employing two thyristors which are controlled using a peaking transformer and phase-shifting circuit. A pulse to the gate of TH_1 during a positive going half cycle of input voltage causes it to become conducting. A pulse to the gate of TH_2 during a negative half cycle causes it to become conducting thus achieving full-wave rectification. Notice that although the pulse to TH_2 occurs during a negative half cycle it is never-the-less towards the gate and conduction commences.

The armature of the d.c. shunt motor is thus fed at a mean voltage which is dependent upon the firing angle of the thyristors. Delaying the firing pulse for 180° results in no conduction and the armature voltage being zero so that the speed will be zero. Providing the firing pulse at the commencement of each half cycle results in the maximum possible

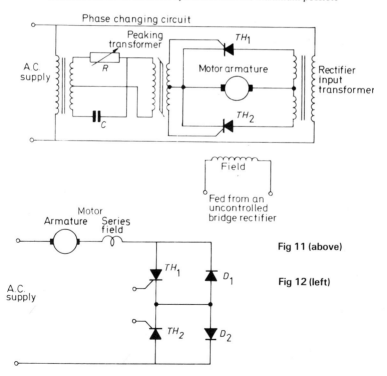

Fig 11 (above)

Fig 12 (left)

169

conduction period and the maximum voltage. This will result in a high speed. Thus control is achieved from a crawl to the maximum speed. The motor field is supplied through an uncontrolled bridge rectifier at constant voltage.

(b) In *Fig 12*, the same control circuit (i.e., transformer, *R*, *C* and peaking transformer) is used but is not shown. A gate pulse during a positive half cycle causes TH_1 to conduct and current flows in the series motor from the supply, through TH_1 and diode D_2 back to the neutral. At the end of the positive going half cycle conduction ceases. A gate pulse during the negative half cycle causes TH_2 to become conducting when current flows in the series motor, TH_2 and D_1. Thus there is control of alternating current to the motor, the speed of which will depend on the mean value of voltage and the mechanical load connected to it.

Problem 3   What dangers are there to using an earthed CRO when viewing the voltage waveforms in a thyristor circuit? How may these dangers be eliminated?

The a.c. supply derived from the public mains has its neutral earthed at the supply transformer. Many oscilloscopes have one of the signal input terminals connected to the casing and to the supply earth. In *Fig 13* it can be seen that

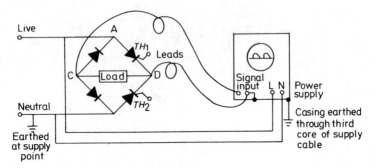

Fig 13

connecting the earthed signal lead to point *D* in the rectifier circuit connects that point to earth. When TH_1 conducts it becomes virtually a short circuit so that the live line of the supply becomes connected directly to earth. This should cause the circuit protection to operate thus clearing the circuit.

The danger may be eliminated by using either of the arrangements shown in *Fig 14*. Isolating the rectifier using a transformer causes it to operate free of earth. Connecting an earthed lead to it at any point has no effect. In the case of a large rectifier the isolating transformer will be large and thus expensive so that the arrangement shown in *Fig 14(b)* will be preferred. Supplying the oscilloscope via an isolating transformer causes it to operate free of earth and its leads may be connected anywhere on the rectifier without danger.

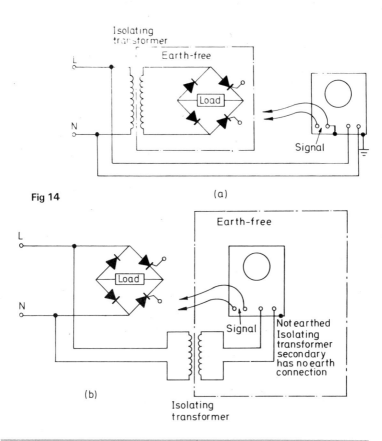

Fig 14   (a)

(b)

Isolating
transformer

C FURTHER PROBLEMS ON THE SILICON CONTROLLED RECTIFIER

(a) SHORT ANSWER PROBLEMS

1 Draw the circuit symbol for the silicon controlled rectifier. Label its terminals.

2 Define the term 'holding current' as applied to an SCR.

3 What advantages are there to using an SCR as a switch as compared with a mechanical contactor?

4 Draw a circuit diagram of a phase-shifting circuit employing a resistor and a capacitor.

5 Draw a set of I_A/V_A for an SCR for a range of gate currents from a value which is in excess of that necessary to cause conduction down to near zero.

6   Define the term 'peak reverse' or 'peak inverse' voltage as applied to an SCR.

7   A single-phase, 240 V a.c. supply is used to feed a 500 Ω resistive load via a single
    thyristor which is triggered 60° after the start of a cycle of the alternating
    voltage. Assuming a sinusoidal voltage, draw two complete cycles of the applied
    voltage waveform together with the waveshape of the resulting load current
    approximately to scale.

8   Sketch the waveshape of a suitable pulse for switching on an SCR.

9   Name a device employing SCRs which enables the power input to a d.c. load fed
    from a d.c. source of power to be controlled without the losses associated with a
    rheostat.

(b) MULTI-CHOICE PROBLEMS (answers on page 213)

1   The action of an SCR may be explained in terms of:
    (i)   two *n-p-n* bipolar junction transistors;
    (ii)   two *p-n-p* bipolar junction transistors;
    (iii) two junction field-effect transistors;
    (iv)   one *n-p-n* and one *p-n-p* bipolar junction transistors.

2   The gate connection in an SCR is in:
    (i)   a *p*-layer; (ii) an *n*-layer.
    The gate must be:
    (iii) positive with respect to the cathode when the anode is positive with respect
           to the cathode,
    (iv)   positive with respect to the anode when the cathode is positive with respect
           to the anode;
    (v)   positive with respect to the cathode when the anode is negative with respect
           to the cathode.
    Select *one* from (i) and (ii) and *one* from (iii), (iv) and (v) to make a correct
    statement.

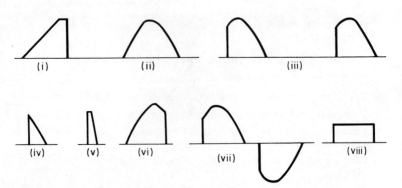

Fig 15

172

3   Select *one* of the waveforms from *Fig 15* (i) to (viii) to fit the description in (a) below. Repeat for (b) and (c).
    (a)   the trigger pulse for an SCR;
    (b)   the output voltage waveform from an SCR, single-phase bridge rectifier with the trigger pulse delayed for 45°;
    (c)   the output voltage waveform from a single-phase, half-wave rectifier with no delay.

4   A single-phase, phase-shifting transformer comprises a stator wound with
    (i)   one winding connected directly to the supply;
    (ii)   two windings, one of which is connected in series with a capacitor;
    (iii) two windings, each with different inductances, one of which is connected in series with a resistor and a rotor which may be rotated through
    (iv)   360° electrical;
    (v)   180° electrical;
    (vi)   is free to rotate through any desired angle.
    Select *one* from (i)–(iii) and *one* from (iv)–(vi) to make a correct statement.

5   As an alternative to the phase-shifting transformer for varying the firing angle of an SCR we may use a resistive/capacitive network. Which of the four diagrams (a)–(d) is correct in *Fig 16*?

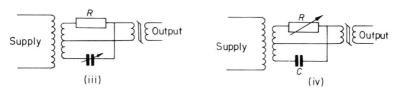

Fig 16

6   From the following five definitions (i) to (v) select one to suit each of the following names (a) invertor; (b) chopper; (c) convertor.
    (i)   a device which inverts the negative half cycle of an a.c. waveform making the output voltage uni-directional;
    (ii)   a device which converts power from a uni-directional source into a voltage and current which are alternating;
    (iii) a device for controlling direct current whilst being fed from a direct voltage source;

(iv) a device for controlling a load in which alternating current flows when fed from an a.c. source;

(v) feeds a load with alternating current at one frequency whilst being fed from an alternating supply at a different frequency.

7 Which of the following will cause a thyristor to change to the non-conducting state from the conducting state when connected to an a.c. supply and supplying current to a load

(i) a gate pulse with negative polarity with respect to the cathode;

(ii) a reversal of the anode/cathode voltage polarity;

(iii) disconnection of the gate circuit;

(iv) the load current being reduced to twice the holding value.

Fig 17

8 Which *two* of the following will cause the thyristor in *Fig 17* to change to the conducting state from the non-conducting state?

(i) short circuiting the load terminals;

(ii) the a.c. voltage changing from negative to positive;

(iii) application of a positive potential derived from a separate circuit between gate and cathode during a positive half cycle of the supply;

(iv) application of a negative potential between gate and cathode during a negative half cycle of the supply;

(v) connecting the gate to the anode through a resistor during a positive half cycle of the supply.

9 Which of the rectifiers shown in *Fig 18* will enable full-wave rectification to be achieved with control of the firing angle during both half cycles of the a.c. input?

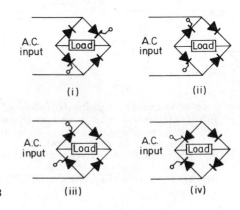

Fig 18

(c) CONVENTIONAL PROBLEMS

1 Draw a circuit diagram showing a phase-shifting circuit controlling thyristors being used to achieve full-wave rectification from a single-phase a.c. supply. Show the directions of the currents in the circuit during both the positive and negative half cycles.

2 A sinusoidal voltage is rectified using:
   (a) a single thyristor giving half-wave rectification and
   (b) a thyristor bridge circuit giving full-wave rectification.
   On two axes show the current waveform to be expected in a resistive load in each case for firing angles of (i) 45°; (ii) 90°; (iii) 150°.

3 Draw a circuit diagram showing two thyristors being used to control the power in an a.c. load circuit when being fed from an a.c. supply. Briefly explain the action of the circuit.

4 What are the advantages of using SCR's to control direct power from a direct source as compared with rheostatic methods?

5 Draw a circuit diagram of an SCR chopper and describe its mode of operation.

6 Suggest a method of interconnecting two alternating systems, one operating at 50 Hz the other at 60 Hz.

7 Why must all but the smallest thyristors be used in conjunction with a heat sink?

8 When controlling direct current from a direct source using SCRs the circuit always incorporates a capacitor. What is the function of this capacitor?

13 Thermionic devices

A SUMMARY OF FORMULAE AND DEFINITIONS ASSOCIATED WITH THERMIONIC DEVICES

1   Atoms consist of a nucleus and orbiting electrons. For a conducting material the mobility of the electrons furthest from the nuclei of the atoms increases as the material is heated and at a particular temperature some of them will have attained sufficient energy to escape completely from the restraining forces exerted by the nuclei.

   To be of use in electronic valves, electrons must be liberated in large numbers from its **cathode** (analogous to emitter or source in transistors) at a temperature below that at which the material melts. The cathodes are made from tungsten wire, coated with oxides of calcium, strontium or barium and these give excellent emission of electrons into a near-perfect vacuum at temperatures around 1000°C.

2   **The diode valve**   *Fig 1* shows a vacuum diode valve. This consists of a cathode, which is heated to incandescence, surrounded by a metal cylinder which is called the **anode**; the whole assembly is encased in a glass envelope exhausted to near-

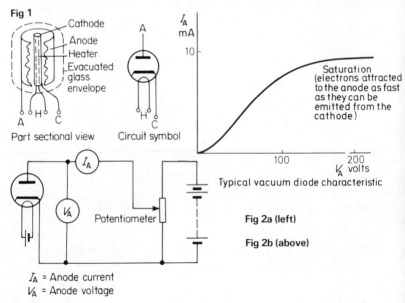

Fig 1

Cathode
Anode
Heater
Evacuated glass envelope

Part sectional view   Circuit symbol

Typical vacuum diode characteristic

Saturation (electrons attracted to the anode as fast as they can be emitted from the cathode)

Potentiometer

Fig 2a (left)

Fig 2b (above)

I_A = Anode current
V_A = Anode voltage

perfect vacuum. The cathode emits electrons which form a space charge around it. In the circuit shown in *Fig 2(a),* the anode (as it is positive with respect to the cathode) attracts electrons from the space charge making it weaker. To replace these, more electrons are emitted from the cathode and a current is established round the circuit. A typical characteristic curve is shown in *Fig 2(b).*

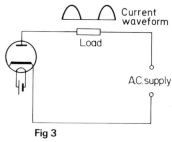

Fig 3

Fig 3 shows the diode connected using an a.c. supply. In this case current flows during the half cycle when the anode is positive but not when it is negative since then it repels electrons. This is a **half-wave rectifier.**

3   **The gas-filled diode**   In the diode valve, with the anode strongly positive, the electrons move through the cathode/anode space at high velocity and are hurled against the anode probably disappearing within it. If a small quantity of gas is introduced into the space, the high-velocity electrons collide with the gas atoms during their travels. If the impact is sufficiently violent, the result of the collision is to liberate an electron from the surface of a gas atom which, since it is now short of one electron, exhibits positive charge and is called a **positive ion.** The liberated electron is accelerated towards the anode and may itself be involved in further collisions liberating more electrons. The ions formed move towards the cathode and there receive electrons turning them into complete gas atoms again.

The gas in the envelope is said to be ionised and once this has taken place, the internal resistance falls to a very low value. When used as a rectifier and connected as shown in *Fig 3*, virtually all the supply voltage is available at the

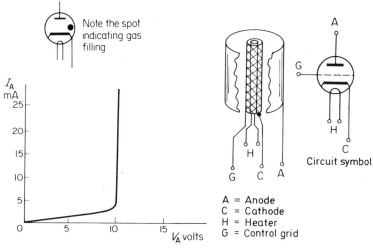

Note the spot indicating gas filling

Fig 4

A = Anode
C = Cathode
H = Heater
G = Control grid

Circuit symbol

Fig 5

177

load and the current is limited only by this resistance. A glow appears inside the valve the brilliance of which is a function of the current flowing. Its characteristic is shown in *Fig 4*.

4 **The vacuum triode valve** *Fig 5* shows a part-sectional view of a triode valve and its circuit symbol. The triode has three electrodes, a cathode and anode (as in the diode valve), and a third electrode called the control grid which consists of a fine wire mesh or helical winding through which electrons can pass. The control grid is close to the cathode and is supplied at a potential which is negative with respect to the cathode. Due to the close spacing, the grid/cathode voltage V_G has

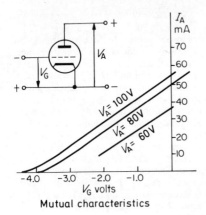

Fig 6

Mutual characteristics

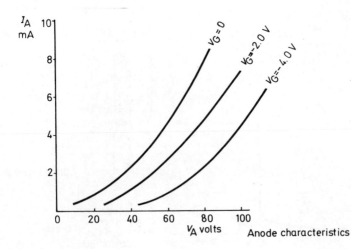

Anode characteristics

Fig 7

much more effect on the anode current than has the anode/cathode voltage, V_A.

Fig 6 shows the mutual characteristics of a triode valve and these are very similar to those for the JFET (see Chapter 11, para. 5 and *Fig 4*). Both devices use a voltage (grid or gate) to control a current (anode or drain). With the triode valve, keeping V_G constant and varying V_A over the working range whilst measuring I_A enables a set of anode characteristics to be plotted as shown in *Fig 7*.

5 **The triode voltage amplifier** This is very similar to the JFET amplifier and the following parts of previous work should be consulted in conjunction with this item (see Chapter 11: Biasing, para. 5; Load line, para. 8; *Problem 3* Decoupling capacitors, *Problem 4*).

Fig 8 shows a triode valve connected as a single-stage amplifier. The grid bias battery is connected with the polarity as shown and has an e.m.f. of magnitude such that the grid can never become positive when the signal is applied. The

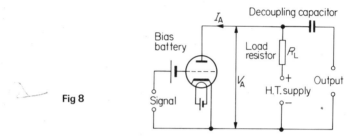

Fig 8

alternating signal gives rise to changes in the anode current I_A and these produce voltage changes across the load resistor. The alternating output is isolated from the high-voltage supply using a decoupling capacitor. Although the changes in I_A are generally only in the milliampere range, the load resistor has a value of several thousand ohms so that substantial voltage amplification is attained. The load line may be drawn in the same manner as for the JFET (see *Problem 3*).

6 **The pentode valve** In a triode valve amplifier, as the grid potential becomes less negative, the anode current increases causing an increased voltage drop across the load resistor; the anode voltage therefore falls. Hence the anode current is less than it would be if the anode voltage were maintained constant.

The pentode valve was developed to overcome this problem. Compared with the triode valve—it has two extra electrodes the screen grid and the suppressor grid. The screen grid is maintained at a constant high positive potential whilst the suppressor grid is connected to the cathode. The effect of these two extra electrodes is to make I_A very nearly independent of V_A and the anode characteristics become as shown in *Fig 9*. (Compare these with *Fig 7* for the triode and *Fig 16* (Chapter 11) for the JFET.)

Making I_A independent of V_A (nearly) gives rise to larger voltage amplification than with a triode valve under similar conditions of high tension voltage and load

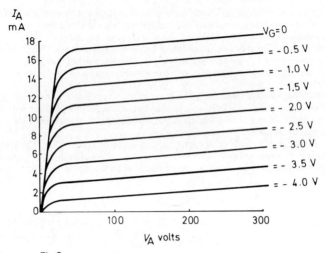

Fig 9

resistance. With a smaller input signal and much larger value of load resistance even better voltage gains are achieved.

Another advantage of the pentode is that the capacitance between the control grid and anode is almost eliminated and as indicated in Chapter 11, para. 10 the presence of capacitance between input and output circuits can cause a reduction in output.

7 **The thyratron valve** The thyratron valve is a triode valve with a small quantity of mercury included in the glass envelope. A test circuit and valve characteristic are shown in *Fig 10*. Consider a voltage E volts applied to the thyratron. The control grid is held negative with respect to the cathode. Starting with $V_G = -8$ V the valve is non-conducting. V_G is made slowly less negative until a certain critical value is reached when the valve suddenly becomes conducting. As with the gas-filled diode, it becomes virtually a short circuit and sufficient current

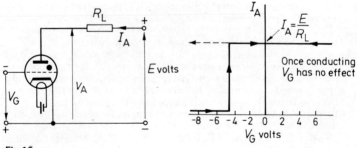

Fig 10

would flow to destroy the valve if this was not limited by the inclusion of a series connected load resistor. The valve can only be shut off by removing or reversing the polarity of the anode voltage.

With the valve fed from an a.c. supply, controlled rectification can be achieved. The grid is held strongly negative until the valve is required to conduct when it is pulsed to zero or just positive to ensure conduction (see also Chapter 12 for work on the thyristor which is the solid state equivalent).

8 **Control of an electron beam**

(a) *Electrostatic* 'Like' electrical charges repel one another whilst 'unlike' charges attract. An electron being injected between two charged plates as

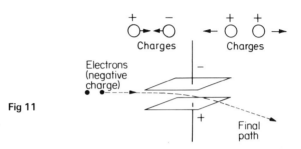

Fig 11

shown in *Fig 11* will be attracted towards the positive plate. The amount of deflection is affected by (i) the entry velocity of the electron; (ii) the plate size and (iii) the potential difference between the plates. Once outside the influence of the electric field between the plates the electron will travel on in a straight line until it is further deflected or it impacts with a surface.

(b) *Magnetic* A movement of electrons constitutes an electric current and when a current flows in a region in which there is a magnetic field, a force is produced. Conventional current flow and electron flow are in opposite directions. The force acting on the conductor in *Fig 12(a)* is downwards. This is for a conventional current flow into the paper or electrons flowing out of the paper.

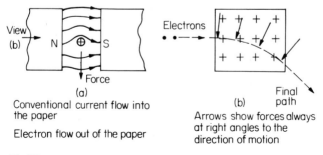

(a)
Conventional current flow into the paper

Electron flow out of the paper

(b)
Final path

Arrows show forces always at right angles to the direction of motion

Fig 12

In the case of a rigid conductor in which the current comprises countless electrons, the force is uniform along its length in the field and it moves directly downwards mutually at right angles to the field and to the current direction. With individual electrons, as soon as one enters the magnetic field it suffers a downward force which changes its direction. The force is maintained at right angles to the direction of travel and it follows a circular path as seen in *Fig 12(b)*.

9   **The cathode ray tube**   The cathode-ray tube comprises, essentially, of a conical glass envelope, evacuated to near-perfect vacuum within which there is:

1   A source of high velocity electrons, the electron gun.
2   A means of focusing the electron beam.
3   A beam deflection system.
4   A fluorescent screen which glows when struck by the electron stream.

The electron gun is very similar to the vacuum diode having a heated cathode but with a flat anode (A_1) in which there is a hole (see *Fig 13*). A cylinder (grid) which is held at a negative potential with respect to the cathode gently repels the electrons tending to keep them on a central path so that most of them pass

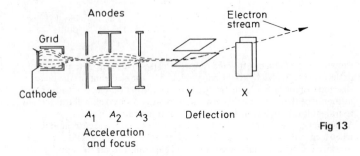

Fig 13

through the anode hole. Making the grid very strongly negative shuts off the flow of electrons so that this potential is made adjustable and affords brightness control. Electrons which pass through the hole in A_1 have before them another cylindrical anode A_2 which, acting with anodes A_1 and A_3, produces electrostatic stresses which focus the electrons into a slightly convergent stream. The degree of convergence is adjusted by varying the potentials of A_2 and A_3 and this will cause the trace on the screen to be thin and sharp or wide and woolly. Deflection of the beam is achieved electrostatically or magnetically.

Fig 14 shows a cathode ray tube employing electrostatic deflection. The X-plates will often be fed from a time base circuit which causes the beam to swing across the screen in a horizontal direction whilst the Y-plates are fed with an alternating signal causing vertical displacement. The trace will then be as in *Fig 14*. In *Fig 15* the beam is deflected by the magnetic fields produced by currents flowing in two pairs of coils, X and Y, mounted externally at the flare in the tube. Relatively large powers are required to provide these fields and because of the inductance of the windings the range of operating frequencies must be limited.

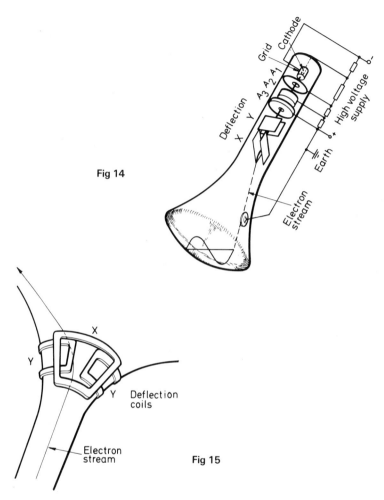

Fig 14

Fig 15

The main application of the type of tube in *Fig 15* is for picture display in television receivers where the frequency of the currents in the Y-coils determines the number of pictures presented per second and that in the X-coils, the number of lines per picture. Magnetic deflection enables the beam to be turned through very large angles so enabling the tube length to be small for a given picture size.

Once the electrons have hit the screen they return to the positive of the h.t. supply via the earthed lead connected to the flare of the tube and hence back to the cathode thus completing the circuit.

B WORKED PROBLEMS ON THERMIONIC DEVICES

Problem 1 Explain why it is that a gas-filled diode conducts more current than a vacuum valve of similar physical size.

In the vacuum diode valve, with the anode strongly positive, the electrons move through the cathode/anode space at high velocity and are hurled against the anode where they are absorbed. Saturation occurs when electrons are attracted through the space as fast as they are emitted by the cathode. This rate of electron emission at a particular cathode temperature is the current limiting factor for the valve.

If a small quantity of gas is introduced into the space, the high-velocity electrons collide with the gas atoms during their travels. If the impact is sufficiently violent, the result of the collision is to liberate an electron from the surface of the gas atom turning it into a positive ion. The liberated electron is accelerated towards the anode and the ion towards the cathode. The liberated electron may itself be involved in collisions liberating further electrons. The gas in the envelope is said to be ionised. Once ionisation takes place there are very many more electrons in the cathode/anode space than in the vacuum valve and its internal resistance falls to a very low value when the current is limited only by the external resistance of the circuit.

Problem 2 Using a triode valve and a load resistor as a voltage amplifier, the voltage gain is significantly less than might be expected from a consideration of the mutual characteristics plotted considering constant anode voltage. Explain why this is.

In the triode voltage amplifier, as the grid potential becomes less negative due to a positive going signal imposed on the negative bias, the anode current increases. This causes an increase in the voltage drop across the load resistor. The anode voltage therefore falls.

$$V_A = E - I_A R_L$$

where, V_A = anode voltage; E = supply voltage; I_A = anode current; R_L = load resistance (see *Fig 8*).

From the characteristics in *Fig 7* it may be seen that a reduction in V_A for any value of V_G causes a reduction in anode current which therefore is less than it would have been if V_A had been maintained constant. The output voltage is a function of I_A and therefore the voltage gain is less than would have been obtained at constant V_A.

Problem 3 A triode valve with anode characteristics as given in *Fig 16* is to be used to amplify a sinusoidal signal with peak value 2 V. The value of the load resistor is 20 000 Ω and the h.t. supply is at 300 V. Draw a load line and using a suitable operating point, determine the value of voltage amplification obtained.

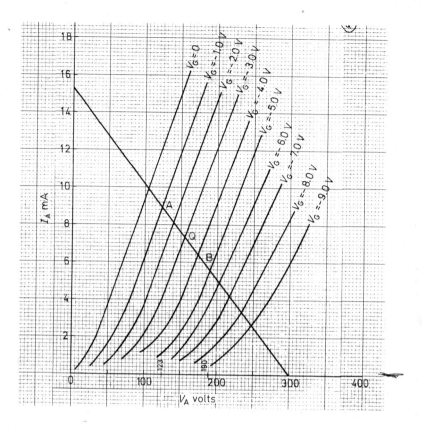

When $I_A = 0$, $V_A = 300$ V (the full supply voltage)

When $I_A = \dfrac{300}{20000} = 15$ mA, $V_A = 0$

The load line is drawn between points: $V_A = 0$, $I_A = 15$ mA and $V_A = 300$ V, $I_A = 0$.
Since the signal has a peak value of 2 V, a suitable bias value would be -3 V.
The operating point Q is shown on the $V_G = -3$ V characteristic in *Fig 16*.
The grid voltage swings between $-3-2 = -5$ V and $-3+2 = -1$ V.
The corresponding values of V_A are 190 V (Point B) and 123 V (Point A)

The r.m.s. value of the signal $= \dfrac{2}{\sqrt{2}} = 1.414$ V.

The r.m.s. value of the output voltage $= \dfrac{190-123}{2\sqrt{2}} = 23.7$ V

Voltage amplification $= \dfrac{23.7}{1.414} = 16.7$

An electron being injected between two charged plates as in *Fig 11* will be
attracted towards the positive plate. The force of attraction is proportional to the
potential difference between the plates. If the entry velocity of the electron is low
it may, in fact, end up on the positive plate when it will be absorbed as at the
anode of a valve. By a suitable choice of entry velocity, plate size and potential
difference the electron may be caused to be merely deflected from its original

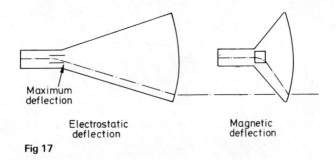

Maximum
deflection

Electrostatic
deflection

Magnetic
deflection

Fig 17

path and once outside the influence of the deflecting field it will travel on in a
straight line.

In the case of magnetic deflection there are no internal parts to the deflection
system and the electrons can be turned through a much larger angle than in the
electrostatic tube with no possibility of absorption. Deflection angles in excess of
60° are quite possible. *Fig 17* clearly shows the difference.

Electrons travelling up the cathode ray tube strike the phosphor coating on the
display end, causing the phosphor to glow. The length of time that the phosphor
continues to glow after being bombarded with electrons is called *persistence* or
afterglow. At any instant only one small point on the screen is being struck by
electrons. The viewer sees a complete waveform on the CRO partly due to the
persistence of vision of the human eye and partly due to the persistence of the
glow on the screen. The same occurs on a TV receiver.

Where many traces of the beam are made each second, the persistence of the
screen needs to be short or we see a trace superimposed on the afterglow of the
previous one. Where changes are occurring, as in the case of the TV picture, long
afterglow would result in us seeing the latest picture superimposed on several

others, each slightly different as they faded away.

(a) The television screen presents twenty-five per second so that a short period of afterglow is essential. Similarly, the laboratory CRO used for examining waveforms which repeat at high frequency needs to have a short persistence if many traces of varying brightness are not to be seen simultaneously.

(b) Where transient phenomena are being examined (once only) or for radar where the trace must persist from one scan until the next, the tube must carry the image long after the beam has passed by.

C FURTHER PROBLEMS ON THERMIONIC DEVICES

(a) SHORT ANSWER PROBLEMS

1   Thermionic emission from a cathode may be increased by raising the temperature. What is the limiting factor?

2   Why does thermionic emission not take place in air?

3   What is meant by the term 'saturation' as applied to a diode valve?

4   What is an ion?

5   When a gas-filled diode or thyratron is carrying current, what external indication is there?

6   How is the energy provided in a triode valve to enable conduction within the valve to commence?

7   What is the essential difference between (a) a diode and a triode and (b) a triode and a pentode?

8   What difference is there between the circuit symbol for a triode and that for a thyratron?

9   On one set of axes sketch the typical shape of the I_A/V_A characteristics for (a) the triode and (b) the pentode valve.

10 A thyratron valve is connected to an a.c. supply with a load resistor R_L in the anode lead. What polarity must the grid/cathode voltage have (a) to prevent conduction and (b) to cause conduction to occur? Assume the values available to be suitable.

11 In a CRO, deflection in the vertical plane is achieved by electrostatic means. Two plates in the horizontal plane are provided, the top plate being positive with respect to the bottom plate. In which direction will the electron beam be deflected?

12 How is the electron beam brought to a sharp focus on the screen of a cathode ray tube using electrostatic means?

13 What part of the electrode system in a CRO affects the number of electrons reaching the screen? (Assume constant cathode temperature)

14 What is 'afterglow' in a cathode ray tube?

15 State two typical colours of the trace on a cathode ray tube.

16 Why is magnetic deflection as opposed to electrostatic deflection employed in TV receivers?

17 Why are CROs which employ electrostatic deflection used in laboratories for testing small pieces of electronic equipment?

(b) MULTI-CHOICE PROBLEMS (answers on page 213)

1 In a vacuum diode valve the charge in the cathode/anode space is:
   (i) made up of ions surrounding the anode;
   (ii) made up of ions emitted by the cathode;
   (iii) made up of electrons emitted by the cathode;
   (iv) made up of electrons emitted by the anode.

2 *Figs 18(a)* to *(e)* show a selection of valve symbols. Allocate each letter to one of the following, which indicates its correct name:
   (i) diode; (ii) gas-filled diode; (iii) triode; (iv) thyratron; (v) pentode; (vi) cold-cathode valve; (vii) tetrode.

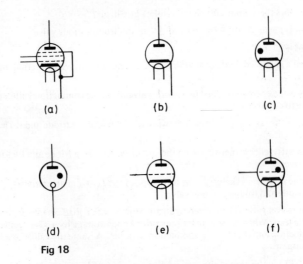

Fig 18

3 When ionisation takes place in a gas-filled valve connected to an a.c. supply:
   (i) the resistance of the valve increases to a high value;
   (ii) the current is limited only by external resistance;
   (iii) the anode/cathode voltage becomes very nearly equal to the supply voltage;
   (iv) conduction takes place during both positive and negative half cycles of the supply;
   (v) the anode/cathode voltage falls to very nearly zero.
   Two of the above statements are correct and state the same fact in different ways. Which are they?

4   A thyratron, correctly connected to an a.c. system, is conducting. Conduction
    will cease:
    (i)   if the grid/cathode voltage is made strongly positive;
    (ii) if the grid/cathode voltage is made strongly negative;
    (iii) if the cathode/anode potential becomes positive;
    (iv) if the grid/anode voltage becomes strongly negative.

5   A triode valve amplifier with load resistor R_L is correctly biased and connected
    to a high voltage direct supply. An alternating signal is fed to the grid circuit.
    Using the words: (i) increase(s); (ii) decrease(s); (iii) remains unchanged,
    complete the following statements.
    As the signal voltage in the grid circuit drives positive;
    (a)   the grid/cathode voltage . . . . .
    (b)   whilst the anode current I_A . . . .
    (c)   causing the anode/cathode voltage to . . . .
    Answer (a) (iii); (b) (ii); etc.

6   A triode valve amplifier with load resistor $R_L = 15\,000\,\Omega$ draws a steady anode
    current of 60 mA. In response to a signal input the anode current alternates
    between 20 mA and 100 mA. The alternating power in the load resistor is:
    (i) 150 W; (ii) 12 W; (iii) 54 W; (iv) 48 W.

7   In a pentode valve the screen grid is held at
    (i)   a positive potential;
    (ii) a negative potential, with respect to the cathode;
    (iii) at the same potential as the cathode.
    Its effect is to
    (iv) return to the anode electrons emitted from the anode due to impacting
          electrons;
    (v)   accelerate electrons from the cathode at a rate independent of the
          anode/cathode voltage;
    (vi) reduce the velocity of impact of electrons with the anode.
    Select *one* from (i), (ii) and (iii) and *one* from (iv), (v) and (vi) to make a correct
    statement.

8   The currents flowing in the two sets of deflecting coils of a magnetically
    deflected television receiver are
    (i)   direct;
    (ii) alternating, both coils carrying currents of the same frequency;
    (iii) alternating, the coils giving vertical deflection having a higher frequency
          than those giving horizontal deflection;
    (iv) alternating, the coils giving vertical deflection having a lower frequency
          than those giving horizontal deflection.

9   The velocity of electrons striking the screen of a cathode ray tube is determined
    by:
    (i)   the grid/cathode voltage;
    (ii) the grid/anode voltage;
    (iii) the cathode/anode voltage;
    (iv) the length of the cathode ray tube;
    (v)   the temperature of the cathode.

10 Electrons travel along the length of a cathode-ray tube having been emitted by the cathode and hit the phosphor to produce a spot of light. The electrons then:
   (i)   are absorbed by the phosphor;
   (ii)   drift back through the vacuum to the cathode;
   (iii) return to the cathode heater through an earth connection;
   (iv)   return to the cathode through an earth connection;
   (v)   return to the positive of the high voltage supply through an earth connection.

(c) CONVENTIONAL PROBLEMS

1 Using the triode characteristics as shown in *Fig 16*, draw a suitable load line and determine the voltage amplification which would be achieved using a load resistance of 12 500 Ω and an h.t. supply at 250 V when the signal has a peak value of 3 V.   [Approx. 12.6]

2 Describe the process of ionisation in a hot-cathode valve.

3 The anode current of a pentode valve may be considered constant at a particular value of grid voltage irrespective of the value of anode voltage V_A.
   For a particular valve: When $V_G = -1.5$ V, $I_A = 17.75$ mA
                                        When $V_G = -1.75$ V, $I_A = 15$ mA.
                                        When $V_G = -2.0$ V, $I_A = 12$ mA.
   Plot the anode characteristics in the form of *Fig 9* using a horizontal axis for V_A from zero to 350 V. Your lines will be horizontal because of the original statement in this question.
       For a load resistance of 17 500 Ω, a supply voltage of 350 V and an input signal of sinusoidal form with peak value 0.25 V, use the load line method to determine the voltage gain when the bias voltage is -1.75 V. What is the value of the alternating power in the load resistor under these conditions?
                                      [Gain 200; alternating power 0.07 W]

4 Describe with the aid of suitable sketches a typical application of (a) a gas-filled diode and (b) a gas-filled triode.

5 Draw a schematic arrangement of a cathode-ray tube using electrostatic deflection and focus. Label and briefly explain the function of each part of the electrode system.

6 What are the essential differences between the thyratron and the thyristor especially concerning the grid/gate conditions for (a) the non-conducting state and (b) the conducting state.
                         [Thyristor must be triggered. Thyratron must be held off]

7 Explain why it is that the pentode valve is able to achieve greater voltage amplification than the triode valve when used in conjunction with the same load resistor.

8 Which solid device has characteristics most similar to those of the pentode valve? Sketch a common set of characteristics labelled twice, once for the pentode and once for the solid state device.

9 Magnetic deflection in a cathode ray tube can deflect the electron beam through a large angle whereas electrostatic deflection can only achieve a few degrees of deflection. Explain why this is and how the difference has influenced the design of television receivers.

14 Photoelectric devices

A SUMMARY OF FORMULAE AND DEFINITIONS ASSOCIATED WITH PHOTOELECTRIC DEVICES

1 **Visible radiations**   Electromagnetic radiations with frequencies between 4×10^{14} Hz and 7.5×10^{14} Hz are detected by the human eye and give the sensations of a range of colours from red to violet respectively. Since light travels at a speed of 3×10^8 m/s, the wavelengths of the radiations, i.e. the distance that light travels in the periodic time of one cycle, are found by dividing the speed of propogation by the frequency.

Wavelength of red light $= \dfrac{3 \times 10^8}{4 \times 10^{14}} = 0.75 \times 10^{-6}$ m

Wavelength of violet light $= \dfrac{3 \times 10^8}{7.5 \times 10^{14}} = 0.4 \times 10^{-6}$ m

2 In 1887, Hertz discovered that light energy caused electrons to become more mobile so that they were able to leave the surface of some substances, whilst in others, voltages could be generated or a change of resistance detected. Similar effects can be produced with heat (see Chapter 13 para. 1).

3 **Photoemissive cells**   The photoemissive cell is a diode comprising a coated metallic cathode enclosed in a vacuum tube and which emits electrons when it is illuminated. The electrons are attracted to an anode which is held at a positive potential and a current is established as shown in *Fig 1(a)*. The current is proportional to the total light flux at the cathode which therefore has to be large and evenly illuminated to give the optimum output. Typical characteristics are shown in *Fig 1(c)*. [*See Chapter 15, para. 6 for definition of light flux and the lumen.*]

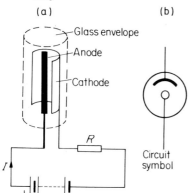

(a)

Glass envelope
Anode
Cathode

R

I

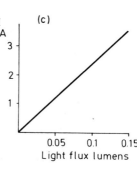

(b)

Circuit symbol

(c)

Photoemissive cell

Fig 1

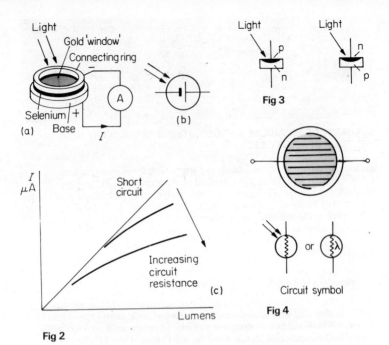

Fig 2

Fig 3

Fig 4

Circuit symbol

Several different cathode coating materials are available each giving its best output when illuminated with light of a different colour. A silver-plated cathode with caesium oxide present has a good response to red light whilst antimony/caesium responds well to the blue/violet end of the spectrum. Adding a small quantity of inert gas to the tube causes a larger current to flow in the external circuit. This is due to ionisation (see Chapter 13, para. 3).

4 **Photovoltaic cells** A selenium cell is shown in *Fig 2*. The selenium is deposited on a base of steel or aluminium and then an extremely thin layer of gold added. Light travelling through the gold strikes the gold/selenium junction and produces an electromotive force. The current in the external circuit is a function of the total light flux incident to the surface of the cell. It is also affected by the external circuit resistance which should be low. Other photovoltaic cells employ a copper oxide/copper junction.

Silicon and germanium *p-n* junctions are also light sensitive and will generate a small e.m.f (*Fig 3*).

5 **Photoconductive cells** The photoconductive cell has the property of variable resistance according to the light intensity at its surface. (*Note: Not* total light flux in the case.) In the dark it may have a resistance of several megohms whilst when brightly lit the resistance will fall to a fraction of a megohm. Large changes in resistance are achieved by arranging the electrodes in the form of interleaved combs. Materials used include cadmium sulphide, cadmium selenide, indium antimonide, lead sulphide and lead selenide (*Fig 4*).

The *p-n* junction may be used as a photoconductive device by reverse biasing it as shown in *Fig 5*. It is then known as a photo-diode and the intensity of the light falling on the junction determines the magnitude of the reverse current flow.

6 **Light-emitting diodes (LED)**   When a *p-n* junction is forward biased using an external battery, light may be emitted from the junction. The quantity and colour of the light are dependent on the current flowing and the material from which the junction is made. The process is called photoluminescence. Junction diodes for this purpose are formed in a similar manner to the photovoltaic selenium cell using gallium arsenide to produce red light, gallium phosphide

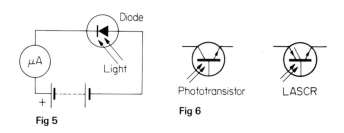

Fig 5

Fig 6

doped with slight impurities to produce red or green light or a combination of both when yellow light is seen. The energy conversion is much more efficient than in the incandescent lamp and an LED of a few mW rating can replace a 5 W indicator lamp without the associated heat.

7 **Phototransistors and thyristors**   The phototransistor has two junctions as in the normal bipolar junction transistor and is so arranged in its capsule that light can shine on the base/collector junction. When so illuminated the transistor becomes conducting, and it requires no electrical connection to its base.

The photothyristor or LASCR (light actuated silicon controlled rectifier) shown in *Fig 6* requires a light input to cause it to become conducting instead of the gate pulse used with the normal SCR.

Both these photo-devices may be built into a small capsule which contains a light source—an LED perhaps. This allows complete isolation of the input signal to the light, from the output circuit. The lamp source operates completely independently of the load and there is no danger of feedback.

B WORKED EXAMPLES ON PHOTOELECTRIC DEVICES

Problem 1   Photoelectric cells may be classified in three groups; (a) photoemissive; (b) photovoltaic; (c) photoconductive. Discuss some of the applications of each of the cell types.

(a) *Photoemissive cells* The output current from a photoemissive tube connected in a circuit as shown in *Fig 1* is very small but the voltage drop across the resistor R is large enough to be used as the bias on the control grid of a pentode valve. Switching the illumination on and off causes the bias value to vary and the valve alternates between the non-conducting and the conducting states. A relay connected in the anode circuit will pull on and drop off according to the light conditions.

A light source may be situated such that a beam of light is projected on to the cell and the arrangement may be used as a burglar alarm or for counting articles passing a particular point as on a production line. Anything interrupting the beam operates the relay which may ring a bell, operate an automatic telephone calling system or pulse a counting circuit, according to the application.

Cinema projection equipment uses the photoemissive cell to convert the varying light output from an optical sound track into sound.

(b) *Photovoltaic cells* The selenium cell has a response similar to that of the human eye and is often used in colour comparators and in commercial light meters in which the output voltage drives a current through a microammeter calibrated in the required units, lux for example.

The *p-n* silicon photovoltaic cells are extremely small and may be used, for example, to read information from punched cards or paper tape for the control of machine tools. A light source above the punched material shines through the holes on to a matrix of cells. Only those which are illuminated produce e.m.f.s and these voltages provide information to control the process.

(c) *Photoconductive cells* These cells are able to detect infra-red radiation. In particular they may be used to detect small variations in radiation from a general background level. Militarily this is very significant since a device to detect the infra-red radiation from a human face, a glowing cigarette end or a gun barrel at a range of hundreds of yards gives very effective night vision.

Civil applications enable hot machine bearings to be detected, hot joints in overhead lines to be located whilst standing on the ground and the condition of thermal insulation of buildings to be detected by an infra-red scan of the outside.

Problem 2 What is a LASCR? Explain how the device is employed as an opto-isolator.

A light actuated silicon-controlled rectifier or photo-thyristor is a four-layer *p-n-p-n* device similar in function to the normal silicon controlled rectifier but which requires a light input to cause it to become conducting instead of the gate pulse used with the normal SCR. It may be used in any of the ways that the normal SCR is used, to rectify alternating supplies, to act as a chopper or invertor or simply as a relay responding to a light signal.

The device is built into a capsule which contains a small light source. There will be four terminals, two for the light and two for the power side of the device. There are also types with only two terminals and a small window to allow for independent illumination.

194

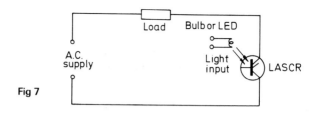

Fig 7

The LASCR allows complete electrical isolation of the input signal from the output circuit. *Fig 7* shows a LASCR controlling a load fed from a single-phase supply.

> *Problem 3* Compare the properties of the light emitting diode with those of a conventional tungsten filament lamp.

When a *p-n* junction is forward biased using an external power supply, light may be emitted from the junction. Using suitable materials red, green or yellow light may be produced (see para. 6).

The forward voltage drop is of the order of 1.3 V and the light output is determined ultimately by the capability of the diode to dissipate the heat produced by the current. The efficiency of conversion is considerably greater than that of the incandescent electric lamp and an LED of a few milliwatts rating can replace a 5 W indicator lamp in equipment such as television receivers where they are used to indicate channel selection, power on etc. The LED can respond to current variations at over 1 million times per second so that it can be used wherever a rapidly changing light output in response to an electrical signal of high frequency is required. The production of sound track on film is an example where the sound frequencies lie between a few herz and about 20 kiloherz. As a comparison, the incandescent light bulb delivers a light output with very little flicker at all frequencies above about 40 Hz.

C FURTHER PROBLEMS ON PHOTOELECTRIC DEVICES

(a) SHORT ANSWER PROBLEMS

1 State the principal colours in the visible spectrum together with the range of frequencies involved.

2 What is a photoemissive cell?

3 On what factors does the current in the external circuit connected to a photoemissive cell depend?

4 What modification (at the manufacturing stage) may be made to a photoemissive cell to increase its output?

5 State two applications of the photoemissive cell

6 What is a photovoltaic cell?

7 On what factors does the current in the external circuit connected to a photovoltaic cell depend?

8 On what factors does the resistance of a photoconductive cell depend?

9 How are particular *p-n* junction diodes biased in order that they will act as photoconductive devices?

10 How are particular *p-n* junctions biased in order that they will act as light emitting diodes?

11 State two applications of a photoconductive cell.

12 Which type of photoelectric cell has applications in the infra-red detection sphere?

13 What difference is apparent externally between a conventional bipolar junction transistor and a phototransistor?

14 State one application of a photothyristor.

(b) MULTI-CHOICE PROBLEMS (answers on page 213)

1 A photoemissive cell correctly connected to an external circuit delivers a current which is proportional to:
   (i)   the number of lumens falling on its anode;
   (ii) the number of lumens falling on its cathode;
   (iii) the anode voltage;
   (iv) the size of the anode;
   (v)   the temperature of the cathode.

2 Adding a small quantity of gas to a photoemissive cell
   (i)   allows it to be operated with a higher voltage supply;
   (ii) increases it sensitivity to ultra-violet radiation;
   (iii) increases its sensitivity to infra-red radiation;
   (iv) increases the current over that for the vacuum tube at a particular voltage.

3 The current in the external circuit connected to a particular photovoltaic cell depends on three of the following:
   (i)   the brightness of the best lit section of its surface;
   (ii) the total light flux falling on its surface;
   (iii) the circuit resistance;
   (iv) the value of the applied voltage;
   (v)   the pressure of the gas filling;
   (vi) the colour of the light at its surface.

4 One type of photoelectric device has a response dependent on incident light intensity in lux. This device is
   (i)   the photoconductive cell;   (iii) the photovoltaic cell;
   (ii) the photoemissive cell;   (iv) the LED.

5 A light emitting diode comprises a *p-n* junction which is
   (i)   forward;
   (ii) reverse biased;
         The colour of the light produced depends mainly upon (iii) the value of the applied voltage
   (iv) the materials from which the junction is made;

196

(v)   the frequency of the supply voltage;
(vi)   the operating temperature.
Select *one* from (i) and (ii) and *one* from (iii) to (vi) to make a correct statement.

(c) CONVENTIONAL PROBLEMS

1   Describe the construction of a photoemissive cell stating the coating materials used on the cathode where (a) ultra violet and (b) red, radiations are to be detected. Suggest a way in which the sensitivity to other colours can be varied.
[Use of filters]

2   Draw a circuit diagram and typical response curve for a photovoltaic cell.

3   Describe the construction and principle of operation of a photoconductive cell. Explain *one* application of such a cell.

4   Discuss the advantages of the LED over the normal filament lamp as a circuit condition indicator (ON/OFF).

5   State and explain one use of the LED where its excellent frequency response is important.

6   Explain with the aid of a circuit diagram the action of two LASCR's used to control a piece of d.c. equipment fed from an a.c. supply. What advantages are there to using LASCR's as opposed to normal SCR's in this particular instance?

7   The gas input to a boiler is controlled using two valves in series. One of these valves is operated using a thermostat. The other valve is held open at all times the pilot (ignition) light is burning. Devise a simple circuit employing a photoelectric cell which could be used to control this second valve, closing it when the ignition light fails. Briefly describe the action of the circuit.

15 Illumination

A SUMMARY OF FORMULAE AND DEFINITIONS ASSOCIATED WITH ILLUMINATION

1 White light may be resolved into a band of colours called the **spectrum** by passing it through a glass prism. The colours in the bands are red, orange, yellow, green, blue and violet. These colours are electromagnetic radiations, similar to radio waves, but have a much higher frequency (see Chapter 14, para. 1).

2 Many solid bodies emit light when raised to a sufficiently high temperature. The ordinary incandescent light bulb, which contains a fine tungsten wire, heated by the passage of an electric current, is a good example of this.

3 The standard light source against which light meters are calibrated is the molten platinum standard. The molten platinum at $1773\,^{\circ}\mathrm{C}$ is white hot and emits light. The **luminance** of the surface of the platinum viewed through a small hole is defined as 60 candelas per square centimetre ($60\,\mathrm{cd/cm^2}$).

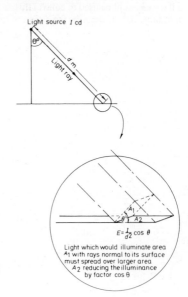

Fig 1

4   Luminance is a measure of surface 'brightness' or how uncomfortable it is to view the source with the naked eye. The sun at mid-day has an estimated luminance of 160 000 cd/cm² whereas an 80-W fluorescent tube has about 1 cd/cm².

5   **Luminous intensity** or light radiating capability (Symbol I) is the product of luminance and area. High luminance over a small radiating area can give the same light radiating capability as low luminance over a large radiating area.

6   A light source with uniform luminous intensity of 1 candela at the centre of a sphere of radius 1 metre gives rise to 1 lumen of light flux on each square metre of surface of the sphere. Since the surface area of the sphere is 4π m² (the radius being 1 m), the total light flux from a 1 candela source is 4π lumens. Since the source is at the centre of the sphere all the light rays fall normally on its surface. The level of surface illumination is called the **illuminance** (Symbol E). The illuminance = number of lumens on each square metre and has the unit the **lux**. For the unit sphere with unit source $E = 1$ lm/m² = 1 lux

7   The solid angle formed by 1 m² on the surface of a sphere of 1 m radius is called the **steradian**.

8   Where the illuminated surface is at a distance d m from the light source and the light rays fall normally on the surface

$$E = \frac{I}{d^2} \text{lux}$$

9   Where the light rays do not fall normally on the surface

$$E = \frac{I}{d^2}\cos \theta \text{ lux} \quad (\text{see } Fig\ 1).$$

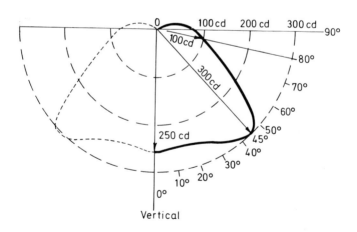

A polar diagram for lamp and fitting

Fig 2

10 By the use of a reflector or prismatic lantern, light may be directed where required. The luminous intensity of the source will now be different in different directions. A **polar diagram** provides information on the luminous intensities in particular directions. In *Figure 2,* the luminous intensity directly downwards (0°) scales 250 cd. At 45° to the vertical the value is 300 cd and at 80°, 100 cd. Values are scaled from the origin, 0, to the point on the curve at the angle required.

11 Where light is reflected at the surface of a highly polished surface, a mirror for example, the reflection is said to be 'specular'. The angle of incidence is equal to the angle of reflection (see *Fig 3*). Where matt surfaces are involved, diffused reflection occurs. Incident light is reflected in many different directions by the slight surface irregularities thus reducing the sharpness of shadows giving a much softer effect than with specular reflection (see *Fig 4*).

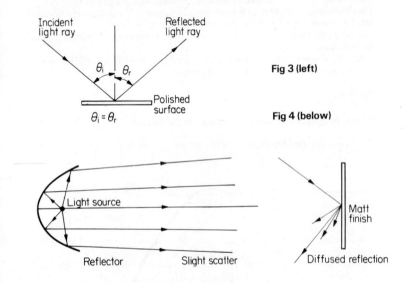

Incident light ray

Reflected light ray

θ_i θ_r

Polished surface

$\theta_i = \theta_r$

Fig 3 (left)

Fig 4 (below)

Light source

Reflector   Slight scatter

Matt finish

Diffused reflection

12 Refraction or bending of light rays takes place when they pass through a prism. This effect may concentrate or diffuse light rays according to the arrangement of the prisms (*Fig 5*).

13 The polar diagram for a particular lighting fitting together with the equation in para. 9 are used to determine surface illuminance due to a single source with no reflecting surfaces nearby, e.g. as in road lighting. If there are two or more sources nearby then the illuminance present is the sum of values due to individual sources. With indoor illumination this method is not suitable since the distances are small and much of the illuminance is due to reflection from floors, walls and ceilings. The amount of light received at a point after reflection depends on the colour, nature and cleanliness of the surfaces involved. It varies with the height of the ceilings and the shape of the room. A coefficient of utilisation is used which has been determined experimentally by the Illuminating Engineering

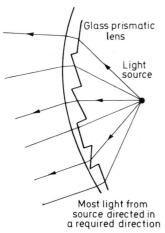

Glass prismatic lens

Light source

Most light from source directed in a required direction

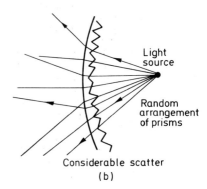

Light source

Random arrangement of prisms

Considerable scatter
(b)

Fig 5

Society for many different combinations of colour and room size. The coefficient of utilisation or utilisation factor is defined as

$$\frac{\text{Luminous flux arriving at the working surface}}{\text{Total luminous flux supplied by the lighting fittings}}$$

14 Where a minimum level of illumination is specified, allowance is made for deterioration of lamps and cleanliness of the installation, by providing a greater level of illumination than the minimum when the installation is new. A **depreciation factor** is used which has been determined by experience. The product of minimum permitted lumen requirement and depreciation factor is equal to the number of lumens to be provided when the installation is new. Sometimes a maintenance factor is quoted which is an alternative way of expressing the same thing.

$$\text{Maintenance factor} = \frac{1}{\text{Depreciation factor}}$$

15 **Types of lamp**
   (i) *The incandescent lamp* A tungsten filament is supported in a glass envelope containing a small quantity of inert gas. It is not very efficient, producing a large amount of heat in addition to the required light. The efficiency varies between 9 lm/W for the 40 W lamp to 14 lm/W for the 500 W size.
   (ii) *The high-pressure mercury discharge lamp* Current flows through mercury vapour contained in a small glass tube. The pressure, when hot, is about 1 bar. To maintain the working temperature the tube is supported in a vacuum flask. The colour of the discharge is basically blue/green and the efficiency is 40 lm/W.

(iii) *The low-pressure mercury discharge lamp (fluorescent tube)*   The discharge is through mercury vapour, as in (ii) but in a very much larger tube and at only a small fraction of the pressure. The output from the mercury vapour is mainly ultra-violet light which is not visible. The ultra-violet light is used to excite a phosphor which is deposited on the inside of the tube. By use of suitable phosphors, light of almost any colour is possible. The efficiency lies between 40 and 60 lm/W according to colour.

(iv) *The low-pressure sodium lamp*   The discharge takes place in a U-tube containing a little neon gas and metallic sodium. The tube is supported in a vacuum flask to maintain the working temperature. The colour of the light is bright yellow and the efficiency of the lamp in the region of 130 lm/W.

(v) *The high-pressure sodium lamp*   Increasing the temperature of the discharge in sodium to about 1000°C and also increasing the pressure causes the light to become much whiter than in (iv) above. It then blends well with incandescent lighting. Under these conditions an alumina containing tube must be used, since glass will melt. The efficiency is 100 lm/W.

(vi) *The halogen lamp*   A little iodine is added to the inert gas in a tungsten filament lamp. Any tungsten evaporating combines with the iodine to form a compound, which does not settle on, and so blacken, the glass envelope. As a consequence this can be made much smaller than in the conventional lamp. The efficiency lies between 15 and 25 lm/W.

16 *Luminaires (lighting fittings)*   Most lamps require some form of shading to prevent glare or to assist in projecting the light precisely where required. Luminaires are used which may be concentrating or diffusing according to the situation. Indoor luminaires may have to be decorative as well as functional. Outside luminaires must be weatherproof as well as being vandal-proof. To minimise maintenance, the surfaces should be self cleaning by the action of wind and rain. Electrical connections to them are generally by means of conduit or mineral insulated cables.

17 The amount of daylight reaching a point inside a building through a window directly from the sky depends on three factors: (i) the area of the sky visible from that point; (ii) the luminance of the sky and (iii) the angle at which it arrives on the surface to be lit.

The luminance of the sky itself depends on three factors, (i) the season of the year, (ii) the hour of the day and (iii) the distance of the room from the equator, i.e. on its latitude. All three of these factors govern the height of the sun above the horizon and hence the luminance.

18 **Room daylighting** may be derived by reflection from external surfaces and the amount of this depends on the state and colour of those surfaces.

19 Increasing the height of windows will allow daylighting to penetrate more deeply into any room.

B   WORKED PROBLEMS ON ILLUMINATION

> *Problem 1*   (a) A metal box has a frosted glass window 1.5 cm^2 in area which is lit from within by a lamp such that it has a luminance of 750 cd/cm^2. What is its luminous intensity in candelas?
> (b) (i) If the window is to have a luminous intensity of 900 cd, to what value must its luminance be changed? (ii) Assuming that the luminance cannot be changed, suggest a method whereby the required luminous intensity of 900 cd could still be achieved.

(a)   In para. 3, luminance is defined as

$$\frac{\text{luminous intensity in candelas}}{\text{area}}$$

Hence, luminance × area = luminous intensity

$750 \times 1.5 = $ **1125 cd**

(b)   (i)   The luminous intensity is now changed to 900 cd,
Hence: new luminance × 1.5 = 900.

transposing: new luminance $= \dfrac{900}{1.5} = $ **600 cd/cm^2**

(ii)   The area of the window might be changed.
thus, 750 cd/cm^2 × new area = 900.

New area $= \dfrac{900}{750} = $ **1.2 cm^2**

> *Problem 2*   A cinema projector employs a lamp with uniform light-radiating capability (luminous intensity) of 1000 cd. The reflector and lens systems, which is used to direct all the available light on to a screen 10 m × 4 m, is 60% efficient.
> Calculate: (a) the total light output from the lamp in lumens and (b) the illuminance of the screen.

(a)   From para. 6, total light output from the lamp = $4\pi \times 1000 = $ **12 566 lumens**
(b)   The area of the screen = $10 \times 4 = 40$ m^2 and 60% of 12 566 lumens is uniformly distributed over its surface. Hence, from para. 6,

illuminance $E = \dfrac{0.6 \times 12566}{40} = 188.5$ lm/m^2

The lumen per square metre is called the lux

$\therefore E = $ **188.5 lux**

Problem 3 Calculate the illuminance of a horizontal surface due to a single lamp with uniform luminous intensity of 2500 cd mounted 10 m above the surface at points:

(a) immediately below the lamp; (b) 5 m from this point on the horizontal surface and (c) 15 m from the original point on the horizontal surface.

Since the lamp has a uniform light-radiating capability, the value 2500 cd may be used throughout.

(a) Immediately beneath the lamp the light rays fall normally on the surface. From para. 8,

$$E = \frac{I}{d^2}$$

and $d = 10$ m. Hence

$$E \quad \frac{2500}{10^2} = 25 \text{ lux}$$

(b) From para. 9, with reference to *Fig 6*, $\tan \theta_1 = 5/10 = 0.5$. Thus $\theta_1 = 26.56°$. This may be obtained by scale drawing if preferred.
  By Pythagoras' theorem: $d_1^2 = 5^2 + 10^2 = 125$

$$E = \frac{2500}{125} \cos 26.56 = \textbf{17.9 lux}$$

(c) Similarly, $\tan \theta_2 = 15/10 = 1.5$. Thus $\theta_2 = 56.3°$.
  $d_2^2 = 15^2 + 10^2 = 325$.
  Hence

$$E = \frac{2500}{325} \cos 56.3° = \textbf{4.27 lux}$$

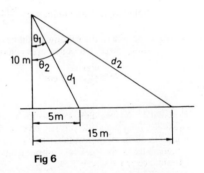

Fig 6

Problem 4 A single lamp in a reflector has a polar diagram as shown in *Fig 7*. The lamp and reflector are mounted 7.5 m above a horizontal flat plane. Calculate the illuminance on the plane (a) immediately beneath the lamp; (b) 10 m from that point on the flat plane.

(a) The lamp is considered to be situated at the origin 0 of the polar diagram. The light illuminating the spot immediately below the lamp is shining directly downwards through zero degrees on the polar diagram. Reading directly from the curve, the luminous intensity in this direction is 600 cd.

$$E = \frac{600}{7.5^2} = \textbf{10.7 lux}$$

204

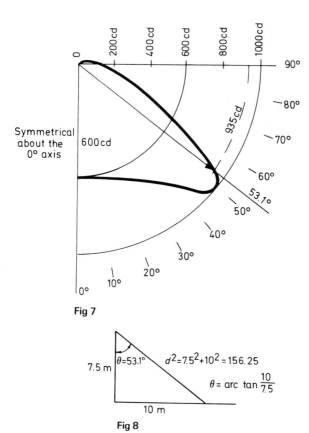

Fig 7

$$d^2 = 7.5^2 + 10^2 = 156.25$$

$$\theta = \text{arc tan } \frac{10}{7.5}$$

$\theta = 53.1°$

7.5 m

10 m

Fig 8

(b) At a distance of 10 m from the first point (see *Fig 8*), the light is projected at an angle of 53.1° from the vertical. From the polar diagram it is found that the luminous intensity in this direction is 935 cd.

$$E = \frac{935}{156.25}\cos 53.1° = \textbf{3.6 lux}$$

Problem 5 A straight row of lamp standards are spaced 30 m apart and each is 8 m high. Each standard carries a lantern with a polar diagram as shown in *Fig 9*.
   Calculate the illuminance 5 m from the base of one standard on a line joining the bases of two standards. Consider only the illuminance from the three lamps nearest to the point.

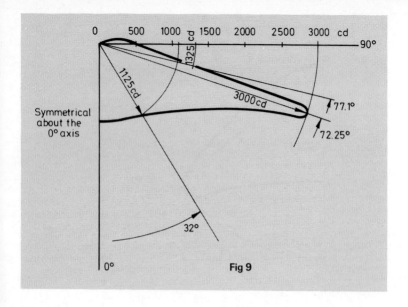

Fig 9

First construct an elevation showing the standards and distances as shown in *Fig 10*.

Now as in *Problem 4*:

$\tan \theta_1 = 35/8$, $\theta_1 = 77.1°$ $\cos 77.1° = 0.223$. $d_1^2 = 35^2 + 8^2 = 1289$

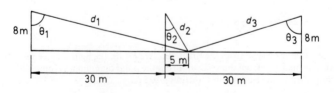

Fig 10

On the polar diagram *Fig 9*, a straight line through the origin at 77.1° from the vertical cuts the polar curve at a value of luminous intensity of 1325 cd.

$\tan \theta_2 = 5/8$, $\theta_2 = 32°$ $\cos 32° = 0.85$. $d_2^2 = 5^2 + 8^2 = 89$

At 32° from the vertical the luminous intensity is 1125 cd (see *Figure 9*)

$\tan \theta_3 = 25/8$, $\theta_3 = 72.25°$ $\cos 72.25° = 0.304$. $d_3^2 = 25^2 + 8^2 = 689$

206

Since the polar diagram is symmetrical about the zero axis, the luminous intensity may be scaled at 72.25° from the vertical as for θ_1 and θ_2. The luminous intensity is 3000 cd.

Total illuminance at the point = sum of the illuminances from the three lamps,

i.e. $\dfrac{I}{d^2}\cos \theta°$. Thus

$$E = \frac{1325}{1289} \times 0.223 + \frac{1125}{89} \times 0.85 + \frac{3000}{689} \times 0.304$$

$$= 0.229 + 10.74 + 1.32$$

$$= \mathbf{12.3\ lux}$$

Problem 6   A workshop 60 m × 40 m is to be illuminated using high-pressure sodium lamps each giving 13 000 lm. The minimum level of surface illumination (illuminance) is to be 120 lx.
   The utilisation factor = 0.65. The depreciation factor = 1.3. (Alternatively, the maintenance factor could be quoted (see para. 14). For this question, maintenance factor = 1/1.3 = 0.77.) Calculate the number of lamps required.

---

120 lux = 120 lumens on each square metre
Hence, total lumens required = 120 × (60 m × 40 m) = 288 000 lumens.
From para. 13,

$$\text{utilisation factor} = \frac{\text{lumens at the working surface}}{\text{total number of lumens from the fittings}}$$

$$0.65 = \frac{288\,000}{\text{total lumens from fittings}}$$

Total lumens from fittings $= \dfrac{288\,000}{0.65} = 443\,077$ lumens

which is the minimum level, so that when new, the installation must provide more than this. Using the depreciation factor, input when
new = 1.3 × 443 077 = 576 000 lumen.
   Note that using the maintenance factor, the same result is obtained by writing:

$$\text{depreciation factor} = \frac{1}{\text{Maintenance factor}} = \frac{1}{0.77}$$

Hence, input when new $= \dfrac{1}{0.77} \times 443\,077 = 576\,000$ lumen

Each fitting provides 13 000 lm, hence the number of fittings required

$$= \frac{576\,000}{13\,000} = \mathbf{44.3}$$

It will be necessary to employ at least 45 lamps and to get a symmetrical arrangement, possibly 48 lamps (6 rows of 8) would be used.

Problem 7   List the factors which determine the illuminance at a point inside a room due to external daylight.

(i)   Area of the sky visible from the point inside the room;
(ii)   The angle at which it arrives at the surface to be lit;
(iii)   The height and width of the window;
(iv)   The season of the year;
(v)   The hour of the day;
(vi)   The latitude of the premises;
(vii)   The degree of overcast, clouds, pollution, etc;
(viii) The direction in which the window faces. For example, north facing never sees the sun.

Problem 8   Describe with the aid of a sketch (i) the ways in which daylight may enter a room through a window and (ii) how the light is distributed once it has entered the room.

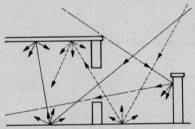

—— Light entering the room directly from the sky
—·—Light entering the room by reflection from
        an external vertical surface
- - - Light entering the room by reflection from   **Fig 11**
        an external horizontal surface

(i)   Light may enter directly from the sky or after reflection by external surfaces. The reflection is generally diffuse and is shown in *Figure 11*.
(ii)   Once the light has entered the room, diffuse reflection takes place again and the degree of re-distribution will depend on (i) the colour and state of the decoration, (ii) whether gloss or matt finish colours are used and (iii) the depth and height of the room.

C FURTHER PROBLEMS ON ILLUMINATION

(a) SHORT ANSWER PROBLEMS

1 Complete the statements:
   (a) Light is emitted by many solid bodies when they are . . . .
   (b) In an incandescent lamp the filament is generally made from . . . . wire.
   (c) The glass envelope of an incandescent lamp contains . . . .
   (d) The efficiency of an incandescent lamp is not very high since a large amount of the energy input appears as . . . . Increased efficiency of light production occurs when the current flows in . . . . instead of a wire.

2 What is the colour of the light from a low pressure sodium lamp? What design change has enabled the colour to be changed to a more pleasing hue?

3 What is the colour of the light from a high-pressure mercury lamp?

4 How is the colour from a low-pressure mercury (fluorescent) tube changed (at the manufacturing stage)?

5 Why is the tungsten iodine lamp much smaller than the equivalent rated normal incandescent lamp?

6 Define the terms: (i) luminance; (ii) light flux; (iii) luminous intensity and (iv) illuminance.

7 Light rays fall normally on a surface 10 m from a source of luminous intensity 500 cd. What is the value of illuminance at the surface? If the surface is now turned through an angle of 15° so that the light rays strike it obliquely, what now is the value of illuminance?

8 What is a luminaire?

9 What are the desirable features of a luminaire to be used outdoors?

10 What is the difference between a diffusing and a refracting lantern?

11 What is the difference between spectral and diffuse reflection?

12 State four factors which determine the amount of daylight reaching a given position in a room.

13 When installing lighting schemes it is often necessary to consider the luminance of the light sources as well as the total lumen requirement. Why is this?

(b) MULTI-CHOICE PROBLEMS (answers on page 213)

1 Luminous intensity is defined as:
   (i) light flux per unit area;
   (ii) luminance × area of the source;
   (iii) illuminance × area of a surface;
   (iv) total lux per unit area

2 A light source has a uniform luminous intensity of 400 cd. It is enclosed in a luminaire which transmits 95% of the light from the source on to a working area. The total light flux received by the working area is (in lumens):
   (i) 5291; (ii) 4775; (iii) 380; (iv) 30.2.

3 A little iodine is added to the gas in a tungsten filament lamp to create the tungsten iodine lamp. The action of the iodine is to:
   (i) make the lamp run cooler;
   (ii) make the lamp run hotter and so increase efficiency;
   (iii) combine with the tungsten evaporating from the filament;
   (iv) decrease the luminance of the source so that it is less uncomfortable to view.

4 Depreciation or maintenance factors associated with the lumen method of lighting calculations depend on TWO of the following. Which are they?
   (i) The height of the ceiling;
   (ii) the amount of dirt which collects on walls and lighting fittings;
   (iii) the colour of the decoration;
   (iv) the size of the room;
   (v) where tungsten lamps are used, the amount of tungsten evaporating from the filament;
   (vi) the shape of the room;
   (vii) the distance between the lighting fittings.

5 Light falls on a surface at 20° to the normal from a source of 600 cd, 3 m distant. The illuminance of the surface is (in lux):
   (i) 71; (ii) 563.8; (iii) 62.65; (iv) 66.67.

6 A uniform light source causes an illuminance of 450 lux on a surface 15 m away when the light rays fall normally on that surface. The luminous intensity of the source is
   (i) 2 cd; (ii) 101 250 cd; (iii) 30 cd; (iv) 6750 cd.

7 Illuminance is:
   (i) a measure of brightness of a light source;
   (ii) the light flux being produced by the platinum standard;
   (iii) the amount of light flux falling on 1 m^2 of a surface;
   (iv) the number of candelas per square centimetre.

8 A diffusing luminaire is used:
   (i) where a soft lighting effect is required;
   (ii) where it is necessary to ensure that the light from a fitting is sent in a particular direction;
   (iii) where the fittings are to be mounted at a considerable height above the working plane;
   (iv) for road lighting.

9 Ten fluorescent fittings light an area of 10 m × 20 m. Each fitting gives 3500 lumens. The utilisation factor is 0.6. The illuminance at the working surface is:
   (i) 175 lux, (ii) 291.6 lux, (iii) 105 lux.

10 At the end of the design life of a lighting installation the total light flux at the working surface is 563 000 lumens. If the maintenance factor is 0.55 and the utilisation factor is 0.6, how many lumens at the working surface will there be when a new set of lamps is installed and the illumination is brought back to 'as-new' condition?
   (i) 1 023 636 lumens; (ii) 309 650 lumens; (iii) 938 333 lumens; (iv) 516 083 lumens.

(c) CONVENTIONAL PROBLEMS

1 A tungsten filament lamp is rated at 100 W and emits 1150 lumens.
   (a) Calculate its luminous efficiency in lumens per watt.
   (b) Assuming uniform radiation, determine its mean luminous intensity in
        candelas.   [(a) 11.5 lumen/watt; (b) 91.5 cd]

2 A room is to be illuminated using tungsten filament lamps with uniform
   luminous intensity of 75 cd. If the total lumens required is 14 137, how many
   lamps are required?   [15 lamps]

3 Discuss the advantages of a fluorescent tube over a tungsten filament lamp both
   having the same total lumen output.
                                        [Low luminance; cool running]

4 (a) Define the terms: (i) luminance; (ii) illuminance; (iii) luminous intensity,
        stating in each case the units used.
   (b) A tungsten filament lamp is suspended 2 m above the centre of a circular
        table of diameter 4 m. The total light output from the lamp is 1800 lumens.
        Assuming uniform light radiating capability in all directions, determine the
        illuminance at the centre of the table. Where, on the table, is the
        illuminance a minimum? What is the value of this illuminance?
                                        [Centre 35.8 lux; edge 12.66 lux]

5 A lamp which has a light radiating capability of 500 cd in all directions below the
   horizontal plane is suspended 2 m above the centre of a games table
   2.5 m × 1.5 m. Determine the illuminance on the table (a) beneath the lamp; (b)
   at each corner of the table and (c) at the centre of the shortest side.
                                        [(a) 125 lux; (b) 66 lux; (c) 76.2 lux]

6 A building 20 m high is to have a vertical wall floodlit using tungsten halide
   lamps in specially designed reflectors. A row of fittings each 7 m from the base
   of the wall and located on the ground are to be used.
   (a) Calculate the luminous intensity required for each fitting along the shortest
        line which would pass through the fitting and just touch the top of the wall
        given that the illuminance at the top of the wall is to be 5 lux.
   (b) What luminous intensity is required in such a direction as to give the same
        illuminance 5 m from the ground?   [(a) 6796 cd; (b) 455 cd]

7 A lamp with luminous efficiency 40 lm/W consumes 65 W. All the light
   produced is directed on to a circular area 2.5 m in diameter. Assuming uniform
   distribution, determine the illuminance of the circular area.   [529.7 lux]

8 (a) Define the terms: (i) maintenance factor and (ii) depreciation factor.
   (b) A new lighting installation comprises 56, 1500 mm long, 65 W fluorescent
        tubes each with an output when new of 3150 lumens. Determine the value
        of light flux at the working surface:
        (i) when the installation is new and (ii) after 5000 hours running given
             that the depreciation factor is 1.15. The utilisation factor = 0.7.
                                        (b) (i) 123 480 lumens; (ii) 107 374 lumens]

9 (a) Define the term 'illuminance'.
   (b) A workshop measures 100 m × 75 m and it is to have a minimum level of
        illumination of 200 lux at the working surface. This is to be provided with
        1500 mm long 65 W fluorescent tubes. Each tube gives 3250 lm when new

211

and they are mounted in fittings each of which contains four tubes. Determine the number of fittings required allowing a utilisation factor of 0.65 and a maintenance factor of 0.75.

Suggest a method of increasing the illuminance locally over benches where fine detail work is to be performed. [237 fittings]

10 An industrial lighting installation provides 235 000 lumens at the working surface at the end of its design life. Allowing a maintenance factor of 0.8 and a utilisation factor of 0.65, determine:
(a)   the total lumens supplied by the fittings when new;
(b)   the total lumens supplied by the fittings at the end of the design life and
(c)   the total lumens at the working surface when the installation was new.
[(a) 451 923 lumens; (b) 361 538 lumens; (c) 293 750 lumens]

11 In summer time an office 25 m long and 16 m wide receives 100 000 lumens by daylighting. This may be considered to be uniformly distributed over one quarter of the width of the office nearest to the windows.
Calculate: (a) the average illuminance over the area covered by daylighting and (b) the number of fluorescent tubes each giving 3000 lumens necessary to give one half of the illumination in (a) over the *remainder* of the office assuming that the daylighting here is negligible. The utilisation factor = 0.7.
(*Note.* The artificial lighting would be used to prevent excessive contrast between the two areas of the office) [(a) 1000 lux; (b) 72 tubes]

12 Discuss the reasons why it would not be desirable to use a high-pressure sodium lamp in the home.

13 Why is the tungsten iodine lamp particularly suited to motor vehicle headlamps?
[Small; centre of focus of reflector]

14 Why are incandescent light bulbs often made from obscured (pearl) glass?

15 What would happen to a low-pressure sodium lamp if its vacuum envelope were holed?

Answers to multi-choice problems

Chapter 1 (page 10): 1 (ii); 2 (iii); 3 (ii); 4 (i); 5 (a) (iii), (b) (i); 6 (iii); 7 (ii).

Chapter 2 (page 28): 1 (ii); 2 (iii); 3 (iii); 4 (ii); 5 (ii); 6 (i) and (iii); 7 (ii); 8 (iii); 9 (ii), (v); 10 (iii).

Chapter 3 (page 40): 1 (ii); 2 (ii); 3 (a) (iii), (b) (ii), (c) (i); 4 (i), (iv); 5 (iii); 6 (i); 7 (iii); 8 (iii); 9 (ii) and (iv); 10 (iii); 11 (iii).

Chapter 4 (page 57): 1 (iii); 2 (iii); 3 (ii); 4 (ii); 5 (i); 6 (iv); 7 (ii); 8 (iii); 9 (iii); 10 (i) and (iv).

Chapter 5 (page 74): 1 (iii); 2 (i), (v); 3 (ii); 4 (iii); 5 (iv); 6 (iii); 7 (i); 8 (i), (iv), (v); 9 (ii).

Chapter 6 (page 97): 1 (i); 2 (iii); 3 (ii); 4 (iii); 5 (iv); 6 (ii); 7 (iii); 8 (iii); 9 (ii); 10 (i) and (iv); 11 (ii).

Chapter 7 (page 111): 1 (ii); 2 (i) and (c); 3 (iv); 4 (iii); 5 (ii) and (iv); 6 (iii); 7 (ii).

Chapter 8 (page 119): 1 (i) and (iv); 2 (i), (iv), (vi); 3 (iii); 4 (a) (ii), (b) (i) and (iii).

Chapter 9 (page 130): 1 (i) = (c), (ii) = (a), (iii) = (e); 2 (iii); 3 Statement (iii) completes sentence 1. Statement (i) completes sentence 2; 4 (iv); 5 (iv); 6 (ii); 7 (iii).

Chapter 10 (page 143): 1 (ii); 2 (iii); 3 (i); 4 (iv); 5 (ii); 6 (ii); 7 (ii); 8 (a) (i), (b) (iv).

Chapter 11 (page 159): 1 (iii); 2 (ii); 3 (ii); 4 (iv); 5 (ii); 6 x = (i), y = (iii), z = (iv); 7 (iii); 8 (i); 9 (a) (ii), (b) (iv); 10 (ii); 11 (iii).

Chapter 12 (page 172): 1 (iv); 2 (i), (iii); 3 (a) (v) Note (iv) is just a possibility but is rather long; (b) (iii), (c) (ii); 4 (ii), (iv); 5 (iv); 6 (a) (ii), (b) (iii), (c) (v); 7 (ii); 8 (iii), (v); 9 (ii).

Chapter 13 (page 188): 1 (iii); 2 (a) (v), (b) (i), (c) (ii), (d) (vi), (e) (iii), (f) (iv); 3 (ii), (v); 4 (iii); 5 (a) (ii), (b) (i), (c) (ii); 6 (ii); 7 (i), (v); 8 (iv); 9 (iii); 10 (v).

Chapter 14 (page 196): 1 (ii); 2 (iv); 3 (ii), (iii), (vi); 4 (i); 5 (i), (iv).

Chapter 15 (page 209): 1 (ii); 2 (ii); 3 (iii); 4 (ii) and (v); 5 (iii); 6 (ii); 7 (iii); 8 (i); 9 (iii); 10 (i).

Index